ARCHITECTS OF FEAR

ARCHITECTS OF FEAR

Conspiracy Theories and
Paranoia in American Politics

George Johnson

JEREMY P. TARCHER, INC.
Los Angeles
Distributed by Houghton Mifflin Company
Boston

Library of Congress Cataloging in Publication Data

Johnson, George, 1952, Jan. 20–
    Architects of fear.

    Bibliography.
    Includes index.
    1. United States—Politics and government.   2. Conspiracies—United
States—History.   I. Title.
E183.J68   1983   320.973   83-9259
ISBN 0-87477-275-3

Requests for such permissions should be addressed to:

Jeremy P. Tarcher, Inc.
9110 Sunset Blvd.
Los Angeles, CA 90069

Manufactured in the United States of America

10   9   8   7   6   5   4   3   2   1

First Edition

To my parents,
Dr. and Mrs. J. E. Johnson

*I must Create a System
or be enslav'd by another Man's*
—WILLIAM BLAKE

Contents

Acknowledgments

Some of the material in this book appeared, in a different form, in copyrighted articles in the *Minneapolis Star;* it is used here by permission of the Minneapolis Star and Tribune Co. Until its demise on April 2, 1982, the *Star* was one of the most exciting, creative newspapers in the country; I would like to thank some of the editors who helped make it that way: Kay Miller, David Early, David Anderson, Zeke Wigglesworth, Robert Ostmann, Michael Finney, Tim McGuire, and, especially, editor-in-chief Stephen D. Isaacs.

Many of my friends and colleagues read parts of the book, helping me make it better: Tom Alexander, David Anderson, Gary Cesarz, Vince Carroll, Linda DeRubeis, Christopher Evans, Stuart Hughes, Cheryl Katz, Alan Lappin, Joan McClelland, Kate Stanley, and Conne Turke. Like all critics of political paranoia, I am indebted to the works of the late historian Richard Hofstadter and sociologist Seymour Martin Lipset.

I'd like to thank editor Stephanie E. Bernstein and assistant editor Leslie Brown for their talent, insight, and commitment to this project, and Jim Martineau and Marshall Tanick for legal advice. I would especially like to thank my publisher, Jeremy Tarcher, for understanding what I wanted to do with this book better than I did myself.

Introduction

Who runs the world? Most of us wonder that at times. Is there a mysterious They, a group of secret conspirators who manipulate world events? Almost as soon as we ask the question, we dismiss it as absurd. We are taught to believe that the world works in more complex and subtle ways.

When, for example, we consider what started World War II, we see many possibilities: the tensions resulting from carving up the Austro-Hungarian empire; the tangle of treaties and secret pacts among the European nations; the effect of the world depression on the German economy; the pressures resulting from German, Italian, and Japanese expansionism. And there are the less tangible factors as well—the character of a nation, the spirit of an age, the pathological drives of leaders seeking power.

Explanations for the way the economy operates are equally elusive. When we ask why prices rise and fall, we are presented with a web of interrelated factors: the rate of production of the nation's factories; the relative size of the gross national product, federal deficit, and money supply; the price of gold compared to the price of the dollar; the fluctuations of the world currency exchange; the balance between U.S. imports and exports; the changing demographic characteristics of the population; the social and psychological aspects of consumption.

In other words, there are no final answers. History and economics are not puzzles to solve. There is no "right" solution, but only models to help us understand. Faced with the world's complexity and uncertainty, we don't stop seeking explanations. The search for order is one of the most elevating of human activities, even though we know it is a quest that can never end. As the amount of information we possess increases, and we are exposed to an accelerating number of theories and conflicting points of view, we learn to absorb into our world view the idea that there are a number of different ways to interpret events—that there is not a single all-embracing system. We learn that knowledge is dynamic, not static—that reality looks different to different people.

This book is about a large number of Americans who reject this pluralistic view. They have taken to an extreme the desire to find connections between events, to find a cause for every effect. They don't react to new information and ideas by adapting. Instead they try to squeeze the world into their systems. They have a deep-seated suspicion that someone is responsible for the world's problems: Communists, Jews, Catholics, bankers, intellectuals, secular humanists—or, simply, Satan. To rationalize their fear and hatred they build elaborate systems explaining all the world's troubles as part of a conspiracy. Inflation, they say, is caused by Jewish bankers plotting to wreck America—or by Communists, or by a combination of the two. World War II is dismissed as a Vatican (or Jewish or Communist) plot.

Most of us at one time or another engage in this kind of thinking. After the Kennedy assassination, many people found it easier to believe in a plot involving the CIA, KGB, and FBI than to accept the seemingly absurd notion that an angry gunman could kill a president and change history. But there is a difference between those who occasionally succumb to the attraction of pat, conspiratorial explanations and the conspiracy theorists examined in this book, who believe everything bad that has ever happened is part of an all-engulfing, centuries-old plot.

The late historian Richard Hofstadter coined the phrase "the paranoid style in American politics" to describe the tradition of casting one's enemies as pawns of a vast, mysterious conspiracy. Paranoia is a psychiatric term for a mental state in which people, seized with a sense of grandeur, believe enemies are scheming against them. A paranoid might, for example, hear imaginary voices and conclude that the FBI is invading his mind with radio waves because he is the last sane person on earth. In political paranoia, people exalt their own race, nation, or religion above all others; they feel persecuted as a group. They imagine that NBC, CBS, ABC, the newspapers, schools, and publishing industry are invading everyone's mind with new ideas, trying to overthrow the old way of life.

In a sense, they are right: society is in constant flux; the media and the schools are agents of change. Those who believe mankind's salvation lies with progress see modernization as an advance; the less enthusiastic see it as inevitable. But those who believe traditions are sacrosanct see change as erosion.

To the conspiracy theorists, the erosion is planned. They see their way of life not as one of many that must contend in the political marketplace, but as the expression of absolute truth. They believe their religion is the one true faith, that American democracy is the one true political system, that laissez-faire capitalism is the one true economic system. In a society that is coming to reject such absolutism for a more flexible, cosmopolitan view, they feel like outsiders. Because they assume the world is divided between forces of good and evil, they consider their opponents not as representatives of a rival philosophy but as dark conspirators.

Political paranoia is most obvious in the conspiracy theories of extremist groups like the John Birch Society and the hundreds of survivalist and right-wing political organizations that form what is known as the radical right. There are at most several hundred thousand Americans who support these groups or subscribe to their publications. But beliefs that are overt among the extremists can be implicit in much larger segments of the population.

I first became aware of how widespread the paranoid style of politics has become when I worked as a reporter for the *Minneapolis Star,* covering what my editors and I called the "idea beat." By writing about philosophy, politics, religion, and science, I tried to penetrate the surface of the daily news to get readers to think about the ideas and beliefs that motivate events. I was interested in uncovering the underlying assumptions that determine the way we perceive the world. I was especially interested in the way reality looks to people whose beliefs are very different from mine.

As I wrote about fundamentalist Protestants, creationists, survivalists, antiabortionists, and members of right-wing political movements such as the Moral Majority and the new Right, I was struck by the degree to which their world views coincide. Although the details of what members of these groups believe vary widely, many of them share a way of thinking that is very similar to the paranoid style. They tend to perceive reality as a tightly constructed system in which good fights evil for control of the earth; in which all problems occur because of satanic plans; in which civilization is declining toward an inevitable Armageddon. As I interviewed members of these groups and studied their writings, I realized that the most important difference between them and their opponents is not so much that they disagree on specific issues, but that they believe the world works in different ways.

As a pluralist who believes there are many possible ways to explain reality, and as a secular humanist who believes that knowledge discovered by humans must take precedence over the biblical word of God, I was considered by members of many of the groups I studied to be an enemy. As a representative of the press, which champions a pluralistic, secular view, I was often eyed with suspicion.

When I interviewed Robert White, leader of a national right-wing organization called the Duck Club, he told me that the *Minneapolis Star* was part of an anti-American plot because its publisher belonged to the Trilateral Commission, an organization that promotes stronger international ties. After I wrote a series of articles about conspiracy theorist Lyndon LaRouche's pronuclear political cult (the people in the airports with the signs that say Feed Jane Fonda to the Whales), his followers denounced me in one of their magazines as part of a conspiracy of elitists that began in ancient Egypt.

White's and LaRouche's reactions were extreme—even

within the fantastic world of political paranoia—but they demonstrated to me the friction that develops when world views collide. Like oil and water, the worlds of absolutists and pluralists are microscopically structured such that it is difficult for them to mix. They are immiscible paradigms—systems of thought that are, by nature, almost mutually exclusive. This book is an attempt to overcome that built-in barrier and help the people caught on each side learn to see how the world looks through alien eyes.

In writing this book, I have tried to avoid becoming a conspiracy theorist myself. As I chart the course of political paranoia, names of leaders of various extremist groups appear on the rosters of other groups, which have traits in common with still others. But what I believe I am mapping is a way of thinking, not a monolithic plot. While these groups share the same style of thinking, many of them differ in the substance of their beliefs. While some conspiracy theorists are anti-Semitic, others, like Jerry Falwell, are strong supporters of Israel. Some conspiracy theorists are anti-Catholic; others are devout followers of the church. Leftists, of course, have conspiracy theories of their own, though generally not as all-embracing and supernatural as the right-wing versions described in this book.

I have also tried to avoid succumbing to the conspiracy theorists' tendency to paint the world black and white. Although political paranoia is destructive, its targets are not all necessarily admirable. I have no desire to defend or condemn groups such as the Trilateral Commission or the Council on Foreign Relations.

And, finally, I do not contend that there are no such things as conspiracies. Consider Watergate, or the Italian banking scandal of 1981, which involved a secret Freemasonic lodge and led to the resignation of the country's prime minister. But even real conspiracies are not the rigid, mechanistic closed systems the political paranoids see. They consist of people, not mindless pawns of evil. They are best understood and combated without the blinders of paranoia.

The purpose of this book is to demystify. At the root of

even the strangest legend there are often seeds of truth. By understanding how history can be rearranged and used as a weapon against enemies, perhaps we can learn the dangers of seeing the world through what William Blake called "mind-forged manacles."

1

The Architecture
of Paranoia

*"We are all sufferers from history, but the paranoid is a
double sufferer, since he is afflicted not only by the real
world, with the rest of us, but by his fantasies as well."*
—Richard Hofstadter,
The Paranoid Style in American Politics, 1963

Right-wing publisher Robert White was flying back from London on a Concorde jet, in 1982, when he found himself face to face with a man he was certain was an agent of "the conspiracy." For the past several days, White, owner of a lucrative company that cleans airport runways, had been working on a project in Saudi Arabia. He was returning to his ranch in Cocoa, Florida, when he saw, sitting two seats in front of him, Lord Carrington, "head honcho of the Trilateral Commission in England." White asked the flight attendant to give the former British foreign secretary a copy of the latest issue of the *Duck Book,* a monthly magazine dedicated to the proposition that the Trilateral Commission and the Council on Foreign Relations are plotting with Communists, international bankers, the Internal Revenue Service, and the Federal Reserve System to cause the collapse of the U.S. economy and absorb it into a dictatorial world government, with the manipulators firmly in control.

Carrington, White reported to his readers, looked back and said, "Thank you." White, who is editor of the *Duck Book* and founder of the national Duck Club movement, handed him a business card with a note scribbled on it: "If you'll read the first page turkey, you'll note that I intend to put a crimp into your one world government crap."

If his lordship was bothered by the faulty punctuation, White didn't care. "I still haven't found an editor who can correct my sentence structure and put the commas in the right place," White wrote to his readers, "but for what I have to say, I don't think it matters a hill of beans."

Dressed in the jumpsuits he wears during public appearances, White looks more like a truck mechanic than a millionaire, but a folksy appearance is important to his appeal. Among the nation's right-wingers he has become a legend. In 1980, after he discovered he was dying of cancer, he sold most of his business and decided to devote the rest of his life and fortune to teach the "little people"—the ducks, as he calls them —how to fight the conspiracy.

While the leaders of the Trilateral Commission and Council on Foreign Relations insist their organizations are simply forums of academic, business, government, and media leaders interested in fostering international cooperation, to White and his followers the groups are the cornerstones of an invisible empire striving secretly to rule the planet. According to a chart that appears regularly in the *Duck Book,* past and present coconspirators include such unlikely cohorts as Barbara Walters, William F. Buckley, Jimmy Carter, Alexander Haig, Andrew Young, Dan Rather, George S. McGovern, and George F. Will. Among the corporations listed as supporters of the Trilateral Commission are General Mills, General Motors, Coca-Cola, Caterpillar Tractor, Procter & Gamble, and IBM.

"These pimps are stealing America," White once told a group of his followers. "They're stealing everything you've got."

Since the media are supposedly part of the conspiracy, White decided the country needed a mass-circulation right-wing journal. He likes ducks (he raises them on his ranch in Florida), so he decided to call his magazine the *Duck Book.* Because he thought he was dying, he offered lifetime subscriptions for $10. "That's my life," he warned readers, "not yours." Each edition is filled with reprints from dozens of right-wing newsletters offering conspiracy theories, tax-resistance tips, and survivalist investment advice. To lighten the tone of the book, White includes cartoons: a duck in a camouflaged helmet carrying a rifle with a bayonet, a duck in an airplane storming Washington. Some editions contain as many as 164 pages of advice and advertisements, all with a common aim: to expose the conspiracy and help the ducks weather the coming apocalypse.

Who reads the *Duck Book*? Judging from the advertisements, subscribers include those interested in gold, diamonds, and silver ("Avoid the collapse of Rocky's Federal Reserve Note"), freeze-dried food ("What If ... Your World Falls Apart!"), combat manuals ("A virtual encyclopedia of extraordinary techniques and tips on how to fight, protect yourself and kill!"), survivalism ("Gun confiscation, monetary collapse, & an American dictator next!?"), and gun silencers ("Tough times ahead ... hunt game undetected"). Sometimes even the bankers try to cash in on the duck movement. The Bank of Boulder ran a full-page advertisement offering a Weatherby Mark V rifle with a wide-angle scope to ducks who would invest $2340 for six years.

According to an article in the *Wall Street Journal,* by 1981 White claimed to have 1358 Duck Clubs around the country, representing more than 100,000 *Duck Book* subscribers, whose fears he planned to harness to a political movement. Soon, he hoped, he would lead an uprising of the extremists, the people who find themselves to the right of Ronald Reagan. For Reagan, White insists, is a puppet of the same conspirators who controlled "born-again" Carter and "that pimp Nixon."

While Reagan supports tax cuts and lower interest rates, many Duck Club members believe he doesn't go far enough. They are convinced that the income tax was invented by Karl Marx to rob the middle class for the benefit of the proletariat and that high interest rates are part of an international banking plot. In the world according to the Duck Club, the federal government, working as a pawn of the conspirators, wastes taxpayers' money on Communist-run social programs like food stamps and welfare. To pay for such antics, the Internal Revenue Service robs the people through taxation. And the government, still unable to pay for its profligate ways, is forced to borrow money from the Federal Reserve, which is controlled by the international bankers. To the ducks, bankers and Communists are working together, stealing money with taxes and inflation, creating wars and depressions—whatever benefits their already enormous wealth.

Although he had yet to break even on his venture, by early 1983 White had published approximately 2 billion pages of *Duck Books*. He was sponsoring Duck Club investment seminars in Costa Rica, London, Hong Kong, and Geneva and trying to raise money to start a right-wing cable television network. His paid circulation dropped to 35,000 when he announced he wasn't dying after all, reneged on his promise of lifetime subscriptions, and started selling the *Duck Book* for $30 a year. But he was still printing as many as 500,000 copies a month (mailing most of them unsolicited) and charging as much as $3000 a page for advertising.

During the 1982 elections, he mailed 770,000 *Duck Books* containing a "hit list" of senators and congressmen he believed were part of the plot. "I hope you ducks will remember these turkeys who gave away our Panama Canal and send them packing back to their law offices," White wrote to his readers. "Surely they have served their elite masters long enough."

Although his plan to capture Congress from the conspirators was a failure, he was looking ahead to 1984, when he hoped he and the ducks would use his organization to elect the first president in decades (perhaps the first president ever) who wasn't one of Them.

THE PARANOID STYLE

White is one of the latest promoters of a conspiracy theory that has been pushed by right-wing extremists since the beginning of the century. According to the scenario, internationalists—whether in the form of the League of Nations, the United Nations, the Communist International, the international banking network, world Jewry, the Catholic church, or, more recently, the Trilateral Commission and Council on Foreign Relations—are plotting to undermine U.S. sovereignty and merge all nation-states into an evil supergovernment. White's success at mass-marketing his version of the legend shows that the paranoid style of American politics didn't die with Senator Joseph McCarthy. In the 1980s, the phenomenon flourishes, often in virulent forms. While the Duck Club promotes an ecumenical approach to political paranoia (in one of White's cartoons, three ducks—a rabbi, a priest, and a minister —offer their benediction: "Bless All the Ducks!"), other organizations use conspiracy theories to persecute ethnic and religious groups.

At the same time White was recruiting ducks for a flight on Washington, the Anti-Christ Information Center of Canoga Park, California, was filling Christian bookstores with a series of fast-selling comic books whose author, the Reverend Alberto Rivera, claims that the Pope runs an international plot to destroy Protestants in a new Inquisition so that he can bring about the godless, one-world religion predicted in the Book of Revelation. Included in Rivera's conspiracy theory are Communists, Nazis, Freemasons, occultists, and the labor union movement.

In Washington, an organization called Liberty Lobby has attracted more than 330,000 subscribers to its weekly newspaper *Spotlight,* which champions the theory that the world is secretly controlled not only by international bankers, Communists, and Trilateralists but also by "Zionists." Liberty Lobby's leaders claim the Nazi Holocaust never occurred but is a myth perpetrated by Israel as a public-relations ploy.

While the leaders of Liberty Lobby couch their rhetoric in euphemisms (they complain about "Zionists," not Jews), members of a confederation of right-wing Christian organizations in Arkansas, Georgia, and Louisiana are less circumspect. They believe that the Jews are scheming to destroy America as a white, Christian nation. "Jews Get The Gas!" read a headline in the *Torch* ("The Revolutionary Newspaper of White Christianity"), published by the White People's Committee to Restore God's Laws. An article in another anti-Semitic newspaper, *Christian Vanguard,* published by the New Christian Crusade Church, posed what the writer considered a philosophical problem: since Hitler killed so many Jews, obviously he had God on his side. Why then was he allowed to lose World War II?

In many extremist groups, bigotry and paranoia go hand in hand. Both are motivating forces behind the survivalist movement, which made national headlines in the early 1980s. The survivalists are so certain an economic apocalypse is being plotted behind their backs that they have stockpiled freeze-dried food and taken up arms. Members of the Christian-Patriots Defense League hold annual military training camps and have made plans to start their own country, in which only white Caucasians would be allowed.

Some members of another survivalist group, the Posse Comitatus, refuse to pay income taxes because they believe the United States government is a puppet of Communists and Jewish bankers. A national leader of the group, LaVerne Hollenbeck, claims to have "quite a few thousand" followers in every state but Hawaii. He told a newspaper reporter that the Federal Reserve "is headed by the Rothschilds of Paris. The Jews do own the banking system, you know. They have a hit man who tells the president of the United States what to do." In February 1983, the federal marshal for North Dakota and one of his deputies were shot to death in a gunfight after they confronted Gordon Kahl, a follower of Posse Comitatus, who was wanted for violating probation. He had been convicted for refusing to pay income tax, which he believed was imposed by the IRS as part of a Communist, satanic plot to destroy the country.

Not all believers in vast, apocalyptic conspiracies are right-wingers. One of the best-funded of the conspiracy-theory think tanks, the National Democratic Policy Committee, is run by conspiracy theorist Lyndon LaRouche, whose politics are so complex that he has been simultaneously accused of being funded by the KGB and the CIA. LaRouche counts among his enemies not only international bankers, the Federal Reserve System, and the Trilateralists, but also Ken Kesey, Bertrand Russell, *Playboy* magazine, Isaac Newton, the Nazis, the Jesuits, the Zionists, the Socialist International, and the Ku Klux Klan. LaRouche and his followers fit these pieces into a complex jigsaw puzzle, complete with its own economic model and electromagnetic wave theory. Despite the extreme nature of his beliefs LaRouche attracted enough political support to qualify for more than $560,000 in federal matching funds for his unsuccessful 1980 presidential campaign.

Some of the fears voiced by today's extremists are familiar themes in the history of political paranoia: the stereotype of Jews as both Communists and bankers was promoted in Germany by Hitler, in the United States by Henry Ford. Fears of world government were sounded by isolationists who opposed Woodrow Wilson's efforts to bring the United States into the League of Nations. In the 1950s, the John Birch Society condemned the United Nations as part of an international Communist plot. Later the society focused its wrath on the Trilateral Commission.

Historian Richard Hofstadter traced the political ideology of many conspiracy theorists back to the radical populists of the late nineteenth century, whose zealous support of the common man sometimes became twisted into paranoia. Many populists not only blamed Wall Street bankers for promoting a tight money policy that hurt farmers, they considered the bankers part of an international plot. Populist sympathy for oppressed farmers and laborers was often limited to the ones who happened to be white, Protestant, and American born. Immigrants —first Catholics, then Jews—were considered soldiers of a conspiracy run from the Vatican or the London offices of the Rothschild banking empire.

Other students of extremist politics have used a sociological approach to analyze political paranoia. Seymour Martin Lipset of Stanford University has shown that the phenomenon often erupts among those who feel their status in society is threatened by rival ethnic, religious, or political groups.

But neither the historical nor the sociological analysis explains why so many conspiracy theorists construct such strikingly similar world views. In case after case, bankers, Communists, the Trilateral Commission, and the Federal Reserve are believed to be acting in consort, plotting an economic disaster that will be followed by a dictatorial world economy, world government, or world church. One conspiracy theory overlaps with another, forming a giant web enclosing centuries and continents: wars, famines, and depressions are believed to be planned in advance; the news and even history itself are considered a stage play to amuse the masses while the real events transpire in secrecy.

The conspiracy theories share not only the same villains, but also a remarkably similar structure. The paranoid tradition is not simply a mishmash of irrational hysterias that have survived in America's political underground. The extremists construct their fantasies according to a coherent set of rules. Since the beginning of our country, fears of conspiratorial elites have been rationalized with superstructures so complex that they have a vocabulary and an internal logic—an architecture—of their own.

One favorite device of conspiracy theorists is to confuse label with object. In conspiracy theories ranging in complexity from the simple bigotry of the Posse Comitatus to the mind games of LaRouche, the conspirators are believed to be evil because they are internationalists. Jews seek to unite their people into an *international* Zionist community; the Vatican controls an *international* church; Communists support an *international* Marxist revolution; bankers run an *international* financial system; Trilateralists support *international* political and economic ties. And so the conspiracy theorists consider members of these groups not only traitors to U.S. sovereignty but coconspirators. It doesn't matter that the motivations of the groups are different, or that the internationalism of Zionism has nothing in common with the endeavors of multinational corporations. Anything international is linked to the same plot.

Using this kind of superficial thinking, conspiracies can be clicked together like Tinkertoys. Complex charts are drawn in which banks, foundations, corporations, political parties, and public-interest organizations are represented by boxes, then connected by lines into patterns as dense as the circuitry on a computer chip. To those who suspect conspiracies, there is nothing unfair about guilt by association. Their minds are rooted in the assumption that the world is divided between good and evil. If you aren't against the conspiracy—or if you don't believe it exists—you are abetting the enemy. There are only two sides to the fight.

In this grid-locked view of reality, no room is allowed for subtle arguments or unconscious motives. In the minds of the conspiracy theorists, the world is a machine and its gears mesh tightly; there is no slack. Everything bad that happens is part of a plot. *There are no accidents*—that assumption is at the root of political paranoia. As the John Birchers warn about Communists or the Posse Comitatus about the international bankers, each assumes a world in which everything—wars, depressions, droughts, and plagues—happens according to plan.

THE ILLUMINATI LEGEND

People who see the world as an arena where good and evil ceaselessly contend assume that events are shaped more by supernatural forces than by the decisions of man. Thus, many conspiracy theorists believe their foes are not simply clever people but possessors of extraordinary powers denied the common man. In some cases, the conspirators are seen simply as members of what Spiro Agnew called the "effete corps of impudent snobs who characterize themselves as intellectuals." They prevail over the forces of good because of an Ivy League education, inside knowledge, and the good-old-boys' network. They are an intellectual, financial elite. In other conspiracy theories, popular during the early 1960s, the conspirators control the minds of the people by brainwashing them in federally funded mental-health clinics or by spiking their water supplies with fluoride, which, one conspiracy theorist wrote, deadens "the rear occiput of the left lobe of the brain [which] contains brain tissue . . . responsible for the individual's power to resist domination."

In the most mysterious of the conspiracy theories, the conspirators' power is said to be derived from ancient secrets that supposedly have been passed down for centuries through a chain of secret societies. The names of esoteric groups such as the Gnostics, Rosicrucians, and Freemasons continually appear in conspiracy theories, along with the Trilateral Commission and the Communist International. Robert Welch, the founder of the John Birch Society, not only believed in an international

Communist conspiracy, but he also thought a group of master plotters called the Insiders or Illuminati controlled the Communists. Articles in the society's magazine, *American Opinion,* suggest the Insiders are heirs of an ongoing occult tradition.

Of course, the belief that history has been shaped by sorcery is centuries old. In its simplest form, the myth is this: since the days of Atlantis, a succession of secret societies has protected occult secrets, passing them down from century to century and elite to elite, always out of the reach of the masses. Those initiated into the mysteries of this esoteric tradition are called Illuminati, or "the enlightened." For almost two hundred years American conspiracy theorists have accused Jews, Catholics, Freemasons, bankers, Trilateralists, secular humanists—and, in the beginning of the American republic, Jeffersonians—of being agents of the Illuminati, the elite at the top of the political pyramid, who supposedly manipulate history by wielding supernatural powers.

A search of the literature purporting to describe Illuminati conspiracies yields hundreds of titles, published from the days of the French Revolution to the 1980s. Documentation in these works relies on pseudoscholarship: pages are heavily footnoted with references to dubious documents; chasms of logic are leaped in a single bound; coincidence is elevated to the status of cause-and-effect. If occult organizations of the twentieth century share ideas with similar groups that existed during the Enlightenment, the Middle Ages, and Golden Age Greece, it is assumed that they are part of a single, monolithic force.

While some conspiracy theorists use the word *Illuminati* as a general term for people supposedly in possession of occult forces, many use it to refer specifically to the Order of the Illuminati, an organization founded in 1776 at a Bavarian university by a rebellious professor named Adam Weishaupt, who wanted to bring the spirit of rationalism and the philosophical Age of Enlightenment to his benighted land. To those who supported religious faith over reason, Weishaupt was considered dangerous. Eleven years after its founding, the Bavarian Illuminati were denounced as subversive by the government and banned. But the legend lived on, and Weishaupt's Illuminati have been written into conspiracy theories that still circulate in the United States. In the 1980s, the John Birch Society sells anti-Illuminati books. The New Christian Crusade Church offers a series of tape cassettes describing Weishaupt's treachery. According to these legends, the symbol for the Illuminati conspiracy appears on the back of the one-dollar bill: an all-seeing eye atop a pyramid, taunting us with its hidden message each time we pay another dollar into a network engineered to keep us in darkness.

It is ironic that the Bavarian Illuminati have become linked to conspiracy theories along with groups interested in occultism. Weishaupt's organization supported the enlightenment of rationality and cosmopolitanism over that of the supernatural. They were Bavaria's secular humanists. But in the minds of the conspiracy theorists, seeming opposites often intertwine. Again, label is confused with object and both kinds of Illuminati—rationalists and occultists—are thought to be plotting together to overthrow established governments and religions. In political paranoia, the powers of reason and magic blur into a single enemy, both on the side of the devil. To the conspiracy theorists, rationalism is as satanic a force as black magic. To fight it, they build complex, teetering structures—the labyrinthine conspiracy theories that are parodies of reason.

THE NEW RIGHT

If political paranoia were limited to extremist organizations, it probably would present little threat to America's pluralistic society. But this world view is embedded deeply and more subtly in a large minority of the populace. Most of America's 30 million fundamentalist Protestants are not paranoid by any means, but their absolutist thinking has the same effect of squeezing reality into a rigid system.

The fundamentalists identify their enemies with Satan and believe the coming of a godless one-world government is foretold in the Bible. They believe the floods, famines, wars, and earthquakes predicted in the Book of Matthew are occurring, and that the Antichrist of the Book of Revelation will soon come to power, promising to lead us out of the confusion with an international empire. But this new world order will deny God and revere Satan. To destroy it, Jesus will make his Second Coming and defeat the forces of evil in the battle of Armageddon.

In many cases, Protestant fundamentalism and conspiracy theory are almost indistinguishable. The Antichrist's kingdom is identified with the United Nations, the Trilateral Commission, international communism, and, in some cases, world Zionism or the Catholic church. Communists are seen as evil because they are atheists, bankers because they are the usurers condemned in the Bible. As believers in "one true religion," some fundamentalists suspect that those of different persuasions —Catholics, Jews, or, more recently, secular humanists—are in the employ of the devil.

Evangelist Hal Lindsey, whose book of biblical prophecy, *The Late Great Planet Earth,* was the best-selling nonfiction book of the 1970s, believes the Trilateral Commission, secular humanism, and occultism are part of the Antichrist's one-world system. The estimated 7 million to 10 million people who regularly watch Christian television shows can tune in to the "700 Club" and hear Pat Robertson, president of the Christian Broadcasting Network, analyze the news according to Lindsey's scenario.

Illuminati-style conspiracy theories are also popular among leaders of the New Right, an alliance of conservative Christian organizations such as Moral Majority and right-wing political groups. Tim LaHaye, who is second in influence only to Jerry Falwell among the leaders of Moral Majority, teaches his followers that an elite of cosmopolitan intellectuals and secular humanists is conspiring to destroy Christianity and bring the United States into an atheistic world order. In his book, *The Battle for the Mind,* LaHaye actually includes Adam Weishaupt among the perpetrators of the plot. Phyllis Schlafly, founder of a New Right group called the Eagle Forum, showed a penchant for political paranoia as far back as 1964, when she wrote *A Choice Not an Echo,* in which she claimed that Rockefeller internationalists secretly run the Republican party, using "hidden persuaders and psychologial warfare techniques."

President Ronald Reagan fosters Illuminati-style conspiracy theories of his own. In a speech in March 1983 to the National Association of Evangelicals in Orlando, Florida, he used the Bible as justification for opposing the nuclear-freeze movement. Communism, Reagan said, is "the focus of evil in the modern world" and so "we are enjoined by Scripture and the Lord Jesus to oppose it with all our might." In an interview in 1981 on the Public Broadcasting System, journalist Ben Wattenberg asked Reagan to explain anti-American demonstrations in Europe. "Oh, those demonstrations," Reagan replied. "You could have used newsreels from the 1960s in America. Yes. Those are all sponsored by something called the World Peace Council, which is bought and paid for by the Soviet Union."

Liberals and conservatives would concede that the Soviet Union has tried to take advantage of Europe's fears of being used as a nuclear battleground. To what degree they have succeeded is a matter for discussion. But to those who see the world in Manichaean terms, debate is impossible. Reagan assumed the protesters were controlled by a force that is absolutely evil. They were not people with conflicting needs and desires but Satan's warriors.

To the anti-Illuminists, enemies are not wrong but evil. People are units, organizations are impenetrable monoliths. If an enemy is believed to be "run" by conspirators, then it is not necessary to fathom his ideas. Opponents are easily dehumanized.

The ideas of those who believe in the Illuminati conspiracy and of those who are accused of being Illuminati reflect the centuries-old battle between absolute truth and relativism, clericalism and secularism, Platonism and Aristotelianism—between the power of faith and the power of reason. It is no accident that the Illuminati conspiracy theory arose during a period we have come to call the Enlightenment or Age of Reason, when philosophy began to eclipse religion.

The war between faith and reason is still going on. The term *Illuminati* rarely appears in news reports of the struggle between creationists and evolutionists, "pro-lifers" and "pro-choicers," fundamentalists and secular humanists. But just as anti-Illuminism is implicit in the beliefs of such groups as the Moral Majority, so are the ideals ascribed to the Illuminati rooted in secular culture.

There are in this country two different intelligences, which pattern reality according to very different rules. Each considers the other an alien mind. In both cases, assumptions are so ingrained that their holders are hardly aware what they are assuming. This blindness makes discourse all but impossible, and the political process of negotiation and compromise breaks down. For both sides, understanding the other is of prime importance. By seeing what it is like to view the world as an immense conspiracy, perhaps the so-called Illuminati can learn to understand their opponents' fears. And by examining the historical roots of their assumptions, maybe the anti-Illuminists can attentuate their constant anger.

2

Philosophers and Magicians

"The [Illuminati] will seek to remain clandestine as much as possible, for whatever is secret and hidden has a special attraction for men; it attracts the interest of outsiders and enhances the loyalty of insiders. . . . It also gives the Order some protection from the impertinent curiosity of spies."
— from the statutes of the Bavarian Illuminati, 1781

If not for the work of conspiracy theorists, Adam Weishaupt and his Order of the Illuminati probably would be all but forgotten. The man who has been immortalized in dozens of right-wing pamphlets, books, and tape cassettes rates only two paragraphs in the *Encyclopedia Britannica*. Over time, the distorted story of the Illuminati has eclipsed the real one.

Weishaupt, who has been condemned by conspiracy theorists for almost two hundred years as an enemy of humanity, was described by Thomas Jefferson as "an enthusiastic philanthropist":

He is among those . . . who believe in the infinite perfectability of man. He thinks [man] may in time be rendered so perfect that he will be able to govern himself in every circumstance, so as to injure none, to do all the good he can, to leave government no occasion to exercise their powers over him, and, of course, to render political government useless. . . .

The means he proposes to effect this improvement of human nature are "to enlighten men, to correct their morals and inspire them with benevolence."

The process by which Weishaupt's rationalistic Illuminati have become linked by twentieth-century conspiracy theorists with both Communists and occultists is a tale worth recounting. In fact, the real story is as fascinating as the twisted versions spun by the conspiracy theorists. In the late eighteenth century, when Weishaupt was introducing philosophy to Bavaria, the line between rational and occult knowledge was not as clearly drawn as it is today—especially among followers of such secret societies as the Rosicrucians and Freemasons. It is largely because of Weishaupt's association with these groups that his Order of the Illuminati has become the centerpiece of contemporary conspiracy theories in which philosophers and magicians are seen as conspirators. And so the story of the rise of the Illuminati legend opens in the early 1600s, when Rosicrucianism began planting seeds that would grow into the paranoid fantasies of the twentieth-century American right.

THE INVISIBLE COLLEGE

In 1614, a document appeared in Germany titled *Fama Fraternitatis or a Discovery of the Fraternity of the Most Noble Order of the Rosy Cross*. It was followed a year later by *Confessio Fraternitatis or the Confession of the Laudable Fraternity of the Most Honorable Order of the Rosy Cross, Written to All the Learned of Europe*. The manifestos claimed to reveal the existence of a secret brotherhood, whose "most godly and highly illuminated father," Christian Rosencreutz, supposedly had traveled the East learning secret wisdom until his death in 1484 at the age of 106. Rosencreutz's disciples offered to reveal his wisdom to those willing to abandon Catholicism and the traditional scientific beliefs of the time. Then, the Rosicrucians promised, "the world shall awake out of her heavy and drowsy sleep, and with an open heart, bare-head, and bare-foot, shall merrily and joyfully meet the new arising Sun." As news of the manifestos spread from Germany to England and France, seekers after the enlightenment of the Rosicrucians published appeals to the brotherhood, asking to join.

In 1616, a third Rosicrucian publication appeared, *The Chemical Wedding of Christian Rosencreutz*. The seven-day ceremony it described could be read as a metaphor for the seven-step process by which the alchemists of that time claimed they could turn lead into gold. As was often true in alchemical writings, the transformation was presented as an allegory: it represented Rosencreutz's journey from the darkness of ignorance to the light of understanding the world's secrets. Although the writer of the manifestos referred to Jesus Christ and God, he made it clear that the knowledge the Rosicrucians promised was largely drawn from two schools of occult wisdom that had been popular during the Renaissance: Egyptian hermetic magic and the cabala of the Jews.

Since the Industrial Revolution of the eighteenth and nineteenth centuries, mankind has developed the belief that, as we accumulate knowledge, we progress toward understanding. But in medieval Europe, truth was more often considered something mankind had lost. Seekers looked to the past instead of the future. The older the knowledge, it was believed, the closer it might be to its source, the gods. Hermetic magic was based on the teachings of several books that, according to legend, were written at the beginning of civilization by Hermes Trismegistus (Thrice-Greatest Hermes), also known as the Egyptian god of wisdom, Thoth. It was Thoth, the scholars of Egypt had taught, who invented the sciences. In the books, astrological and alchemical teachings were combined with a world view in which the universe consisted of ten concentric spheres through which the soul must ascend to be regenerated from matter to pure spirit. As students of the hermetic texts pondered this image, they noticed how similar it was to that of the cabala.

The cabala, the other source of Rosicrucianism, was a system of Jewish mysticism that developed in Spain during the twelfth and thirteenth centuries but had its roots in teachings that went back at least as far as those of the Greek hermetics.

Cabala means "that which is received." According to tradition, the cabala was secretly taught by Moses as an esoteric supplement to the Old Testament. While the Bible was written for the masses, the cabala was intended for a scholarly elite. Initiates were said to have transmitted the knowledge orally from generation to generation for hundreds of years.

The cabalists took literally the biblical declaration that in the beginning was the Word. They believed God's Word generated the cosmos, and that the ten numerals and twenty-two letters of the Hebrew alphabet were the elements of which the world was made. The most holy word was the Tetragrammaton, the four letters of the name of God: YHVH or JHVH, which the uninitiated pronounced Yahweh or Jehovah. To the cabalists this sacred word was not to be uttered. They also believed that mystical teachings were hidden in the pages of the Bible—encoded to keep the information secret. By transforming the letters of biblical verses into numbers, performing calculations, and replacing words with ones of equivalent value, a secret story was said to unfold. Behind the revealed God of the Bible was a hidden God, described as the divine nothing, or the infinite. Surrounding this hidden God were ten spheres of "emanations" through which the void, in successive stages, became the world.

In both hermetic magic and the cabala, matter was seen as fallen godstuff, inferior to pure spirit. But in every object of creation was a spark seeking to free itself from its prison. Like the spheres of hermetic magic, those of the cabala came to be seen as tiers through which one's soul must travel to reach the holy light. As in the seven steps of alchemy, lead would, step by step, become gold.

To those who felt oppressed by the hardships of the material world, the hermetic-cabalistic system of the Rosicrucians offered a vision of harmony. All the world was alive, connected by a web of sympathies in which gold resonated with the sun, silver with the moon, iron with Mars, copper with Venus. Metals were believed to have sexual charge: sulfur was male, mercury female. They lived in the ground, aspiring to become gold. The earth was filled with a spirit that could be distilled into the magic philosopher's stone, to aid in the transformation of both rocks and souls. In an age when knowledge was often considered the monopoly of ecclesiastical authorities, the Rosicrucian manifestos offered the allure of a universe whose secrets were not only exciting and mysterious but accessible; through study and contemplation men could become as learned and powerful as priests and kings.

In 1623, seven years after the appearance of *The Chemical Wedding,* placards appeared in Paris announcing that the Rose Cross brothers were making "a visible and invisible" stay in the city. The order had come to be called the Invisible College, half because of its elusiveness, half as tribute to its mystical aims. But, as prospective members waited in vain for the writers of the manifestos to show themselves, the belief that there really was a secret brotherhood waned. Whether or not the Rosicrucians existed, supporters of the Catholic church began weaving the supposed society into conspiracy theories. In 1623, *Horrible Pacts Made between the Devil and the Pretended Invisible Ones* was published in Paris, claiming that a worldwide network of thirty-six Rosicrucians was tempting Catholics to renounce their faith.

Whether there really was a Rosicrucian society in the seventeenth century remains a mystery. A Lutheran theologian later admitted writing *The Chemical Wedding,* and historians suspect he wrote the other Rosicrucian works as well, perhaps as an attempt to reconcile ancient occult knowledge with Protestant Christianity. Although Christian Rosencreutz may never have existed, the Rosicrucian manifestos were influential. Many later groups called themselves Rosicrucians and claimed to be descended from the original sect. Today an international occultist organization based in San Jose, California, uses the name Ancient and Mystical Order Rosae Crucis, but a direct connection between later Rosicrucians and the writers of the manifestos is untraceable. It seems now that the original Rosy Cross Brotherhood existed only as a name and an idea. However, Rosicrucian philosophy—and its promise of ancient secrets—spread from Germany to England, where it influenced the Freemasons, who would become the subjects of still more conspiracy theories.

THE MASONIC CRAFT

Freemasonry is, according to its official definition, "a science of morality, veiled in allegory and illustrated by symbols." Since it was originally chartered in England in the early eighteenth century, the movement's members have met in secret lodges, conducting initiations, acting out rituals, and studying the complex mix of biblical, medieval, occult, and rationalist ideas that are part of the Masonic tradition. The aim of Freemasonry is to use its symbols and stories to teach its members the meaning of such virtues as honesty and cosmopolitanism and to help them lead noble lives, in concert with their fellow men. As members learn these Masonic "secrets," they rise through a hierarchy of degrees, each with its own symbols and rituals. While Freemasonry in the United States has come to be thought of as little more than a social organization for town fathers and businessmen, during the eighteenth century the Masonic lodges were havens for men who wished to study Enlightenment philosophy, occultism, and other ideas not sanctioned by the Catholic church.

That so controversial a movement grew out of a medieval union of English stoneworkers is one of the stranger developments of history. But there were needs and talents unique to the masons of the Middle Ages that foreshadowed Enlightenment ideals. Guilds representing other trades—coopers or blacksmiths, for example—were rooted in the towns, but the masons were migratory. Wherever a castle or cathedral was to be constructed, masons gathered, disbanding when the work was done. A system developed to ensure that a man seeking work was a skilled mason and member of the guild. By sharing secret signs, symbols, and passwords, masons were bound into an amorphous union. By agreeing to deal honestly and help one another, they became a brotherhood. Keeping rein on the secrets of the trade served as a method of quality control—and, as with modern trade associations, a monopoly developed that guaranteed employment by limiting the number of practitioners.

Early on, Masonry developed an aura of mystique. Its members possessed a power based not on royal or ecclesiastical authority but on knowledge, not only of stonecutting and mortaring but of the mysteries of ancient Greek geometers. The masons of the fourteenth and fifteenth centuries were as much architects as laborers. To the uninitiated, their work seemed holy. Since ancient Egypt, large stone edifices have been monuments to power, celebrating the magic of priests or the divine right of kings. As outsiders watched, men—some armed with chisels and mallets, others with compasses, rulers, levels, and squares—made temples grow from the ground.

By the early seventeenth century, the reverence for Masonry became so strong that gentlemen and professionals who knew nothing about stonework began to join Masonic lodges. These members became known as "accepted" or honorary masons. Some were attracted by the ideals of brotherhood: they thought the lodges would be good social clubs. Others were intrigued by the idea of being part of a tradition flavored with such a strong sense of antiquity. As the number of honorary masons grew, the movement began to have increasingly less to do with construction. Freemasons contemplated the possible esoteric meanings of Masonic secrets and developed a mythology tracing Masonry's lineage to the builders of Solomon's Temple and the Tower of Babel. Adam was described as the first Grand Master of Masonry. Enoch was said to have preserved the Masonic symbols by engraving them on columns before the flood.

By 1717, when four lodges in London joined to form the United Grand Lodge, the transition from so-called "operative" to "speculative" Freemasonry was complete. For the rest of the century, the lodges became homes for those who sought a brotherhood not based on class or bloodline but on the camaraderie of all mankind. In 1723, the English Freemasons published a Book of Constitutions, declaring that the organization would tolerate all religions.

The rituals of speculative Masonry, practiced by the 6 million Freemasons in the world today, still reflect these ideals. A stone, symbolizing man in the natural state, is to be shaped, polished, and fit into the building, which symbolizes the brotherhood of man. A first-degree Mason is responsible for "preparing stones." Upon initiation he is given a gavel, which symbolizes conscience; a chisel, which symbolizes education; and a twenty-four-inch ruler, which symbolizes the hours of the day. After studying more Masonic lore, an initiate becomes a second-degree or Fellow Craft Mason and is given a square (morality), a level (equality), and plumb (rectitude) to help build spiritual walls. Third-degree Master Masons are given a trowel to help cement the blocks together. The tool represents brotherly love. Other symbols, such as the pencil and compass, remind Masons that a Great Architect designed the universe according to a harmonious plan. Geometry is revered as an expression of these natural laws. Pythagoras and other ancient geometers are honored. One of the Masonic symbols is based on his theorem about right triangles. Another symbol—the all-seeing eye of Providence—is often inscribed inside a triangle.

Today the Masonic ideals seem commonplace, but by posing practical rules of conduct based on fraternity and equality rather than divine decree, the masons of eighteenth-century Europe were quietly opposing authority based on absolute truth. God, they believed, was an architect, not an autocrat. The Masonic lodges became havens for freethinkers to discuss controversial ideas. Members shared the belief that Freemasonry could promote a brotherhood that would transcend the boundaries of nation, social class, and religion. Freemasons in France, England, Germany—even in the United States—idealized themselves as members of an international movement.

In the eighteenth century, such cosmopolitanism was a radical notion, and only the more liberal rulers and aristocrats became Masons. Those who sought to keep power confined to established channels—the bloodlines of royal families or the chain of command that ascended from priest to bishop to cardinal to pope—saw Freemasonry as a threat. After all, anyone could join, If a member learned the symbols and rituals and practiced the Masonic ideals of honesty and fraternity, he could aspire to the highest degrees of the organization.

Freemasonry, wrote historian James H. Billington, was "a moral meritocracy—implicitly subversive within any static society based on a traditional hierarchy. Men of intelligence and ambition in the eighteenth century often experienced within Masonic lodges a kind of brotherhood among equals not to be found in the aristocratic society outside."

Although theoretically open to commoners, in practice the lodges came to be dominated by an elite of freethinking princes, Enlightenment philosophers such as D'Alembert and Voltaire, clergymen, and citizens of the upper class. In England, Freemasonry was not only tolerated but respected. Between 1737 and 1907, sixteen princes were Freemasons; four of them became kings. In the principalities of Germany, Freemasonry flourished—especially where liberal Protestants were in power. But in Catholic-dominated countries such as Bavaria and France, the rulers were very suspicious of what was being discussed in the lodges. To Catholics, Masonry was the latest heresy. In 1738, Pope Clement issued the first of a series of papal denunciations of Freemasonry, and as late as 1918, the Code of Canon Law forbade Catholics from joining "Masonic sects or any other similar associations which plot against the Church." To entrenched monarchs, the Masonic interest in egalitarianism was as threatening to their power as the study of Enlightenment philosophy was to the dogmas of the faith.

THE ESOTERIC TRADITION

Freed from the strictures of the Church, Freemasons sought truth on their own. While some concentrated on the rationalism and materialism of the Enlightenment philosophers, others turned their attention to the occult. They hoped to find secrets that had been known long ago and forgotten—or suppressed by the priests. As Freemasons studied the ideas of ancient and medieval cults, they began to embroider the legend that Freemasonry began in biblical times. They developed the myth that the Masonic secrets and symbols, which supposedly were given to Adam in the Garden of Eden, were passed along to the builders of the Egyptian pyramids, who worshiped the goddess Isis, then to ancient Greek cults such as the Pythagoreans and the Eleusinians. From these groups, the Masonic lore supposedly traveled through the ages via a chain of secret societies such as the Gnostics, Cathars, Knights Templar, and Rosicrucians. By contemplating the symbols of these an-

cient groups, many Freemasons hoped to discern esoteric secrets: new explanations for the way the world worked.

It was understandable that Freemasons were attracted to
the society of Pythagoras, a philosopher who lived from 580
B.C. to 500 B.C. Pythagoras taught his followers that numbers—as manifested in musical vibrations, the proportions of
geometry, and the motions of the stars and planets—reflected
the harmony of the universe. Pythagoras' students lived together in a communal society, practicing asceticism and purify-
ing their minds by learning geometry, arithmetic, astronomy,
and music. After five years of study, the members of the outer
circle, the *exoterici,* were initiated into the inner circle, or *esoterici,* where they learned mystical doctrines based on the relationships between numbers. Pythagoreanism was more a religion
than a science, but it presaged later attempts to explain the
universe mathematically.

The Freemasons also revered Pythagoras as a political revolutionary. He and his followers gained positions of power in
several Greek city-states, attempting to apply their idealistic
beliefs to government. But the experiment failed. Led by an
enemy of Pythagoras, a group of citizens rebelled and massa-
cred the philosopher-kings.

The Eleusinian cult, the next link in the esoteric chain,
was a pagan Greek religion that dated from the sixth or seventh
century B.C. The Eleusinians celebrated the myth of Persephone, the goddess of vegetation, who lived imprisoned in the
underworld but was allowed to return each spring to the earth's
surface. Like Persephone upon her return from darkness, and
the seeds that were planted beneath the surface of the earth, the
followers of the Eleusinian cult were annually reborn into light.
At a ceremony called the Lesser Mysteries—held near Athens in
spring—initiates purified themselves in the river Ilissus, ready-
ing themselves for the main event of the year, which was held
in autumn. During these Greater Mysteries, as they were
called, members walked fourteen miles to the temple in Eleusis
for four days of secret ceremonies. It has been speculated that
the rites involved reenactment of the Persephone myth, with a
priest and priestess copulating to symbolize the fertility of the
earth. But that might be antipagan propaganda. Despite what-

Egyptian Isis Worshipers
↓
Pythagoreans
↓
Greek Mystery Cults
↓
Gnostics
↓
Cathars
↓
Knights Templar
↓
Rosicrucians
↓
Freemasons

The Myth of the Esoteric Tradition

ever preliminaries did exist, toward the end of the ritual, members were led through caverns (to symbolize the underworld), then into an upper chamber flooded with torchlight. To the Masons, the Eleusinian rites symbolized their own search for enlightenment.

From the Pythagoreans and Eleusinians, the Freemasons often traced their tradition to the Gnostics, a rebel religious group condemned as heretics by the Catholic church during the first two centuries A.D. The Gnostics supposedly passed the Masonic secrets to the Cathars, another group of heretics, who were slaughtered by the Catholic church in the thirteenth century. According to legend, the Cathars gave the secrets to the Knights Templar, a chivalrous group whose members were condemned and burned to death in the fourteenth century by King Philip of France and Pope Clement. The king felt threatened by the wealth and power the Templars had accumulated during the Crusades, while the church blamed them for losing Jerusalem to the Moslems. Templars who survived the Inquisition were said to have taught the ancient secrets to the Rosicrucians, who then supposedly gave the secrets to the Freemasons.

As with most legends, the myth that teachings have been

handed down through a series of secret societies may contain
seeds of truth. Later occult societies certainly were influenced
to some extent by the doctrines of their predecessors. The
Rosicrucians' hermetic-cabalistic view of the universe as concentric spheres is similar to that of the Gnostics. The Gnostics,
Pythagoreans, and Cathars believed, like the Rosicrucians, that
each human contained a spark of the divine. And there are signs
of Rosicrucian influence in Masonry. A poem published in
1638 refers to Masonry as "the brethren of the Rosie Crosse."
A Masonic pamphlet published in 1676 gives notice "that the
Modern Green-ribbon'd Caball, together with the Ancient
Brotherhood of the Rosy Cross; the Hermetick Adepti and the
company of Accepted Masons intend to dine together on the 31
of November." It is unknown exactly what the relationship
was between Rosicrucianism and Freemasonry, but the craft
became infused with an interest in alchemy and hermetic-cabalistic symbols. One of the most well-known Masonic symbols,
a "G" in a triangle, may be a modern-day corruption of the
ancient symbol for the Tetragrammaton: the Hebrew letter *yod*
surrounded by a triangle.

Direct connections between the various secret societies,
however, existed largely in the imaginations of Freemasons,
who identified with these groups because they seemed to share
the spirit of brotherhoods formed to seek truth on their own.

As the body of occult legends and symbols grew, the
number of degrees in Masonry proliferated, especially in Germany and France. Soon there were more than thirty. By 1750,
the Rosicrucian spirit was commemorated in French Masonry
by a Rose Croix degree. At about the same time, an Order of
the Gold and Rosy Cross was formed in Germany. The Oriental Rite of Memphis, founded in Paris in 1814, eventually
claimed ninety-seven degrees, including Commander of the
Luminous Triangle, Sublime Sage of Isis, Doctor of the Sacred
Fire, and Sublime Master of the Luminous Ring. Conservative
Masons regarded the new degrees and occult interests as cor-
ruptions of what started as a fairly simple system. The Masonic
hierarchy was becoming as complex as the concentric spheres
of the hermetic-cabalistic universe. There seemed to be an al-

most endless number of tiers through which a member must ascend to attain spiritual regeneration.

It is strange that the Freemasons, whose members included such rationalists as Benjamin Franklin, Voltaire, and George Washington, took an interest in teachings that included what we now consider mysticism. But in the eighteenth century, the difference between the scientific and occult was only beginning to become distinct. Men who found Freemasonry a vehicle for the new spirit of exploration were as likely to examine reprints of hermetic texts as recent works on materialism. Empiricism had not yet dominated the scientific mind. Even Isaac Newton was far from being a strict materialist, mixing his scientific and mathematical studies with an interest in biblical prophecy and alchemy. Included in his library were English translations of the first two Rosicrucian manifestos, although a note he wrote in the book may indicate that he considered the movement a hoax. In her study, *The Rosicrucian Enlightenment,* historian Frances Yates showed that Francis Bacon, revered now as an early champion of experimental science, was influenced by Rosicrucian mysticism, and that the Royal Society, the prestigious scientific organization, may have been founded by Rosicrucian sympathizers. To avoid being victims of a witch hunt, Yates suggested, the members played down their more controversial beliefs.

Even Descartes, whose mechanistic description of the universe was a forerunner of modern science, was attracted to mysticism. Ironically, his decision to seek the mysteries of nature in mathematics came to him in a visionary dream while he was serving as a soldier in Germany. It was around that time that he heard about the Brotherhood of the Rosy Cross. Like others interested in cosmic secrets, he sought to join the order, waited in vain to be contacted, and finally gave up.

THE ORDER OF THE ILLUMINATI

By the late 1700s, when Adam Weishaupt founded the Order of the Illuminati, there already was a tradition of independent thinkers who opposed the dogmas of the Catholic faith by looking to both new and ancient ideas. Weishaupt was fascinated by the old secret societies, considering them ideal models for a modern organization dedicated to introducing Enlightenment philosophy to the backward country of Bavaria.

The philosophers Weishaupt revered opposed the church by attempting to define a morality independent of religion. They replaced God's decrees with social contracts and rationalist systems of ethics. Some of the philosophers were deists: like the Freemasons, they saw God not as an autocrat who should be worshiped but as an architect or mathematician, whose perfect creation should be appreciated through science and philosophy. Others were avowed atheists. All of them supported egalitarianism and cosmopolitanism, believing that man, not God, was the measure of all things.

Outside Bavaria, these revolutionary ideas were spreading. In nearby Berlin, Frederick the Great, the liberal king of Prussia, had been corresponding with the anticlerical writer Voltaire for twelve years. In France, the philosophers Diderot and D'Alembert were beginning work on their *Encyclopedia,* a celebration of reason and science over faith. But in Bavaria the Jesuits were still firmly in control. As spiritual allies and confessors of the country's rulers, they had been entrenched in Bavarian politics for years. They considered French philosophy a danger to the religious doctrines that were the basis of their power.

But, by the time Weishaupt was a young adult, the Jesuits were finding it harder to keep new ideas from crossing the Bavarian frontier. In 1745, a relatively liberal ruler, Maximilian Joseph, came to power. Weishaupt's godfather was appointed curator of the University of Ingolstadt and began introducing books that had been banned by the Jesuits. In 1772, his godchild joined the faculty as a professor of law.

It wasn't long before the Jesuits became disturbed by Weishaupt's philosophical interests and his outspoken opposition to the church. In 1775, the rift widened when the twenty-seven-year-old professor was appointed to the chair of canon law, which had been held by the Jesuits for ninety years. Weishaupt, denounced as a freethinker, began to organize a secret society to oppose the power of the church.

The purpose of the Order of the Illuminati, as described

in its statutes, was "to encourage a humane and sociable outlook; to inhibit all vicious impulses; to support Virtue, wherever she is threatened or oppressed by Vice; to further the advance of deserving persons and to spread useful knowledge among the broad mass of people who were at present deprived of all education."

Through the Illuminati, Weishaupt hoped to build a world where the divisions of class, religion, and nation were overcome and all people were united in a universal brotherhood. Like the French philosopher Rousseau, Weishaupt envisioned a day when mankind would regain a natural state of equality and happiness, uncorrupted by organized religion and class distinctions.

Because of the repressive church-state hierarchy he was opposing, Weishaupt knew he had to keep his society secret. Like the Freemasons, members met in secret lodges. Students were awarded ranks and titles reminiscent of those of Freemasonry. Because of his love for antiquity, he decided to adopt the methods of indoctrination and discipline used by the Pythagoreans and Eleusinians. Perhaps Weishaupt, who prided himself in his hatred of superstition, felt that introducing rationalist philosophy to eighteenth-century Bavaria required adepts as dedicated to their studies as the Pythagoreans, and that inspiring students to become enlightened required the appeal of secrecy and ritual that had infused the Eleusinian Mysteries.

On May 1, 1776, he founded the Order of the Illuminati as a cult of reason. Like the Pythagoreans, Weishaupt's followers began as *exoterici,* studying their way, ring by ring, to the inner circle, the *esoterici,* or enlightened. As the disciples ascended the ranks, the preoccupation with ritual and symbolism gradually diminished, giving way to the study of philosophy and the development of an egalitarian morality. Initiates started with the philosophical classics, working their way up to the more radical French thinkers. Eventually, as the hierarchy grew more complex, initiates could aspire to learn what Weishaupt called the Lesser Mysteries and the Greater Mysteries, finally becoming Areopagites, named after the members of the ancient high court of Athens. Step by step, the initiates would rise

from the darkness of false power and be reborn—illuminated—
through reason.

While training their followers, the Illuminati leaders enforced a sense of obedience and intrigue like that of their opponents, the Jesuits. When exchanging letters, they protectively
encoded information. Illuminati leaders and the locations of
lodges were referred to by secret names borrowed from ancient
times. Weishaupt took the name Spartacus, leader of a revolt of
slaves. In correspondence, Ingolstadt was sometimes referred
to as Eleusis. To protect the society from infiltration, members
kept each other under surveillance and filed reports with their
superiors. Members in the lower ranks weren't allowed to
know the identities of those on the tiers above them. Only the
Areopagites were supposed to know that Weishaupt was the
Illuminati's leader.

While members knew they were part of an organization
dedicated to studying philosophy, it was only when they had
become advanced in their training that they learned the society's ultimate aim: by spreading Enlightenment philosophy, recruiting influential members, and working their way into government posts, members would bring about a bloodless
revolution, redeeming the world from the tyrannies of church,
state, and superstition.

Weishaupt's strict disciplinary measures and fascination
with subterfuge seemed to contradict his dream of universal
brotherhood. Enlightening Bavaria and the world was so con-
suming a mission that he took to heart the dictum of his enemies, the Jesuits, that the end justifies the means. He was tired,
he wrote, of those who "go into ecstasies over antiquity, but
are themselves unable to do anything." What was needed, he
believed, was a "force to put into practice what has long been
affirmed by our minds." The object was "neither to conquer
territories nor to impose authority, nor to gather riches . . .
[but] the more difficult conquest of individuals."

It is not enough, wrote Weishaupt, that followers be
passively obedient: "Their total confidence without reserva-
tion, their enthusiasm, must be gained." Then they could be
trained to become an elite, a vanguard to lead the people out of
darkness.

The organization started with five members. Three years

later there were five Illuminati lodges, including one in Munich, and about sixty members. Then an influential German diplomat named Baron Adolf Francis Knigge joined the order and helped Weishaupt with a plan to infiltrate European Freemasonry. Knigge toned down the movement's anticlericalism and made the organization less despotic. He added new layers to the hierarchical pyramid, providing a system of ranks through which Masons could become Illuminati and Illuminati could enter the already elaborate circuitry of Masonry.

The Masonic lodges were, for Weishaupt, fertile recruiting grounds. During the next eight years, the order expanded to Austria, Switzerland, Italy, Bohemia, and Hungary. By the time it reached its peak in 1784, it had, according to varying estimates, as many as 2000 to 4000 members, mostly students, merchants, doctors, pharmacists, lawyers, judges, professors, government officials, and even a few renegade priests. Dukes, princes, counts, and barons became Illuminati. The philosopher Herder, the poet Goethe, Prince Metternich's father, and Beethoven's teacher, Christian Neefe, all were Illuminati. According to some accounts, Mozart and Schiller also were members.

THE ILLUMINATI SUPPRESSION

Although, in Freemasonry, philosophy and occultism often intertwined, sometimes there were conflicts between Masons who preferred one approach to the other. At a conference called in 1782 in Wilhelmsbad, Germany, to resolve disputes between various Masonic movements, Weishaupt and the Illuminati sided with the rationalists against those who preferred the mystical traditions of the Rosicrucians. The Illuminati believed Freemasonic mysticism should be eclipsed by philosophy and reason. But the neo-Rosicrucians of Germany feared Enlightenment rationality as a challenge to their beliefs. Some Rosicrucians became so reactionary in their opposition to reason that they sought political protection by allying themselves with conservative kings. When the reactionary King Frederick William II succeeded the liberal Frederick the Great as ruler of Prussia, he bowed to the wishes of his Rosicrucian advisers and instituted religious edicts censoring rationalist writers, including Immanuel Kant.

In their opposition to the occult strains of Freemasonry,

some of Weishaupt's Illuminati became fanatics themselves, concocting a conspiracy theory in which the Jesuits supposedly introduced occultism into Freemasonry to undermine the movement. It was true that after the pope temporarily disbanded the Jesuits in 1773, some members joined the conservative Rosicrucians in their efforts to oppose the rationalist influence of the Illuminati. But it seems that Weishaupt's followers were betraying a touch of paranoia, perhaps because their movement was threatened by internal dissension and pressure from the Bavarian government.

Shortly after the Wilhelmsbad conference, Knigge, the man responsible for spreading the Illuminati's influence into Freemasonry, resigned after Weishaupt refused to make the society more religious and mystical. And, in 1784, the Bavarian rulers began a campaign to eliminate the organization.

The liberal ruler of Bavaria, Maximilian Joseph, had been succeeded by a conservative regime, led by a duke named Carl Theodore. When the duke's sister received a letter, apparently from an Illuminati defector, accusing the order of deriding religion and patriotism and of working for the Austrian government, Carl Theodore became suspicious of a plot to take over Bavaria. Encouraged by his confessor, a Jesuit and Rosicrucian named Ignaz Frank, Theodore issued an edict banning all unauthorized societies.

By 1785, when a second edict was released that explicitly condemned the Illuminati and Freemasons, Weishaupt had left the country, ostensibly because of a dispute with Jesuits who opposed his attempts to introduce books on skepticism and biblical criticism into the university library. He stayed for a while with a fellow Illuminatus in Regensburg. But the friend —by an act of God, the clergy said—was struck and killed by lightning. Weishaupt then moved to Gotha, where the duke was an Illuminatus, and began writing pamphlets defending his order. But the purge had begun.

A Bavarian commission in charge of interrogations discovered that Weishaupt's goal of infiltrating the government and educational establishment had been a minor success. Students, professors, and officers of the church and state were dismissed for being Illuminati. Sympathizers were considered security risks and removed from their posts in government. In 1786, the house of a former member who had fled the country was raided and Illuminati documents were seized, including books, papers, and more than two hundred letters exchanged by Weishaupt and his followers.

In the furor surrounding the Illuminati scandal, Weishaupt's plans for a peaceful revolution sounded like sedition. The sinister aura surrounding the society was enhanced by the revelation of secret symbols and initiation rites. The public was shocked by writings favoring atheism and the right to commit suicide. There were instructions for counterfeiting seals and making secret inks. Descriptions of chemical experiments sounded suspiciously like attempts to make poison. The papers revealed that Weishaupt, while seeking a papal dispensation to marry his sister-in-law (his first wife had died), had got the woman pregnant and was seeking a means of abortion. The papers were edited by a commission consisting largely of Illuminati defectors and published by the Bavarian government. On August 16, 1787, Carl Theodore issued a third edict: any member found guilty of recruiting for the order would face death by sword. The Order of the Illuminati officially ceased to exist, and the Illuminati conspiracy theory began.

The legends coined during the Illuminati supression would be recycled for almost two hundred years, flourishing whenever people feared new ideas. In the late eighteenth century, pamphlets were printed whose contents appeared later in books that were cited in footnotes to still more books. A bibliographic chain had begun. Before 1790, more than fifty works about the Illuminati were published, many claiming that the society had not dissolved after its banishment but had gone underground.

One early example of an Illuminati conspiracy theory, *Exposure of the Cosmopolitan System,* was published in Leipzig in 1786. In the book, a young man proudly tells his father that he has joined a Masonic lodge and become initiated into its cosmopolitan vision. "You are either a loyal subject or a rebel," the angry father replies, "there is no third possibility." When the son learns that Masonry has been infiltrated by the Illuminati, he becomes disillusioned and confronts a leader of the group: "You mean to make universal this religion of pure reason—this joyless, formless, heartless metaphysical creation which has emerged from some dry brain?"

"Precisely," his superior replies.

In an interesting twist of logic, the writer of the book, a Protestant, speculated that the Jesuits were part of the Illuminati. In countries firmly under Vatican control, he claimed, the Jesuits championed dogma and superstition. In apostate nations they promoted the Enlightenment "with the deliberate purpose of blinding the people through an excess of light." Those who had left the Church to become Protestants would be stripped by philosophy of the belief that anything was holy or absolute. Faced with the void of pure reason, they would return to the comfort of the Church.

As the Illuminati conspiracy theory spread from Germany to France, its convolutions became even more complex.

3

Thomas Jefferson, Illuminatus

"Shall we, my brethren, become partakers of these sins? Shall we introduce them into our government, our schools, our families? Shall our sons become the disciples of Voltaire, and the dragoons of Marat; or our daughters the concubines of the Illuminati?"
—Timothy Dwight,
president of Yale University, 1798

Before the French Revolution began in 1789, the seeds of the Illuminati conspiracy theory had been scattered, in the form of pamphlets, in Germany and France. Then the fear aroused by the revolt of the commoners against the French monarchy and its ally, the Catholic church, compelled supporters of this so-called *ancien régime* to arrange the bits and pieces of the Illuminati legend into stories of elaborate plots. Surrounded by what seemed to them like chaos, the supporters of the church-state alliance hoped to find a system to explain a world that seemed to them turned upside down. Many of the conservatives couldn't understand what—besides a satanic conspiracy—could be motivating the revolutionaries in their attacks on church and king. During the first year of the revolution, the commoners established their own government and curbed the powers of the clergy, aristocracy, and monarchy. Almost immediately afterward, the revolutionary government nationalized church property. A year later, religious orders were sup-

51

pressed. In the churches, the revolutionaries replaced statues of saints with ones honoring such philosophers as the anti-Catholic Voltaire. A new calendar was instituted, replacing Christian holidays with feast days celebrating Virtue, Genius, Labor, and Reason instead of saints. To supporters of the old established order, the revolution seemed to be fulfilling agendas set earlier in the century by the Enlightenment philosophers. It was comforting for the conservatives to think the turmoil was the result of a plot by a small elite rather than the result of inexorable change. Then the conspirators could be eliminated and the old order restored.

First the French conspiracy theorists blamed the church's old enemy, the Freemasons, for engineering the revolution. With anti-Illuminati propaganda floating around Europe, Weishaupt's society was soon written into the plot. His hopes for a cosmopolitan brotherhood based on reason instead of faith was interpreted as a conspiracy to overthrow all nations and churches and tie them into an international, atheist state.

It was true that leaders of the revolution, such as Lafayette and the Duke of Orleans, were Masons, as were such radical philosophers as D'Alembert and Voltaire. The Club Breton, forerunner of the revolutionary Jacobin Club, had been formed by Masons. And the *Cercle Social,* publisher of a revolutionary journal, was influenced by Weishaupt's Illuminati. Its founder, Nicholas Bonneville, was a Mason. In Paris he had met Christian Bode, an Illuminati leader who had come to speak to a Masonic lodge. Bonneville called on Freemasons to support the revolution. He even advocated membership in Masonry as a requirement for holding public office.

As with other Freemasons, Bonneville's republican ideals were mixed with an interest in mysticism and ancient secret societies. He believed the father of the revolutionary spirit was Pythagoras, who "brought from the Orient his system of true Masonic instruction to illuminate the occident." Bonneville was so enamored of Weishaupt's movement that he was accused of making "the title of citizen a grade of Illuminism." He conceived of his own revolutionary elite, the *Cercle Social,* as the center of a flame that would radiate outward in "magic circles," illuminating mankind. A member of Bonneville's group, Sylvain Marechal, glorified Pythagoras in a six-volume work called *Voyages of Pythagoras*, claiming that one of the ancient Greek mystic's rules for revolution was that "the history of an entire people often lies entirely in the life of a handful of men."

Because of their reverence for geometry, Freemasons had long honored Pythagoras. Now Masonic triangle symbols appeared in revolutionary seals. Marechal identified himself by the initials HSD (*l'homme sans dieu*, "man without God") and sometimes inscribed them inside a triangle. To the revolutionaries, geometrical symbols invoked the idea of a Pythagorean harmony that would be achieved when they established their new secular orders. Geometric simplicity would replace the roccoco style of the aristocrats.

The paranoia of supporters of the *ancien régime* was inflamed by other Illuminati connections. The Duke of Orléans's physician was an ex-Illuminatus. An ex-Illuminatus named Jakob Mauvillon was a friend of another revolutionary leader, Count Mirabeau, and helped him write a book praising rationalist goals. A revolutionary journal written by Italian students who had studied in Bavaria praised Weishaupt's Illuminati as "the company which Count Mirabeau has compared to the Priests of Eleusis."

Historians examining the causes of the French Revolution agree that Freemasons played active roles—but as individuals with a common spirit, not as agents of a conspiracy. While Masonic ideals contributed to the revolutionary fervor, many Freemasons remained staunch supporters of the establishment. One Masonic lodge produced revolutionary politicians, including two who voted in favor of executing the king. Yet six members of the lodge were themselves guillotined, as was the Duke of Orléans. But to those who couldn't understand the revolution as a spontaneous uprising, Freemasonry seemed the likely vehicle of a plot.

As early as 1791, a French priest, the Abbe Lefranc, compiled anti-Masonic writings and published a description of a Protestant-Freemason plot. The legend was expanded that year by the notorious Count Cagliostro, a magician and healer who charmed the upper classes of Paris and invented his own Egyptian-Masonic rite. When he was arrested later in Italy by the Inquisition and accused of heresy and fraud, he claimed to know of a worldwide Illuminati-Freemason conspiracy to overthrow the French royalty and the papacy. Cagliostro's story is now dismissed by historians as a failed attempt to gain leniency; he was given a life sentence and died in prison. But his accusations about the Illuminati were quickly published in Italian, French, and English. The following year, Lefranc picked up on the Illuminati strain, weaving it into his conspiracy theory.

In 1796, a new version of the Masonic conspiracy theory appeared that included the Knights Templar, the crusaders who were vanquished in the fourteenth century by King Philip of France and Pope Clement. According to this version of the theory, the Templars' leader, Jacques DeMolay, had vowed his revenge for the destruction of his order while he was in prison —coincidentally, on the site of the Bastille. DeMolay's descendants, the Masons, supposedly were carrying out his wishes by starting the French Revolution.

As proof, the conspiracy theorists pointed to the existence in French Freemasonry of Templar "Grades of Vengeance" that commemorated DeMolay, who was seen as a kindred spirit in the fight against the powers of church and state. In their rituals, Freemasons symbolically avenged his death. (In the United States, DeMolay's name lives on through the efforts of the Order of DeMolay, a nine-degree Masonic organization for teenage boys.)

As the revolution proceeded, attempts to explain the seeming madness became more elaborate. The DeMolay conspiracy theory came to include Oliver Cromwell, the Jesuits, Cagliostro, and the Assassins, an Islamic sect of hashish-smoking killers who supposedly had become allies of the Templars during the Crusades. Another priest, Abbe Fiard, attributed to the conspirators powers of wizardry. To the conspiracy theorists, the magicians were in league with the philosophers. As evidence they cited an anti-Illuminati book published in 1788 called *Essai sur la secte des Illuminés,* by the Marquis de Luchet; he was a rationalist who was helping Prince Henry of Prussia, the brother of Frederick the Great, fight the conservative political influence of the mystical Rosicrucians. By *illuminés,* Luchet meant mystics. But the term was confused with Weishaupt's Illuminati.

With so many conspiracy theories circulating, it was only a matter of time before a more fully developed anti-Illuminati history evolved. In the 1790s, a Frenchman, Abbe Barruel, and a Scotsman, John Robison, compiled the assorted theories into two international best-sellers: *Memoirs of Jacobinism* and *Proofs of a Conspiracy Against All the Religions and Governments of Europe, Carried On in the Secret Meetings of Free Masons, Illuminati, and Reading Societies, Collected From Good Authorities.*

Robison, a mathematician, professor of natural philosophy at the University of Edinburgh, and general secretary of the Royal Society of Edinburgh, was so respected a scientist that he was asked to contribute to the third edition of *Encyclopedia Britannica* articles on the telescope, optics, hydrodynamics, magnetism, seamanship, and music. Although he had been inducted into English Freemasonry, he considered it a system of trivial rituals, an excuse for men to socialize. He was astounded to pick up a German magazine and learn of the strange developments in European Freemasonry. He read the Illuminati documents published by the Bavarian government and a journal produced in Vienna by an ex-Illuminatus who had given up his chair of language and literature at the university to write against his former colleagues.

The result of Robison's research was a book in which he approached the subject of a world conspiracy with the cool detachment of the British empiricist, the skeptical man of letters. He wrote with pride of how sensible, "homespun" British Masonry was corrupted by the French love for pageantry and the German fascination with mysticism. As he described grown men flocking to Masonry in hope of learning the secrets of raising ghosts and transmuting metals, he assumed an air of bemused detachment. He tried to be fair. He could see how, in France, government and religious oppression might have compelled men to secrecy. He could understand that the excesses of the Catholic church could drive men to denounce all religion.

But when he came to the story of Weishaupt and the Illuminati, he abandoned his even tone. He was shocked at the letter published by the Bavarian government in which Weishaupt asked an associate for help in finding an abortionist for his pregnant sister-in-law. He gloated over correspondence in which Weishaupt complained of the loose morals of some of his associates. Robison was equally disgusted with Weishaupt's idea that reason alone would make men happy, that cosmopolitanism and equality were unquestionably good.

God made men unequal, Robison wrote, and the world worked correctly when everyone was in his place. Certainly there were abuses of power, but Weishaupt's Illuminism would ensure "that the innocent rich may be robbed with impunity by the idle and profligate poor." Robison's ideal society was that of Britain, a limited monarchy where people were free but knew their stations.

Proofs of a Conspiracy was published in 1797. By 1798, four editions were in print. During the next two years the book was translated into French, German, and Dutch. It would be republished in 1967 in the United States by the John Birch Society, becoming a source for present-day conspiracy theorists. But in its day it was eclipsed by the four-volume work of Abbe Barruel. Between 1797 and 1798, Barruel's *Memoirs of Jacobinism* was published. Written in French, it was reprinted in five volumes in Hamburg, Augsburg, and Braunschweig, Germany; London; Hartford, Connecticut; New York; and Elizabethtown, New Jersey. The book was eventually translated into Polish, Dutch, Portugese, Spanish, and Italian.

Barruel was a Jesuit. During the early part of the French Revolution, he wrote pamphlets opposing the anticlerical reforms. When the revolution became too violent, he fled to England and began formulating his theory of a conspiracy of French philosophers and Illuminati. Barruel believed that the "Sophisters of Impiety" (Voltaire, D'Alembert, Frederick the Great, and Diderot), the "Sophisters of Rebellion" (Voltaire, Montesquieu, and Rousseau), and the "Sophisters of Impiety and Anarchy" (the Bavarian Illuminati) were part of an ongoing attempt to overthrow not just the French Catholic church and monarchy but all religions. And, Barruel wrote, the conspirators aimed at the *"entire, absolute and universal overthrow of all PROPERTY whatever."*

Barruel devoted one volume to each of the factions; the fourth volume showed how the conspiracy culminated in the radical Jacobin Club, which supposedly masterminded the revolution. Like Robison, Barruel recycled the story of Christian Bode, the Illuminatus who visited a French Masonic lodge, carrying Weishaupt's spark to French Masonry and igniting the revolution. To add historical perspective, Barruel tied the medieval Templars and Cathars into the plot. By the time he wrote his book, French armies were engaged in battles all over Europe. Barruel saw them as exporters of revolution. "As the plague flies on the wings of the wind," he wrote, "so do their triumphant legions infect America   God grant that the United States may not learn to their cost, that Republics are equally menaced with Monarchies; and that the immensity of the ocean is but a feeble barrier against the universal conspiracy of the Sect!"

THE NEW ENGLAND ILLUMINATI SCARE

The year after it was published, copies of *Proofs of a Conspiracy* arrived in New York and Philadelphia. By November, Barruel's *Memoirs of Jacobinism*, translated into English, were being serialized in the *Connecticut Courant,* published in Hartford, and Boston's *Massachusetts Mercury.* To the Federalist politicians and Congregationalist clergy, who formed what was known as New England's Standing Order—a church-state alliance of aristocrats who distrusted democracy—the Illuminati conspiracy theory became something of a sensation.

The members of the Standing Order believed the country was best ruled by an educated, moneyed elite who knew what was best for the people. They believed democracy would lead to mob rule. As heirs of the Puritans, the Congregationalists hated French Enlightenment philosophy, which they believed championed not only secularism, but also atheism and anarchy. The Federalists believed that government by the people was dangerous. They thought the passions of the masses must be reined in by leaders cognizant of what Federalist John Adams called "eternal and immutable laws of justice."

"All communities divide themselves into the few and the many," the Federalist Alexander Hamilton wrote.

> The first are the rich and wellborn, the other the mass of the people. . . . The people are turbulent and changing; they seldom judge or determine right. Give therefore to the first class a distinct, permanent share in the government. They will check the unsteadiness of the second, and as they cannot receive any advantage by a change, they therefore will ever maintain good government.

At other times, Hamilton was even less restrained in his attack on democracy. "The people!" he once exclaimed. "The people is a great beast!" He considered the French Revolution a sign of the atrocities this beast could commit. Revolutionaries espousing the ideals of the Enlightenment philosophers had executed King Louis XVI and Marie Antoinette, as well as thousands of citizens deemed counterrevolutionaries by Robespierre and Marat. As news of this "Reign of Terror" crossed the Atlantic, members of the Standing Order became convinced that the minds of the French had been infected with a madness that was filtering to the United States.

Since the end of the American Revolution, a spirit of secularism had been challenging the old Puritan religious order. Thomas Jefferson's Democrats (or Democratic-Republicans, as they were called then) opposed the notion that Congregationalism should continue to be the state-supported religion of Massachusetts and Connecticut. While Jefferson and his followers deplored the violence of the French Revolution, they agreed with its ideals.

In 1798, an annual convention of Massachusetts's Congregationalist clergy condemned "those atheistical, licentious and disorganizing principles which have been avowed and zealously propagated by the philosophers and politicians of France." The Federalists began to fear a conspiracy between France and the Jeffersonians to overthrow the Standing Order, just as the French revolutionaries had toppled the *ancien régime*. The democratic societies that formed in the United States in support of

French ideals were compared to the Jacobin Clubs, effectors of the Reign of Terror. Jefferson, who made no secret of his admiration for the French Enlightenment, was denounced as the Antichrist. It was in this spirit that in 1798, President Adams secured passage of the Alien and Sedition Acts, giving him power to deport aliens suspected of "treasonable or secret machinations" and punish citizens who were illegally conspiring, assembling, or publishing false, scandalous, and malicious writings.

When the conspiracy theories of Robison and Barruel arrived in the United States, members of the Federalist-Congregationalist alliance began invoking the specter of a worldwide Illuminati plot as justification for suppressing dissent. Adams's wife, Abigail, encouraged her friends to read Barruel. In April 1798, the Reverend Jedediah Morse, a leading spokesman of the Standing Order, bought a copy of Robison's *Proofs of a Conspiracy* in Philadelphia. In the book he read that, according to Robison's estimate, eight Illuminati lodges had formed in England, two in Scotland, and several in the United States.

On May 9, when President Adams called for a day of fasting and prayer for the endangered republic, Morse stood before the congregation at the New North Church of Boston and said: "As a faithful watchman I would give you warning of your present danger."

> Secret and systematic means have been adopted and pursued, with zeal and activity, by wicked and artful men, in foreign countries, to undermine the foundations of this Religion, and to overthrow its Altars. . . . These impious conspirators and philosophists have completely effected their purposes in a large portion of Europe, and boast of their means of accomplishing their plans in all parts of Christendom.

The conspirators, of course, were the French. But behind their plans, Morse told the congregation, were Adam Weishaupt's Illuminati. Since its establishment in Germany more than twenty years before, Morse said, this secret society had aimed "to root out and abolish Christianity, and overthrow all civil government." The Illuminati approved of suicide and promiscuity, he said, and condemned patriotism and private property. They infiltrated schools, newspapers, and literary societies with their ideas. They had plotted the revolution in France. Now they had bases in America: the democratic societies. The publication of Tom Paine's *Age of Reason* was, he said, part of the plot.

Once the sermon was published, newspapers in Boston, Philadelphia, Hartford, and New York began debating whether there was indeed an Illuminati conspiracy. On June 19, the Reverend David Tappan, a divinity professor, warned the Harvard senior class about the Illuminati, who "while deluding mankind with a beautiful picture of virtue . . . were themselves stained with vices of the most gross, savage, and monstrous complexion." On July 4, Timothy Dwight, who, as president of Yale University, was so high in the Standing Order that he was referred to as Pope Dwight, warned the people of New Haven of a conspiracy of infidels who were plotting to turn New England's churches into "temples of reason."

On the same day, Dwight's brother, Theodore, spoke in Hartford against the Illuminati, suggesting that Jefferson might be one of them. When a Lutheran minister wrote to George Washington about the plot, Washington replied that he had indeed heard of "the nefarious and dangerous plan and doctrines of the Illuminati" but that he was certain American Freemasonry, of which he was a leader, was not involved.

For months the debate continued. Morse suggested that the American Society of Irishmen, a group of exiled Irish republicans, was an Illuminati front. When the *American Mercury* of Hartford, Connecticut, published its annual New Year's Day poem, it included the verse:

> From Anno Lucis *till out time*
> *Masonic Treason's been a crime:*
> Now Robison's *in every pocket,*
> *And up he's flown to fame, like [a] rocket.*

But a backlash was developing. Newspapers printed letters demanding that Morse prove his claims. In August and September, he wrote eleven articles in the *Massachusetts Mercury* in reply, but he was unable to demonstrate the existence of

American Illuminati. Although he had been careful to write—
in a footnote to his first Illuminati sermon—that he did not
believe American Masonry was involved in the conspiracy,
members of the lodges felt threatened by the scare. When leaders of the Vermont Grand Lodge protested to President
Adams, he assured them they weren't under suspicion. But he
expressed concern that Masonry's "wonderful power of enabling and compelling all men . . . to keep a secret" conceiv-
ably could result in insurrection.

In 1799, Adams called for another day of fasting, warning
that the "most precious interests of the people of the United
States are still held in jeopardy by the hostile designs and insidious acts of a foreign nation." On April 25, to commemorate
the fast, Morse delivered another Illuminati sermon. "[T]he
subtil [sic] and secret assailants are increasing in number," he
warned, "and are multiplying, varying, and arranging their
means of attack." He told of a French plot to invade the United
States from the island of Santo Domingo with an army of
blacks who would incite a race riot in the south. Then he began
building toward the climax of his speech.

"It has long been suspected that secret societies, under the
influence and direction of France, holding principles subversive
to our religion and government, existed somewhere in this
country." The effect of his words must have been dramatic. It
is difficult to read the rest of his sermon without thinking of
the speeches that, a century and a half later, were given by
Senator Joseph McCarthy.

> I have now in my possession [Morse said] complete and in-
> dubitable proof that such societies do exist, and have for
> many years existed, in the United States. I have, my breth-
> ren, an official, authenticated list of the names, ages, places of
> nativity, professions, &c. of the officers and members of a
> Society of *Illuminati* . . . consisting of *one hundred* members,
> instituted in Virginia, by the *Grand Orient* of FRANCE. This
> society has a deputy, whose name is on the list, who resides
> at the Mother Society in France, to communicate from thence
> all needful information and instruction.

Using this network, Morse said, the Illuminati sowed political discord and attacked the church-state establishment by circulating "baneful and corrupting books," spreading "infidelity, impiety, and immorality," and making "systematic endeavours . . . to destroy, not only the influence and support, but the official existence of the Clergy."

The evidence, supplied by Morse's friend, Secretary of the Treasury Oliver Wolcott, was a letter from the French Provincial Lodge of Wisdom Number 2660 of Portsmouth, Virginia, which was chartered by the Grand Orient, an international Masonic organization with headquarters in France. The letter was written to another lodge in New York to convey congratulations for receiving "new Constitutions and Regulations"; it ended with the hope that "the Grand Architect of the Universe bless your labours, and crown them with all manner of success." Included in the letter was a list of members of the Portsmouth lodge and references to affiliated lodges in Petersburg, Virginia, and on the island of Santo Domingo. Because the lodge in New York was called the Union Number 14, Morse concluded that, counting the other three lodges mentioned in the letter, there were at least seventeen Illuminati fronts. Because there were 100 names on the Virginia lodge's membership list, he concluded there might be 1700 Illuminati in the United States.

"I suspect that I have disturbed a hornet's nest," Morse wrote to Wolcott. "Happily I am fearless of their sting." Four editions of his sermon were published, in Charlestown, Boston, Hartford, and New York.

But Morse's evidence had come too late and wasn't very convincing. By now the Illuminati debate had turned against him. The Democratic-Republicans were attacking the scare as Federalist propaganda. In September, the *American Mercury* printed an account of a letter to Morse from Christopher Ebeling, a German geographer and historian, who said *Proofs of a Conspiracy* was a ridiculous, inaccurate book that was not taken seriously in Europe. Earlier that year, the *Columbian Centinel* had published a letter from another German, identified as provost of the College of Weimar, who said his countrymen were surprised that Americans were excited about a legend that had died out nine years ago in Germany. Morse wrote an inquiry to a Virginia congressman, who replied that the Wisdom Lodge was considered reputable and harmless. Although it consisted largely of Frenchmen, he wrote, they were honest and industrious.

During the next few years, the Democrats tried to turn the tables. An Episcopalian clergyman wrote that it was the Standing Order that was the dangerous elite, and that Timothy Dwight was chief Illuminatus. Abraham Bishop, a New Haven Democrat, attacked the Standing Order in a work called *Proofs of a Conspiracy against Christianity, and the Government of the United States; exhibited in several views of the union of church and state in New-England.* As orator of Yale's Phi Beta Kappa Society, Bishop was to give a speech during commencement, but it was canceled when officials saw an advance copy. He obtained a hall himself and delivered his address, "The Extent and Power of Political Delusion," saying:

> Robison and Barruel can deceive us no more. The seventeen sophistical work-shops of Satan have never been found: not one illuminatus major or minor has been discovered in America, though their names have been published, and though their existence here is as clearly proved as was their existence in Europe.

In a letter to Bishop James Madison (President Madison's cousin), Jefferson described a volume of Barruel's work that he had seen as "the ravings of a Bedlamite":

> As Wishaupt [sic] lived under the tyranny of a despot and priests, he knew that caution was necessary even in spreading information, and the principles of pure morality. . . . This has given an air of mystery to his views, was the foundation of his banishment . . . and is the color for the ravings against him of Robison, Barruel, and Morse. . . . [I]f Wishaupt had written here, where no secrecy is necessary in our endeavours to render men wise and virtuous, he would not have thought of any secret machinery for that purpose.

THE LEGEND SPREADS

By the early nineteenth century, the ideas of liberty, fraternity, and equality that had inspired the French Revolution were spreading across Europe. As a second generation of revolutionaries fought to replace monarchies with nation-states, many of them were influenced not only by Masonry's ideals of brotherhood but by its geometric and occult imagery. Many of the rebels described revolution as a fire, burning the old religious and royal orders so that a new secular order could arise. Some of the revolutionaries used Masonic-like secret societies to organize uprisings. In many cases, the revolutionaries arranged their secret societies using the concentric-circle structure of Weishaupt's Illuminati: level by level, initiates were introduced to the inner circle and became indoctrinated with revolutionary ideals that were often equated with light. Level by level, they scaled the pyramid to become the elite, the intelligentsia that would ignite the flames and destroy the established order. For their seals, the societies used triangles, radiating eyes, and concentric circles. They considered themselves part of a tradition, as bearers of ancient light.

After Robespierre's Reign of Terror was quelled in 1794 by the formation of a more conservative government, a revolutionary named Francois-Nöel Babeuf tried to overthrow the new regime with his "Conspiracy of Equals." His attempt failed, but one of his co-conspirators, a young Italian nobleman named Filippo Buonarotti, kept alive the idea of the secret society as a revolutionary device—a vanguard to lead the uprisings that the masses were not yet enlightened enough to seek. Buonarotti was exiled to Geneva in 1806, where he spent the last two decades of his life trying to form an international organization to foment nationalist revolutions. He called his group the Sublime Perfect Masters. Its symbol was a triangle of three dots surrounded by a circle. Buonarotti is believed to have been a Mason, and possibly a member of an Italian lodge influenced by the Illuminati. At least he shared an interest in the mix of rationalist, revolutionary, and occult ideas that was the hallmark of European Freemasonry. One grade of his society included initiation into Rosicrucian philosophy.

In his quixotic attempt to coordinate revolutions, Buonarotti had many possibilities from which to choose. Influenced by the French, Italian revolutionary societies formed, adopting such Masonic-sounding titles as the Knights of the Sun, the Astronomica Platonica, and the Centri, whose directing body was said to be the "solar circle." The Carbonari used triangle imagery in their initiation ceremonies. Similar societies were involved in revolutions in Spain and Greece. Reverence for Pythagoras spread as far as Russia, where, in 1818, a revolutionary "Society of Pythagoras" was formed in the Western Ukraine, later evolving into the Society of the United Slavs. The Decembrists, who revolted against the Russian czar in 1825, used Masonic lodges and symbols.

Perhaps this spread of secret societies was the result of a feedback effect: the paranoid writings of those who blamed Freemasonry for the French Revolution gave other rebels the idea of forming their own lodges to overthrow their *anciens régimes*. The appearance of these new societies made the conspiracy theorists more paranoid, providing new publicity for the myth.

Ultimately, Buonarotti's attempt to unite these movements failed. The connections between them remained ones of spirit, symbols, and ideas. But those who could not conceive of commoners uniting on their own against the divine rule of kings used the Buonarotti legend as the basis of new versions of the Illuminati conspiracy theory. In 1823, an aide to Buonarotti was arrested in Italy. Documents he was carrying described Buonarotti's efforts to work with revolutionary societies in Italy and France. The aide later wrote that Buonarotti also had sent emissaries to Germany, Russia, and Poland. To the conspiracy theorists, it looked as though Geneva were headquarters for all the revolutions they couldn't explain, the center of a plot for what would come to be called "one-world government." The conspiracy-theory industry flourished with tracts on Buonarotti's supposed Illuminati connections. The Vatican excommunicated the Carbonari, associating them with Freemasonry.

For the rest of the decade, the Illuminati legend continued to grow. When German émigrés in Paris, and later London, formed a revolutionary secret society called the League of the Just, which evolved into the Communist League, there were disciples of Buonarotti among them. To those who insisted on replacing notions of subtle influence with thick, black connecting lines, the revolutionary spirit looked like a plot.

In the United States, where Freemasonry remained little more than a social organization, the Illuminati conspiracy theory was revived in 1826. William Morgan, an ex-Mason who was writing an exposé of the organization, was abducted and never seen again. His presumed murder at the hands of Freemasons became the focus of a grass-roots anti-Masonic movement popular among conservative Protestants, abolitionists, and prohibitionists. In 1830, the Anti-Masonic Party of Massachusetts passed a resolution claiming that an investigating committee found evidence of "an intimate connection between the high orders of Free Masonry and French Illuminism." By that time there were also Anti-Masonic parties in New York, Vermont, Pennsylvania, and Rhode Island. Six state senators and seventeen assemblymen from New York were elected on the Anti-Masonic ticket. The governors of Vermont and Pennsylvania were members of the party.

Just as the Federalists used the Illuminati scare to rally the masses against the Jeffersonian Democrats, the National Republicans, who were the Federalists' heirs, took advantage of anti-Masonry to build a popular base. During the next several years, the populist Anti-Masons merged with the elitist National Republicans to form the Whigs and fight the successors of the Jeffersonians, the Jacksonian Democrats.

While all this was going on, Adam Weishaupt remained in exile, where, according to the 1907 edition of the *Catholic Encyclopedia,* he recanted and returned to the Church before his death in 1830. Five years later, Jedidiah Morse's son, Samuel F. B. Morse, the inventor of the telegraph, wrote *Foreign Conspiracy Against the Liberties of the United States.* Morse feared an Austrian conspiracy. Metternich had agents—the Jesuit missionaries, Morse wrote—who were plotting to bring the country under the rule of the Hapsburg Empire. "The serpent has already commenced his coil about our limbs, and the lethargy of his poison is creeping over us," Morse wrote. "We must awake or we are lost."

With Samuel Morse's anti-Catholic diatribe, the conspiracy theory had come full circle. The Catholic church, which had begun the Illuminati panic in Bavaria and helped promote the Illuminati conspiracy theory of the French Revolution, soon became firmly written into the plot. This was only one of the strange twists anti-Illuminism took as it developed, book by book, into the twentieth century. In 1924, an Englishwoman named Nesta Webster published *Secret Societies and Subversive Movements,* one of several books in which she traced the Illuminati conspiracy back to ancient mystery religions and forward to include socialism, communism, and Judaism. In 1933, Edith Starr Miller, writing under the name Lady Queensborough, carried on the tradition by publishing *Occult Theocracy,* a two-volume work with 107 chapters, each devoted to a cult, heresy, secret society, or movement: the Gnostics, Knights Templar, Assassins, Knights of Malta, Rosicrucians, Anabaptists, Mormons, Knights of Columbus, Christian Scientists, Fabian Society, Independent Order of Oddfellows, Knights of the Ku Klux Klan, American Civil Liberties Union, League of Nations, Mafia, and the International Bank.

"The aim of the societies," she wrote, has been "the concentration of political, economic, and intellectual power into the hands of a small group of individuals." She included a nine-page bibliography and an index in which the names of Freemasons are marked by a triangle made of three dots, the names of Jews by a Star of David.

In the 1930s, the reverend Gerald B. Winrod, an admirer of Hitler and the head of a Protestant fundamentalist organization called Defenders of the Christian Faith, published a pamphlet called *Adam Weishaupt, A Human Devil,* linking the Illuminati to both the Catholics and the Jews. By the 1980s, most of the books mentioned in this chapter were available from right-wing booksellers in the United States. Researchers were publishing magazines and books expanding the Illuminati conspiracy theory to greater proportions than ever before.

4

The Great Pyramid Game

"The Illuminati plan for world conquest ... was a diabolical masterpiece of Luciferian ingenuity that would take the lives of hundreds of millions of human beings and cost hundreds of billions of dollars in its accomplishment."

—Des Griffin,
Descent Into Slavery?, 1980

Eighteenth-century mathematician Pierre Simon Laplace once boasted that, given the positions of every object in the universe, a mind powerful enough could devise a formula to calculate the unfolding of history. "For such an intellect," Laplace wrote, "nothing could be uncertain; and the future just like the past would be present before its eyes."

This dream of a perfectly understandable clockwork world is now in question. On the cosmic scale, time and space have been found to bend relativistically; inside atoms, particles seem to move at random, not by predictable rules of cause and effect. Even the weather has proved so complex that it takes the largest, most powerful computers to process the information required just to make short-range forecasts.

In the face of such uncertainty, conspiracy theorists like Des Griffin remain undaunted. He is certain he has found a grand system to account for the turmoil he believes surrounds him: an economy wrecked by inflation, a morality corrupted by the sexual revolution, an America that has lost prestige abroad and is becoming more socialistic every day.

"To most people," he wrote in his book, *Fourth Reich of the Rich*, "the whole world is a jumbled mass of conflicting and confusing ideologies without rhyme or reason—or purpose! That is true—ON THE SURFACE!"

But Griffin believes he has seen through the veil and glimpsed the workings of the machine. "Did we fall accidentally into our present hideous national trauma—or were we deliberately pushed?" he wrote. "Did it come about as a consequence of natural degeneracy or as the result of a CONSPIRACY?"

The answer, he believes, is obvious. In the mechanical world Griffin takes for granted, accidents don't happen. He is fond of quoting Gary Allen's right-wing classic, *None Dare Call It Conspiracy:*

> If we were merely dealing with the law of averages half of the events affecting our nation's well-being should be good for America. If we were dealing with mere incompetence, our leaders should occasionally make a mistake in our favor. We . . . are not really dealing with coincidence or stupidity, but with planning and brilliance.

For more than twenty years, Griffin has been studying the conspiracy and sharing his findings with other believers. On a night in early 1982, he was on his way to a speech—titled "Adam Weishaupt, A Human Devil"—in which his fellow conspiracy theorist, John Townsend, would explain the nation's woes as the latest developments in an ancient conspiracy that had begun in the Garden of Eden and was supposedly run by a group called the Illuminati. The occasion of the presentation was a weekly meeting of a Los Angeles–area tax-revolt group called Your Heritage Protection Association, whose members are so sure the country is imperiled that they wear their American flag pins upside down—a traditional sailors' signal of distress.

Conspiracy theorists have been citing each other's work for so many decades that a folklore of paranoia has developed. While the details of right-wing conspiracy theories vary, de-

pending on which political movements, organizations, or religious groups they are designed to attack, many of them share a
distorted version of history based on the legend of the Illuminati. Griffin's books capture this myth in painstaking detail. Since much of the speech would be based on Griffin's own
works, he wouldn't learn anything new. But the meeting was a
chance for him to sell his books and experience the sense of
fellowship that comes from knowing others share your world
view.

To Griffin, every word he'd be hearing was the truth. Or,
as he wrote the word in his books, the TRUTH. He wasn't
talking about relativistic truth or situational ethics, the truths of
man, but absolute truth revealed from on high—perfect, untar-
nished, and unquestionable. When philosophers write of absolute truth, it is customary that the word be capitalized to distinguish it from lesser varieties. Griffin prefers to write each letter
of the word in the upper case. Like much of the literature of
paranoia, his books are filled with capitalized sentences punc-
tuated with exclamation points. Sometimes even that typogra-
phy proves too quiet for him, so he italicizes his capital letters.
It is the literary equivalent of yelling.

Des Griffin is tired of being ignored. For years he sat back
and watched the world listen to the experts—the technocrats
and intellectuals who said they had the answers.

"You've got shrinks, psychologists, penal experts, law
experts, sex experts," Griffin complained. "If experts were the
answer we'd have a model society. But marriages are breaking
apart, the economy is in turmoil. . . . Obviously something
is wrong."

He resents the implication that the world is supposed to
be too complicated for a self-taught man like Des Griffin to
fathom. The complexity, he believes, is a smoke screen, a
conspiracy to hide the truth. And the Illuminati—the experts of
experts—are the authors of the plot. It started, he believes, with
the priests of ancient Babylon, who controlled the masses by
presenting themselves as keepers of divine knowledge, secrets
the people were not to know. Now, he believes, we are enslaved by the priests of reason and their deliberate obfuscation.

"I believe virtually everything is plain, simple, logical, understandable," Griffin said. "If it isn't, it can't be any good." There is good and there is evil. Learn to distinguish them, he believes, and you won't need rulers to tell you what to do.

To spread the word, Griffin established Emissary Publications to produce his books and sell other conspiracy literature. To help finance his endeavors, he works at a regular job during the day. He won't say where. He won't say how much money he earns from his books. As much as he despises secrecy, he seems to feel that in a world run by conspirators it is only prudent to be clandestine.

Griffin arrived at the Van Nuys municipal airport, where the speech would be delivered, and unloaded boxes of books from his car. In the back of the meeting room, members of Your Heritage Protection Association were selling Liberty Lobby's weekly newspaper, *Spotlight,* and copies of *None Dare Call It Conspiracy*. A young man with a beard was distributing literature urging citizens to avoid taxes by starting their own churches. Also available were registration cards for the National Rifle Association and subscription cards for the *Duck Book*. Many members of the audience were in their twenties and thirties. One young man wore a T-shirt bearing the legend "Only the Strong Survive."

In addition to his own works, Griffin was selling such anti-Illuminati classics as Nesta Webster's *Secret Societies and Subversive Movements,* first published in 1924, and the John Birch Society's edition of John Robison's 1798 book, *Proofs of a Conspiracy Against All the Religions and Governments of Europe, Carried on in the Secret Meetings of the Free Masons, Illuminati, and Reading Societies*.

Also for sale was *Adam Weishaupt, A Human Devil,* by Gerald Winrod, the book from which the title of the evening's speech was taken. For three dollars each, an audience of fifty would hear Townsend, a forty-three-year-old electronics engineer for Hughes Aircraft, who, at various times, had been a follower of est, Eastern religion, Carlos Castaneda, and the Libertarian party. Recently he had begun studying the Illuminati conspiracy. He was so alarmed at what he had learned about the coming cataclysm that he invested in freeze-dried food and gold.

Townsend opened the talk with Your Heritage Protection Association's version of the Pledge of Allegiance: ". . . with liberty and justice for all—*who fight for it!*" Then he began delineating the Illuminati conspiracy.

THE WORLD ACCORDING TO TOWNSEND

The plot began with an angry angel, Lucifer, and his plan to wrest from God the control of the universe. "I will scale the heavens, I will set my throne high above the stars of God," he said, in the words of the biblical prophet Isaiah. "I will . . . make myself like the Most High." As punishment for his hubris, he was expelled from heaven. "Your beauty made you arrogant," God said. "[Y]ou misused your wisdom to increase your dignity."

Since Lucifer couldn't rule heaven, Townsend said, he fled to earth and schemed to make it his own. The name Lucifer comes from the Latin word for "bearer of light." Since the first days of creation, he has seduced men with the notion that by becoming enlightened—whether with philosophical learning or occult powers—they could lord it over their fellow beings and challenge the wisdom of God. With Lucifer, the Angel of Light, began the Illuminati conspiracy, an attempt by evil elites to exploit the masses by tricking them into worshiping those who claim to possess extraordinary powers. From the days of the Garden of Eden, Lucifer has been the force behind the conspiracy, Townsend said. He is the embodiment of absolute evil, whom most people refer to as Satan.

In the form of the serpent, Lucifer tempted Eve with the fruit of the tree of knowledge and the promise, "You shall be as gods!" As punishment for challenging the power of the Almighty, the human race was driven from paradise. When, under Lucifer's tutelage, mankind became even more corrupt, God punished it again with the Great Flood. But when Noah's ark landed, Lucifer was waiting on shore.

First he recruited Noah's grandson, Cush, to help him build a godless world government that would be symbolized by the Tower of Babel, built so high it would reach the heavens—a monument to the power of man over God.

God became so angry at this latest affront that he cursed mankind by destroying its unity. Until this time mankind spoke one language. God decreed that from then on men would speak many tongues, making it more difficult for them to join in another attempt to usurp divine authority.

But Satan did not give up easily. He passed his evil powers to Noah's great-grandson, Nimrod the hunter, king of Babylon, a pagan so powerful that his people worshiped him instead of God. Nimrod was so corrupt that he married his mother, the beautiful and evil Semiramis.

Semiramis and her followers started their own religion, convincing the people that she and her priests were divine.

"They set up confessionals so all the followers of the religion had to confess their sins to the priest," Townsend said.

> That way she knew what everyone was doing. She told her followers that only she and her priests could understand the great mysteries of God. . . . Her priests went into action with this propaganda scheme. They were the masters of lies, magic, and illusions. They set up idols of this mother holding the son. It began to appear everywhere. And she became accepted as the Queen of Heaven.

At this point, an observer familiar with the various paths of the Illuminati legend might have sensed that Townsend had reached a fork in the trail. Depending on which branch he chose, he could link either Catholicism or Freemasonry to the plot. The image of Nimrod and Semiramis suggested the baby Jesus and the Virgin Mary, whom Catholics call the Queen of Heaven. The power of the Babylonian priests was reminiscent of that of the Catholic church, but directly attacking a mainstream religion was imprudent in a public gathering. After hinting at possible Illuminati roots of Catholicism, Townsend developed the anti-Masonic theme instead.

There is, in fact, a wealth of literature that could be used to link ancient civilizations such as Babylon to Freemasonry. In their attempts to establish the antiquity of their movement, early members of Masonic lodges unwittingly aided the conspiracy theorists by developing the mythology in which ancient biblical builders were the first Freemasons. Few Masons still believe these stories, but by taking these fancies as history, conspiracy theorists like Townsend can spin elaborate plots. It seems strange that such traditional enemies as Catholics and Masons both could be candidates for inclusion in the same conspiracy. But in the Illuminati conspiracy theory, such conflicts are said to be illusions—beneath the surface, opposing forces are in secret accord.

Townsend continued with a leap of logic typical of conspiracy theorists: Semiramis's worshipers had to take a secret oath. "That was the beginning of secret societies," he said. Then he set out to describe the tortuous route by which the powers of Lucifer supposedly traveled from ancient Babylon to twentieth-century America.

After Babylon fell, Townsend said, the Egyptian civilization arose—and it too was controlled by Lucifer. The satanic cult of Semiramis was replaced by one that worshiped Horus, god of the sun. The symbol for this pagan god was an eye inside a triangle.

Townsend reached for his billfold.

I'd like you to get out a one-dollar Federal Reserve note. If you'll look on the back you'll see that there's a pyramid. At the top of that pyramid you'll see that there's a little triangle, and it has an eye in it. That's the all-seeing eye of Horus. That typifies the sun. It's the all-seeing eye of Freemasonry. That pyramid appeared on your one-dollar Federal Reserve notes back around 1933. That was the symbol that they had managed to finally take control of your money system.

One of the rules for constructing conspiracy theories is that symbols may be used to forge links not easily made by the laws of cause and effect. In a few minutes, Townsend would explain the sequence of events that led to an Egyptian cult symbol supposedly finding its way to the United States. Step by step, he would describe the details of what he believed was our Illuminati heritage. But for the moment, the image of a radiating eye atop an Egyptian temple was a powerful connecting device. As the spectators stared at the backs of their dollars, Townsend hoped they felt the mystery of ancient connections, the hint of a centuries-old plan that might just explain why their money was eroding in value, taxed so that the government could spend more money, fuel inflation, and make the dollars worth even less. He hoped his listeners would feel the crushing weight of being on the bottom tier of a pyramid, manipulated by an elite that exploited them as stealthily as pharaoh did his slaves.

And why was the eye on the dollar's pyramid radiating light?

"Lucifer," Townsend reminded his listeners, "was the bearer of *light*." The ancient Egyptians, builders of pyramids, were sun worshipers. Solar worship, Luciferian light, *Illuminati*. The pieces of the puzzle were snapping together.

"It's a black light of satanic illumination. It's rooted in black magic and occultism. There are seducing spirits capable of impregnating human minds with the doctrines of evil, doctrines of devils. . . . It's like an onrushing torrent pouring through the centuries."

For thirty centuries, Townsend said, Lucifer's torch had been passed through a sequence of Illuminati fronts, including the Gnostics, Cathars, Knights Templar, Rosicrucians, and Freemasons. Every step of the way, a secret elite preserved the tradition of controlling people through deception.

As in the days of the French Revolution, secret societies and heretic cults appear in many twentieth-century American conspiracy theories. Often these Illuminati legends begin with the mythical Atlanteans, then go on to include the sequence of secret societies popularized by the Freemasons' myth of the esoteric tradition. In part, the myth has remained alive because leaders of contemporary groups such as the California-based Rosicrucian Order claim that they are indeed heirs to ancient occult secrets. The Rosicrucians advertise in popular magazines, offering to teach the wisdom of the ancients by mail. Members pay eighty-four dollars a year in dues, eventually ascending to the rank of Illuminati. The group's aim is benevolent; its leaders simply want to preserve and teach the body of occult knowledge—the cabala, astrology, alchemy, tarot, hermetic magic, the I Ching, et cetera—that has accumulated over the centuries. To the skeptic, these beliefs are disproved fantasies. But to both followers of the occult and those who think occultists are plotting against them, the secrets are considered real and powerful. They are assumed to include the ability to use psychic powers and magic to predict events and control minds.

In some Illuminati conspiracy theories, the conduit for the ancient secrets goes directly from the Gnostics to Ignatius Loyola, founder of the Jesuits. Others trace the Illuminati tradition back to the cabalistic magic of the ancient Jews. But in all the various constructions, the paths converge in Ingolstadt, Bavaria, on May 1, 1776, when Adam Weishaupt founded his Order of the Illuminati.

With Weishaupt, Townsend explained, Lucifer's attempt to use black magic to take over the world gave way to a new plan. Now he would use a different kind of satanic illumination —the light of reason—to undermine all religions and states and establish one-world government. The name of this atheistic, secular order, Townsend said, is inscribed beneath the pyramid on the dollar bill: *Novus Ordo Seclorum*. The Roman numerals for 1776, which appear on the pyramid's base, do not refer to the date of the Declaration of Independence, Townsend believed, but to the founding of Weishaupt's secret society. To Townsend, it is no accident that Communists hold their parades on May Day.

"[Weishaupt] had the ability to mold humans and bend them to his will," Townsend said. "He set forces in motion which wrecked whole nations and destroyed millions of lives, *hundreds of millions of lives*. . . . The plot was carried on with such secrecy that his name was scarcely known."

He asked the audience:

How many of you have heard of Adam Weishaupt? Not too many of you, and you're the people who *know*. Your friends, neighbors, and relatives don't know—ask them. *His name was scarcely known*. That's one underlying rule of all secret societies. The real author of that secret society is never known.

They never show themselves. They use men as carpenters use tools, to build for the future, mold generations to come.

As conspiracy theorists are fond of pointing out, Weishaupt structured his organization like a pyramid. On the bottom level were the Novices, who reported to the Minervals, who reported to the Illuminated Minervals. Eventually, thirteen ranks were established. Thirteen levels, as on the dollar-bill pyramid. As initiates learned new powers and secrets, they ascended the steps of the pyramid, coming increasingly closer to the light.

By infiltrating Masonic lodges, Townsend explained, Weishaupt and his Illuminati plotted the French Revolution — the triumph of godless reason over the tradition of church and king.

"Starting in 1789, when lightning struck on the surface of France, it was merely the visible effect of hidden causes which had been carefully planned and timed by the conspirators. It was Illuminism in action," Townsend said.

During the next century, Weishaupt's light flowed through a network of secret revolutionary societies, including the League of Just Men, which hired Karl Marx to write the *Communist Manifesto,* calling for the dissolution of nations into an international, godless state—a new Tower of Babel. But Lucifer didn't work only with Communists to establish his one-world kingdom. Another elite, the international bankers, was also part of the plot. First Lucifer used black magic, then the powers of reason. Now he would use the power of money to further his one-world aims. As with Catholicism and Freemasonry, the apparent opposites of communism and international banking were, Townsend believed, symbiotic. Even revolutionaries needed money. By financing them, the bankers would benefit. And, under the guise of socialism, the people would be taxed and controlled, individualism suppressed, private property abolished. People would be more manageable pawns. When one-world government was finally achieved, the bankers would find it that much simpler to run the world economy.

Banking, Townsend said, was invented by Nimrod. He

persuaded his subjects to leave their gold in the temple for safe-keeping. Clay tablets were issued as receipts. Soon he realized he could loan out gold and earn interest. Then he discovered that, by producing more clay tablets, he could loan many times more gold than he actually possessed. He had created wealth out of thin air. He learned the power a creditor has over his debtors. Banking is, after all, the ultimate pyramid game. The little banks pay interest to the big banks, which pay interest to bigger banks. Each block on the pyramid feeds fewer blocks on the level above. Step by step, the wealth becomes concentrated. By the time the money has risen to the top, a fortune has been made.

The first Illuminati banker, Townsend said, was Amschel Mayer Rothschild. In the late eighteenth century, he stationed each of his five sons in a different country, where they became lenders to kings and controllers of history. During the Battle of Waterloo, the Rothschilds began to develop their strategy of profiting from wars. Through an agent stationed at the battlefield, Nathan Rothschild discovered that Napoleon was losing the battle. He went to the London exchange and started selling off the English currency he owned. Other traders, assuming that Rothschild knew what he was doing, figured England must be losing at Waterloo. They started dumping their English currency, too. As a result of all the selling, the price of the pound bottomed out. Rothschild bought back all the English money at a discount and won control of the English economy.

According to Townsend's story, the Rothschilds tried to put the United States in their debt by financing the Civil War. When Abraham Lincoln tried to foil their plan by printing greenbacks to pay the North's war debts (instead of borrowing Rothschild money), he was assassinated.

In fact, said Townsend, the Rothschilds and their allies— Kuhn Loeb and Company, J. P. Morgan, the Warburgs, the Schiffs, and the Rockefellers—found wars so profitable that they created them. World Wars I and II and the Vietnam War were started by international bankers. "You haven't fought a war *they* didn't set up for you," he told his audience. In the Illuminati legend, even enemies in battle often turned out to be unwitting allies in the conspiracy.

While the bankers benefited from wars, Townsend explained, the turmoil also furthered the aims of the one-worlders. World War I destabilized Russia, allowing the Bolshevik Revolution to succeed. By fostering chaos, the Illuminati made the world more susceptible to cries for international government. President Woodrow Wilson fell into the trap when he tried to convince Congress to let the United States join the League of Nations. Wilson failed, but the country was manipulated later into joining the United Nations, which, Townsend noted, is built on land donated by the Rockefellers.

Bankers could create not only wars but depressions. The Panic of 1907 frightened the U.S. Congress into accepting a plan by the bankers to establish a central bank to control the economy. Thus the Federal Reserve System was inaugurated and made independent of the president or Congress.

Now the Illuminati had an outpost in the United States, a system to suck America's wealth into their worldwide economy. By surrendering its constitutional right to coin money to the Federal Reserve System, a deceived Congress ensured that the United States would be forever in debt to the conspirators. When a president ran a deficit because of an Illuminati-made war, he could no longer print greenbacks as Lincoln did. He would have to borrow money from the Federal Reserve System to cover the debt. By creating the Great Depression, the Illuminati paved the way for Roosevelt's New Deal. The bankers benefited from the interest they earned on all the money Roosevelt spent, and the United States moved another step toward one-world socialism.

Until Roosevelt's reign, Townsend explained, there had been a limit on the power of the Federal Reserve System. The money that it created and loaned to the government had to be backed by gold. Roosevelt eliminated the gold standard. Like Nimrod, Roosevelt made the people turn in their gold. From then on, the Federal Reserve could print unlimited amounts of money, loan it to the government, and charge interest. The bank was creating something out of nothing—money out of thin air. It was a power as mysterious as that of priests and magicians. In commemoration of their triumph, the Illuminati had their symbol engraved on the dollar bill.

In the 1970s and 1980s, the plot continued. Through the Trilateral Commission, which was started by David Rockefeller under the pretense of improving international relations, the bankers trained leaders such as Henry Kissinger, Zbigniew Brzezinski, and Jimmy Carter to be agents of the plot. To make sure the conspirators wouldn't be exposed by the media, the Trilateralists recruited influential journalists. They hired intellectuals—experts—to write studies promoting one-world government.

And so, Townsend told his audience, we are in the grip of a conspiracy of elitists—occultists, rationalists, Communists, and millionaires. World War III is on the drawing board: the ultimate Illuminati-engineered catastrophe, which will finally scare the world into accepting the one-world government Lucifer has tried so long to establish.

Townsend was ready for his conclusion.

> The information about some of this stuff has been so well-suppressed that you can only get bits and pieces about the conspiracy. But you've got to be looking. When you get enough bits and pieces it fits into a puzzle. Pretty soon you begin to see the picture.
>
> How many of you in this room believe there's a conspiracy to set up a one-world government?

Almost every member of the audience raised his hand. They were tired of bankers, politicians, and professors telling them what must be done for their own good. They were tired of being enslaved by priests of money and reason.

> I want to ask you to go out from this meeting tonight and be willing to be *un*reasonable. Don't let them con you with "reason is stronger than faith." Be willing to be unreasonable. No matter how much your friends try to stop you from telling it the way that it is, go on and tell it.

SOLVING THE PUZZLE

By the time the speech ended, many members of the audience appeared tired but soothed by the feeling that they had been let in on secrets. The government that was taking their

money, the bankers who had refused them loans—all were part
of a plot that was unknown to most of society. But as they left
the meeting, many of the listeners looked dazed by information
overload. They had been overwhelmed with data. How were
they to evaluate it all? Those who wanted to research further
could find similar material in Des Griffin's books or in those
Townsend had named during the lecture. There is a library's
worth of anti-Illuminati literature, some available by mail
through Griffin's company and such firms as Angriff Press of
Hollywood, California; Alpine Enterprises of Dearborn, Michigan (publisher of a journal called *Conspiracy Digest*); or Omni
Publications of Hawthorne, California. A list of the books sold
by these companies is like a map of the anti-Illuminati mind:
*The Federal Reserve Conspiracy, The Federal Reserve Monster, The
Federal Reserve Hoax, The Green Magicians, Lincoln Money Mar-
tyred, Red Fog Over America, Lightbearers of Darkness, The Plot
Against Christianity, Invisible Government, Pawns in the Game,
Freemasonry and the Vatican, Judaism and the Vatican, The Vatican
Moscow Alliance, Trilaterals Over Washington, The Cult of the
All-Seeing Eye.* But the problem with such literature is its cir-
cularity. The books cite each other as references, forming a
tangle of closed loops.

Even if they searched their public libraries, curious members of the audience would find what they might consider
verification for Townsend's version of reality. For it is not so
much his facts that are contradicted by historians as his interpretation.

Religious historians do indeed trace many of the rituals
and symbols of the Roman Catholic church to ancient religions
of Egypt and Babylon. Some speculate that the image of Mary
with her child Jesus is a Christian version of Isis and Horus,
and there was an Egyptian symbol called the eye of Horus.
Although there is no evidence that Weishaupt's Illuminati used
the symbol, it was adopted by Freemasonry to represent the
"all-seeing eye of Providence." Later, a similar symbol was
included on the back of the great seal of the United States, and
from there it was transferred to the back of the one-dollar bill.
Many of the founding fathers were Freemasons and sympa-
thized with Masonic aims of universal brotherhood, but shar-

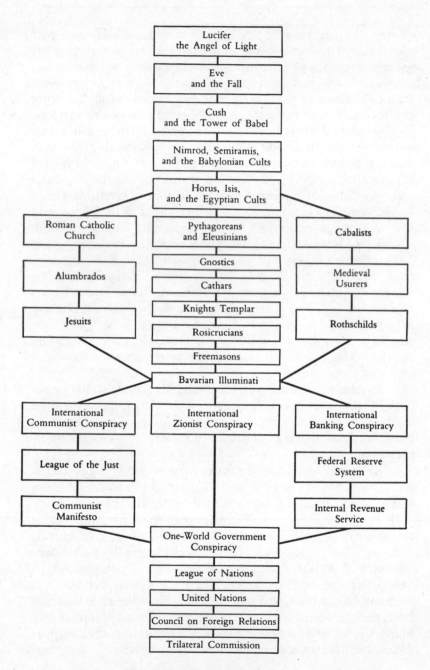

The Illuminati Conspiracy Theory

ing symbols and ideas is different from participating in a plot.

Tales of the Rothschilds are the stock of the conspiracy-theory trade. While the Waterloo legend is untrue, there is no doubt that the family was powerful, crafty, even conspiratorial. With brothers stationed in London, Paris, Frankfurt, Vienna, and Naples—the financial centers of Europe—the Rothschild banking dynasty helped shape history by lending to governments. Using carrier pigeons and messengers on horseback, the Rothschilds ran an intelligence network that was the best and fastest in Europe. It has even been documented that Rothschilds banked on both sides of World War I. When the allies won, the Rothschilds's Austrian branch appeared to be near ruin. But by forming an alliance with J. P. Morgan in the United States, the French Rothschilds manipulated the price of the franc, helping their Vienna branch earn enough profit on the international currency market to recoup much of its war losses.

Conspiracy theorists can easily find examples of bankers influencing world events and taking advantage of wars, but that doesn't mean they created them as part of a satanic plot as old as the planet.

Townsend was using a common technique of conspiracy scholarship: he snowed his audience with what seemed a preponderance of evidence. Point by point, listeners could check the statements and find that, taken in isolation, many of them were true. Some listeners might come to believe that if the facts were true by themselves, then so was the way Townsend had strung them together into the rigid, mechanistic network of the Illuminati conspiracy theory.

To the conspiracy theorist, academic historical analysis is Illuminati fog. When historians study war, they analyze variables, pondering the nature of opposing forces and how they enhance or cancel each other. They consider economic, sociological, psychoanalytic, geographic, and cultural influences. They recognize that there are many different ways to pattern the facts into interpretations. No answers are final, for it is thought that history is a relationship between the observing culture and the culture that is observed.

In Townsend's world, history is nothing but the interplay of good and evil, and truth is as well defined and unchanging as Isaac Newton's laws of physics, before they were turned to rubber by Einstein. Everything, as writer Des Griffin said, is very simple. There are no accidents, for everything is planned.

The Illuminati conspiracy theory manifests currents that have flowed through two hundred years of American history: populism, isolationism, anti-intellectualism. Most important, the anti-Illuminists see the universe as a great machine, much like the one described by the mathematician Laplace. But it is a machine that runs according to a different physics. Laplace was an atheist. When Napoleon received a copy of Laplace's *Mecanique Celeste,* he criticized the mathematician for not mentioning in his work the existence of God. "I have no need of this hypothesis," Laplace replied. His gods, mathematics and causality, were so integrated in the way he saw the world that he wouldn't think to identify them. They were part of the background, the epistemological air he breathed. To Griffin, Townsend, and the writers of the scores of anti-Illuminati books, God is at the helm of the celestial machinery, and Satan sits at the controls of the conspiracy.

5

The Computer in the Vatican

"Anti-Catholicism has always been the pornography of the Puritan."
—Richard Hofstadter,
The Paranoid Style in American Politics, 1963

Since colonial times, Protestants have been afraid of a Catholic conspiracy: a grand plan to take control of America and integrate it into a world empire run by the Pope. It wasn't until this century that most Protestant denominations quelled these fears, and the Vatican stopped condemning Protestants as heretics. During the Second Vatican Council of the early 1960s, the Catholic church liberalized its attitude toward other churches and expressed hopes of forming a spiritual union with all forms of Christianity. The result was the current ecumenical movement, in which Catholics and Protestants are trying to resolve their differences and work together as Christians.

But to many members of the fundamentalist wing of Protestantism, the medieval Inquisition is a more powerful memory than the Vatican II reforms. They believe that their version of Christianity, based on a literal interpretation of the Bible, is the one true religion. Just as they believe the world was created in seven days, as described in Genesis, they believe it will end according to the scenario outlined in the Book of Revelation: an Antichrist will come to power and enslave the world with an international satanic kingdom. Martin Luther and John Calvin, leaders of the sixteenth-century Protestant revolt against Catholicism, denounced the Pope as the Antichrist and the Catholic church as his international kingdom. Among segments of American fundamentalism, this belief survives.

Most fundamentalist leaders do not openly condemn Catholicism. Television evangelist Jerry Falwell tries to recruit conservative Catholics to join Moral Majority and fight the rise of secularism in the United States. But, occasionally, signs of Protestant anti-Catholicism become public. When Pope John Paul II visited England in 1982, a group of militant Protestant demonstrators waved Bibles and called him "Antichrist." In 1981, the *Los Angeles Times* reported that a Southern California group called Mission to Catholics was distributing an anti-Catholic pamphlet written by Bob Jones, chancellor of Bob Jones University, the largest fundamentalist college and seminary in the country. In the tract, Jones condemned Pope Paul VI as the "archpriest of Satan, a deceiver, and an antichrist." The *Times* reported that Mission to Catholics had received financial support from Scott Memorial Church, a multimillion-dollar complex that includes four grammar schools, two high schools, and the Christian Heritage College. Scott Memorial's pastor is Tim LeHaye, a Bob Jones University graduate and a founder of the Moral Majority.

In recent years, the most outspoken fomenter of anti-Catholic paranoia has been a fundamentalist extremist named Alberto Rivera. Through the Anti-Christ Information Center of Canoga Park, California, Rivera denounces the Catholic church as the Antichrist's one-world kingdom and attempts to link it to the Illuminati conspiracy theory. Rivera claims to be a former Jesuit priest. He regularly speaks at fundamentalist churches in various states, preaching against Catholic subterfuge and trying to raise the $100,000 he believes it will take to realize his dream: the construction of a retreat for nuns and priests he hopes will escape from the Catholic church. Among the items he offers for sale is a tape cassette, *Escape From a Catholic Convent, "Sister Charlotte's Testimony"*, in which a woman claiming to be an ex-nun tells gothic stories of torture and murder in the dungeons of her cloistered order, and of sexual molestation by priests.

Rivera's views are so extreme that most fundamentalists would disown them. But by joining forces with Jack T. Chick, a well-known publisher of fundamentalist comic books, Rivera has gained a national audience for his attempt to reignite the anti-Catholic bigotry that has existed in the United States since the Puritans reached the Atlantic shore.

Since the early 1970s, Chick Publications, of Cucamonga, California, has produced more than a dozen comic books and a series of hand-sized tracts sold by the thousands in Christian bookstores in the United States, Canada, England, Australia, South Africa, and New Zealand. In many of the bookstores, Chick's publications command a display rack of their own. Bible students buy his tracts in bulk to distribute during prose-lytizing efforts, making them a common sight on college campuses.

One Chick comic, *Angel of Light,* is based on a detailed description of the Illuminati legend, beginning with Lucifer and the Garden of Eden. In *Sabotage?* a character claims that Catholicism was invented by Lucifer and is descended from pagan, occult religions. In the comic, the Pope is accused of using the ecumenical movement to pave the way for the coming of the Antichrist's one-world church and government. Freemasons are denounced as allies in the plot.

The anti-Catholic theme reaches a crescendo in Chick's series of comic books detailing the supposedly true adventures of Alberto Rivera. In *Alberto, Double-Cross,* and *The Godfathers,* Rivera rehashes age-old legends of priests keeping nuns as concubines and seducing girls in confession boxes. Throughout the comics, cartoons of the contorted faces of priests, nuns, and victims of the Inquisition capture the fear and hatred Rivera believes is the essence of the Catholic church. The illustrations include pictures of a nun who has been whipped so severely that her back is encrusted with blood.

Shortly after the Rivera series began to appear in the early 1980s, the Catholic League for Religious and Civil Rights denounced it as "religious hate literature." Two of the comics were banned in Canada as "immoral and indecent." It was the first time a Canadian customs law designed to control importation of pornography was used to bar religious material. *Our*

Sunday Visitor, a national Catholic newspaper, had offered a $10,000 reward to anyone who could prove that Rivera's charges were true. After complaints from the Christian Booksellers Association, Chick resigned his membership, claiming that the group had been infiltrated by Catholics.

While many Christian bookstores reacted to the bad publicity by dropping Chick's anti-Catholic material, his tracts and comic books attacking evolution and the occult and predicting the coming of Armageddon are still widely sold. In 1980, Chick's company was said to have grossed $1 million from his publications, most of which sell for less than a dollar.

Chick and Rivera countered their critics by including them in a conspiracy theory. In a tract called *My Name?. . . In the Vatican?*, they claimed that the Catholic church was conspiring to suppress the dissemination of *Alberto* by intimidating booksellers. According to the booklet, the name of every Protestant is stored in a large computer in the Vatican in preparation for another Inquisition.

CARTOON ADVENTURES

Alberto begins in Spain in 1942, when young Rivera is forced by his family to join a seminary. On the opening page of the comic, the hero is shown being dragged, sobbing, into the clutches of the Jesuits to begin his training as an espionage agent for the Vatican. Several pages later, he is assigned to infiltrate Plymouth Brethren, Pentecostal, Baptist, and United Evangelical churches. He describes how he supposedly sabotaged Protestant congregations in Spain and Latin America by posing as a member and encouraging dissent. He tells how he planted rumors that Protestant pastors were involved with narcotics, tax evasion, and illicit sex. Ministers who refused to yield to blackmail were killed or made crazy with drugs. After destroying an interdenominational seminary in Costa Rica, Rivera says, he was rewarded by being ordained a Jesuit priest and being taught the darkest secrets of the Catholic church. Nuns in the confessional admitted to him that they had been guilty of lesbian encounters and of love affairs with priests, that their illegitimate babies had been suffocated and buried in convent basements. In one scene—at a secret black mass in northern Spain—Rivera kisses the ring of a high Catholic official and sees it is marked with a Masonic symbol: a "G" inside a triangle made of drafting tools. In fact, Rivera says, he soon learned that the Jesuit General was a Mason working with the Illuminati.

In Rivera's conspiracy theory, the Illuminati existed as early as the sixteenth century in the form of a heretic Spanish cult called the Alumbrados, or "the Enlightened." Ignatius Loyola, the Spanish mystic who founded the Jesuits, was secretly an Alumbrado, Rivera believes, "enlightened" with satanic powers. The Alumbrados, he says, were the forerunners of Adam Weishaupt's group. Rivera believes that Weishaupt was, like himself, a double agent. While he pretended to oppose the Church, he was secretly furthering its aims: to absorb all religions into "one-world church" and all political movements—communism, socialism, Masonry, anarchism, and labor unionism—into "one-world government." The ruler would be the Pope, the Antichrist of Revelation.

In the final scenes of *Alberto*, Rivera tries to reveal his discoveries and is incarcerated in a mental asylum. Then he accepts Jesus as his savior and becomes a Protestant. A sympathetic priest allows him to escape. Rivera flies to London to rescue his sister, a nun who is being held against her will in a convent, where she is flagellated as penance for Christ's suffering. The details are described in *Double-Cross*, the sequel to *Alberto*. In another Rivera comic, *The Godfathers*, Jesuits are blamed for coaching Marx and Engels to write the *Communist Manifesto* and for instigating the Bolshevik Revolution in an attempt to retake the Russian Orthodox church. World War II is explained as a plot in which Hitler was a Vatican agent used to exterminate Jews. All these machinations are supposedly part of the master plan to bring on the Antichrist's reign. Everything, Rivera believes, can be explained as part of the Catholic-Illuminati plot.

"I don't believe in accidents," Rivera has said. "I believe that accidents are promoted by cause and effect. . . . [S]omebody did something for the accident to take place. . . . People must understand that history is manipulated. If they go to ex-

amine every war, everything has already been caused. There is
a cause . . . that sparked the fire."

THE JESUIT PLOT

Modern historians (as well as most Catholic and Protestant theologians) believe the Antichrist predicted in Revelation
refers to the Roman emperor Nero. The book apparently was
written after Christ's death to comfort Christians persecuted
by Nero's "one-world government," the Roman empire. But
Rivera, like most fundamentalists, believes Revelation refers
not to the past but to the future. In his attempts to turn fundamentalist theology against Catholicism, Rivera is tapping a tradition that has existed for hundreds of years. While eighteenth-
century Catholics feared an international plot of conspirators
enlightened by rationalism or occultism, Protestants have his-
torically seen the Catholic church as an all-powerful conspiracy
infused with satanic powers. For centuries, Jesuits have been
depicted as key agents of the plot.

In the late twentieth century, Jesuits have become known
as a force for modernism in the church. Included in their ranks
are such radicals as Vietnam protester Daniel Berrigan. But for
centuries Jesuits were famous for an unquestioning loyalty to
the Pope that bordered on fanaticism.

The Society of Jesus, as the Jesuits are officially called,
was founded in 1540 by Ignatius Loyola, who used his *Spiritual
Exercises,* a manual of practical mysticism, to instill in his followers a fervid devotion to the Vatican's cause. As special
agents of the Pope working to counter the Protestant Reformation of the sixteenth and seventeenth centuries, Jesuits developed a reputation for wiliness, zealousness, and intrigue.

By serving as confessors to royalty, Jesuits influenced
European politics. In an undercover effort to reintroduce Catholicism to Protestant England, where it had been banned,
Jesuits communicated in code and disguised themselves as army
officers, gentlemen, servants, and tailors. They developed a
reputation as men for whom means were justified by ends: in
the fight for what they believed was absolute truth, the laws of
man could be circumvented. Because of their dedication—hundreds of them were killed during missionary work in Asia,
Africa, and the Americas—they were seen by critics as zom-

bies, brainwashed by the *Spiritual Exercises* to do Rome's bidding.

By the late eighteenth century, the order's image had become so menacing that Jesuits were being expelled from countries all over the world. In Portugal, Jesuits were accused of plotting to kill a king. Such charges were not new. The "Black Popes," as the Jesuit generals are still called, had been accused of plotting the assassinations of William of Orange, Henry III and Henry IV of France, and Elizabeth I of England. As educators and friends of the rich and powerful, members of the order were developing an image as an elite, and were condemned in terms that made them sound very much like Illuminati.

In a popular book published in French, Spanish, Italian, and German, Jesuits were charged with "seditious machinations against every government in Europe" and of "surpassing Machiavelli in their diabolical plots" while "committing crimes worse than those of the Knights Templar." By 1773, when the Vatican was pressured into temporarily disbanding the order, a body of anti-Jesuit literature had developed. Members of the society were said to possess a diabolical talent to mold minds, a power that conspiracy theorists would later attribute to Communists and the secular-humanist media.

The Wandering Jew, an international best-seller published in 1844, is described by historian David Mitchell as the book that "set the fashion for a whole series of highly profitable anti-Jesuit thrillers." In the book, a character complains of "the darkness of this Company of Jesus, founded with the detestable and impious aim of destroying, by a homicidal education, all will, liberty, and intelligence in the people."

When persecuted Jesuits emigrated to the new United States, they were opposed both by Federalists who considered them enemies of Protestantism and by Democrats who believed they were agents of an ecclesiastical tyranny. In 1814, two years after the society was restored by Pope Pius VII, John Adams wrote to Thomas Jefferson:

> I do not like the resurrection of the Jesuits. Shall we not have regular swarms of them here, in as many disguises as even the King of the Gipsies himself can assume? . . . If ever any

congregation of men could merit eternal perdition on earth
and in hell, it is the Company of Loyola.

Jefferson replied: "Like you I disapprove of the restora-
tion . . . for it makes a retrograde step from light towards darkness."

"BREAK THE POPE'S NECK"

By the time Jefferson and Adams made their statements
against the Jesuits, anti-Catholicism was already a well-estab-
lished American tradition. In elementary school, history students are taught that America's spirit of free worship dates as
far back as 1649, when Lord Baltimore, the Catholic proprietor
of the colony of Maryland, passed the Toleration Act, calling
for people of differing religions to live in peace. But Baltimore
promoted the legislation out of fear of persecution from Protestants who were becoming the majority in the colony, which
had begun as a haven for Catholics. Amid rumors of a Vatican
plot to kill dissenters, Baltimore was banished from the colony,
and the Toleration Act was replaced with a law stating that
"none who profess to exercise the Popish religion, commonly
known by the name of Roman Catholic religion, can be protected in this province." England wouldn't approve so extreme
a measure, but it did allow Catholics to be banned from public
office.

England had been an enemy of the Vatican since 1534,
when the Pope would not approve Henry VIII's divorce. British fears that the Catholic powers, France and Spain, would
defeat England and return it to Catholic control were brought
to America by the colonists. With French settlements to the
north and Spanish enclaves to the south, the British-Americans
felt they were being surrounded by Catholics. The few Catholics among them often were seen not as fellow citizens but as
agents of a Vatican-run plot.

In Massachusetts, the Puritan government called for the
banishment of Catholic priests. Those returning were to be executed. In 1696, the New Hampshire legislature required citizens to swear an anti-Catholic oath; and in Georgia, an inspec-

tor was appointed to bar Catholic immigrants who, it was
feared, would aid a Spanish invasion from Florida. Virginia
legislators, roused by fear of a Catholic-Indian plot "to cut the
throats of the Protestants," passed laws forbidding Catholics to
be witnesses, to be guardians, or to settle in large groups.
Shortly afterward, all Virginia Catholics were disarmed. In
Pennsylvania, Catholics were required to register with the authorities.

By the mid-1700s, a popular New England family game
was called "Break the Pope's Neck." Each November 5 was
dubbed "Pope Day": an effigy of the pontiff was paraded
through the streets and burned. The practice continued until it
was denounced in 1774 by George Washington, who was hoping to enlist the aid of Canada, then a largely Roman Catholic
country, in the revolution against England.

These anti-Catholic beliefs were held by a people who,
for the most part, had never seen a Catholic. In the 1830s and
1840s, when Catholics began to immigrate in large numbers to
the United States, the threat began to seem less abstract and the
conspiracy theories multiplied. Protestants were afraid Catholic
workers would compete for jobs and drive down wages. They
justified their hatred by depicting Catholicism as a force of absolute evil.

Speakers claiming to be former priests and nuns toured
the country, titillating Protestants with stories of scandals behind the walls of convents and monasteries. Books such as
Female Convents: Secrets of Nunneries Disclosed and *Jesuit Juggling:
Forty Popish Frauds Detected and Disclosed* popularized tales of
infant skeletons found buried beneath convents and of priests
seducing women in the secrecy of the confessional. The oppor-
tunities available to a celibate man alone in a dark room with a
young woman intrigued and disgusted readers. After taking
advantage of his visitor, it was thought, the priest could promise to absolve her of sin. *Awful Disclosures of the Hotel Dieu
Nunnery of Montreal,* by Maria Monk, sold 300,000 copies before the Civil War, making it a likely candidate for the best-
selling contemporary book in America before Harriet Beecher
Stowe's *Uncle Tom's Cabin.*

As Catholic immigration increased, the fear of Catholicism grew so strong that it soon erupted in violence. In 1829, homes of Irish Catholics in Boston were stoned for three days. In 1833, five hundred citizens raided the Irish section of Charlestown, burning down houses to punish the community for the actions of a group of drunken Irishmen who had beaten to death a "native American." America's Protestant culture was so saturated with the image of the Pope as biblical Antichrist that persecuting his subjects became almost respectable. "The average Protestant American of the 1850s had been trained from birth to hate Catholicism," historian Ray Allen Billington wrote.

> [H]is religious and even his secular newspapers had warned him of the dangers of Popery. . . . Venders of books against Rome penetrated into every corner of the nation. . . . Children whose primary instruction was from one of the primers in common use were accustomed to crude engravings of Protestant martyrs and to sentiments . . . that Popery included everything that was vicious and vile.

In an article in an 1835 edition of *Western Monthly* magazine, a writer complained that "the abuse of the Catholics . . . is a regular trade, and the compilation of anti-Catholic books . . . has become a part of the regular industry of the country, as much as the making of nutmegs, or the construction of clocks."

Images of Pilgrims and minutemen were adopted as insignia of militant Protestant organizations whose members were called "native Americans" or nativists. Accounts of anti-American Catholic plots became increasingly elaborate. Samuel F. B. Morse warned that Jesuits were directing the settlement of Catholic immigrants, strategically placing them for a Vatican-controlled revolution. In *Plea for the West,* published in 1835, Lyman Beecher, father of Harriet Beecher Stowe, wrote that Catholic schools were part of a plot to claim America's rich frontier for the church of Rome. As a revivalist preacher in Boston, Beecher helped arouse a spirit of anti-Catholicism that climaxed with the burning of a Massachusetts convent in 1834.

A decade after the convent burning, thirteen people were killed in three days of anti-Catholic rioting in Philadelphia.

Two Catholic churches were burned and a third was the site for a cannon and musket battle between nativists and the militia, which had been called to quell the disturbance. New York nativists, fearing the Philadelphia riots were the outbreak of a Catholic war on Protestantism, planned a large anti-Catholic demonstration in Central Park. By ordering the Catholic churches in the area surrounded by thousands of armed parishioners, the New York bishop possibly averted a riot.

Anti-Catholic violence was the work of a minority of Protestants, but it was fueled by sentiments common enough to decide elections. In 1844, anti-Catholic political groups elected six congressmen in New York City and Philadelphia and the mayors of New York and Boston. The Whigs were finding an alliance with the nativists as natural as the one their predecessors, the National Republicans, had made with the anti-Masonic movement. In both cases, parties run by a conservative upper-class elite took advantage of the mass support the nativists provided.

By 1854, annual immigration had quintupled over ten years, reaching a level of more than 427,000. To combat the changes these new settlers were causing in the makeup of American society, the anti-Catholic American party, nicknamed the Know-Nothings, was formed by the Order of the Star-Spangled Banner, a national secret society complete with lodges, passwords, and initiation rituals. When members were asked for details about the organization, they were to say that they knew nothing. Meetings were announced by distributing white paper hearts; red hearts were a danger sign.

After the fall elections, the governor and all state officers of Massachusetts were Know-Nothings, as well as the entire Massachusetts senate and all but two of the 378 members of the state house of representatives. The Know-Nothings claimed major victories in Delaware and Pennsylvania. "About seventy-five congressmen were sent to Washington, pledged to carry the nation into a war against the Pope and his minions," historian Ray Billington wrote. A year later, Know-Nothings added Rhode Island, New Hampshire, Connecticut, Maryland, Kentucky, New York, and California to their list of victories.

Newspapers were predicting a Know-Nothing president would be elected in 1856. But the party was unable to fulfill its promise. In the presidential election, one-fourth of the voters supported the Know-Nothings. Then the party began a fast decline as a force in national politics.

But anti-Catholicism lived on. After the Civil War, Northern Catholics were denounced as traitors by such leading papers as *Harper's Weekly*. A former Catholic priest wrote a book, *Fifty Years in the Church of Rome,* in which he blamed Jesuits for Lincoln's assassination. More than a century later, the book was reprinted by Chick Publications, which also offers a comic-book version of the story.

By 1895, an anti-Catholic organization called the American Protective Association claimed 2.5 million followers. It fought for "true Americanism" and immigration restrictions. To publicize its goals, it sponsored lectures by former nuns and priests and used forged documents to prove Catholic plots. The organization distributed a counterfeit encyclical in which Pope Leo XIII instructed American Catholics "to exterminate all heretics." Fears of such a massacre led the mayor of Toledo, Ohio, to call out the National Guard. The association claimed that bank failures and labor strikes were part of a Vatican conspiracy to take over the United States, and they denounced the Democrats as a party controlled by foreigners.

In the first decades of the twentieth century, stories of Catholic subversion were popularized by the *Menace,* an Ozark weekly that, by 1914, had a circulation of more than 1 million. In the 1920s, the Ku Klux Klan, which had between 3 million and 6 million members, warned of a Catholic plot to take control of the United States government. The Klan attributed the assassinations of presidents Lincoln, Garfield, and McKinley to a Vatican plot. According to one Klan theory, President Harding had been killed by "telepathic thought waves generated in the brains of Jesuit adepts."

In 1920, Tom Watson, whose *Watson's Magazine* promoted anti-Catholic conspiracy theories involving the Knights of Columbus, became a United States senator. By then, Jewish immigrants were becoming as visible as Catholic immigrants had been the century before, and Watson directed some of his efforts toward uncovering what he thought were Jewish plots. He also condemned Wall Street, the oil companies, and the United States Steel Corporation as enemies of the common people.

Watson was an example of what was becoming a confusing political phenomenon: the populist who combined leftist sentiments with a belief in a conspiracy against white Protestants. When Watson died in 1922, Socialist party leader Eugene V. Debs called him "a great man, a heroic soul who fought the power of evil his whole life long in the interest of the common people [who] loved and honored him." At his funeral was an eight-foot-high cross of roses sent by the Ku Klux Klan.

THE RIVERA HOAX

In his 1980s version of anti-Catholic paranoia, Alberto Rivera claims the Vatican has developed more subtle techniques to subjugate the United States. By promoting the ecumenical movement, he believes, the Jesuits make it appear that the differences between Protestants and Catholics are minor. By penetrating the schools with Jesuit-influenced history books, the Catholics supposedly train children to accept Catholicism as the sister and not the enemy of Protestantism. (That Protestants and Catholics both celebrate Thanksgiving is to Rivera part of the plot.) By encouraging religious plurality, Catholics are eroding America's Protestant culture, Rivera believes, and replacing it with a secular-humanistic system in which all beliefs are of equal value. When the barrier between the two forms of Christianity has been dissolved, Rome will reimpose its control and Protestantism will become a footnote to Catholicism.

Most Catholics may be unsuspecting Roman agents, said Rivera in an interview, but they are all potential traitors:

"[O]nce that he pleads his alliance to the flag of the Vatican and to the Pope of Rome and to the canon laws, he has already another constitution, another flag, and another country."

Because he believes he is one of the few men who can expose the conspiracy, Rivera is convinced that Jesuits are trying to destroy his credibility. He blames the conspirators for an investigation by the magazine *Christianity Today,* which concluded that Rivera was never a Jesuit priest and that two of his children (including one who died in infancy) were born while he was supposedly under the vow of celibacy. The article stated that Rivera did not have a sister who was a nun in England and that he had been wanted by police on charges of writing bad checks, stealing a credit card, and using an automobile without authorization.

"The [Jesuits] have been after my life since I left Madrid in 1967," Rivera said. He claimed that they fired into his house and at his car, tried to run him off the road, and attempted to kidnap his wife and children.

Often, he said, they've used poison. "So many times that I cannot even count I felt the effect. . . . I collapsed in many instances when I was about to preach in public auditoriums. I collapsed in the street. I collapsed while I was driving once. . . . Doctors have used medicines to distort my mind."

He believes he is alive only because God is not ready for him to die.

"I'm here to do no more than what Jesus Christ did," Rivera said. "I'm here not because I am the light. I'm here because I carry the light. . . . The accusations and slanders have made my convictions stronger than ever."

In an issue of a newsletter published by the Anti-Christ Information Center, publisher Jack Chick defended Rivera against the charges in *Christianity Today*. He claimed the car and credit card were given to Rivera by Vatican agents pretending to be brethren who wanted to aid his ministry. When Rivera crossed the state line, they called the police.

"The Pharisees couldn't give Pilate legitimate evidence either," Chick wrote, "so they had to find another way." He reminded readers that the Vatican supposedly conspired to destroy another of his colleagues, a young man by the name of John Todd.

Todd made national news in 1978 when he spoke to fundamentalist churches throughout the nation, claiming that until being saved by Jesus he had been a witch and a Grand Druid high priest in the Illuminati. As a member of the "Council of Thirteen," he said, he was a tier beneath the Rothschilds in a worldwide conspiracy of international bankers who were in league with the devil. Todd believed Jimmy Carter was the Antichrist. As part of the Illuminati takeover, guns would be confiscated, a false fuel shortage created, and all Christians tortured and murdered. Their names, he said, were stored in computers. The Christian Broadcasting Network, preacher Jerry Falwell, and the Maranatha "Jesus rock" company were part of the plot. Todd advised Christians to store weapons and food to survive the planned devastation.

Todd said his conversion to Jesus came after reading one of Chick's tracts. Chick met Todd in 1973 after the young man had appeared on Christian television shows, becoming a celebrity among Southern California's fundamentalist fringe. Like Rivera, Todd had traveled the fundamentalist circuits for years, working in a Christian coffeehouse and as a storefront preacher. Chick published Todd's story and used him as an adviser for two comics warning of the dangers of the occult. In one of them, *The Broken Cross,* a teenage girl is picked up hitchhiking by hippie devil-worshipers who sacrifice her during a black mass.

Christianity Today reported that Todd, while preaching for Jesus, was practicing witchcraft on the side and seducing teenage girls. The article quoted preachers who had turned against Todd after first being entranced by his story. According to the report, even the National Church and School of Wicca, an organization of witches, denounced Todd as a fraud.

Rivera said he accepted Todd's description of the conspiracy, with one modification: the witches in the plot are run by the Jesuits.

POSTSCRIPT

While Protestants have become the main designers of Illuminati conspiracy theories in the twentieth century, Catholics haven't completely abandoned the craft. In the late 1930s, the Sunday afternoon radio broadcasts of a Catholic priest named Father Charles Coughlin drew an audience estimated in the tens of millions. The core of his following consisted of Irish Catholics, who had been in the United States long enough to feel nativist sentiments of their own. Coughlin preached that the United States was being destroyed by a conspiracy of bankers,

Jews, and Communists. He combined his political paranoia with populist beliefs, calling for a state-controlled economy and a guaranteed annual wage for anyone willing to work. Coughlin was praised in the Nazi newspaper *Der Sturmer*. In 1938, he supported Nazism as a defense against communism. According to Coughlin's conspiracy theory, Adam Weishaupt founded communism. The priest also believed that international Masonry was involved in a plot against Benito Mussolini, who was once honored in Coughlin's magazine, *Social Justice*, as Man of the Week.

Later in the century, followers of another conservative Catholic leader, the French archbishop Marcel Lefebvre, developed a different Illuminati theory—one that attacked their own church. In the early 1980s, there are about two hundred churches and missions in the United States defying the Pope by celebrating the old Latin Mass and ignoring the Vatican II reforms. About half of these Catholic traditionalists are served by priests from Lefebvre's Society of St. Pius X seminary in Oyster Bay Cove, New York. While Rivera and his fundamentalist followers see Vatican II as part of an Illuminati plot to disarm Protestantism, Lefebvre's Catholics believe it is a conspiracy of Protestants and Freemasons to corrupt the purity of the Church.

The traditionalists believe that in modernizing the Mass, the Vatican II council changed its meaning. For example, the old Mass, decreed by the Council of Trent in 1570, stated—in Latin—that Christ's blood is shed "for you and for many." In the English version of the new Mass, the blood is shed "for you and for all men"—even Protestants, the traditionalists complain.

This consorting with the enemy is as upsetting to Catholic traditionalists as it is to Alberto Rivera. "I'm a very orderly person," said a lay leader in a traditionalist church that follows Lefebvre. "I have a very orderly mind. It doesn't make sense to me that there can be one hundred and one ways to achieve your eternal reward. You get a dozen priests together and not one would agree on anything having to do with doctrine or dogma. You get a dozen of *our* priests together and they would all agree."

Like the Protestant fundamentalists, the Catholic traditionalists believe their religion is the receptacle of absolute truth; they dismiss their enemies as part of an international satanic plot. Traditionalists believe it was bad enough that, in writing the reforms, Protestants were consulted. But, according to a tract distributed by a group called the Catholic Doctrine Center of Green Bay, Wisconsin, the archbishop in charge of rewriting the Mass was a high-ranking Freemason.

Catholics for Tradition, of Monroe, Connecticut, distributes a tract called *The Dream of Vatican II,* containing what it claims are secret Masonic writings that describe a plan to infiltrate the church and bring about "the destruction forever of Catholicism." True Mass Tapes of Milwaukee, Wisconsin, sells, in addition to cassette tapes of the old Mass, recordings of Pope Leo XIII's encyclical condemning Freemasonry, and works called *Papacy and Freemasonry, V-2 Betrayed Christ—Rome under Enemy Occupation, The Robber Church—How They Did the Inside Job,* and *The Protocols—World-wide Judeo-Masonic Plot.* (*The Protocols of the Elders of Zion,* a document now believed to be a forgery, describes an international Jewish conspiracy.)

Lefebvre himself has said that Freemasons "celebrate Black Masses and are in league with the devil." Father Clarence Kelly, leader of Lefebvre's movement in the United States, wrote *Conspiracy Against God and Man,* in which he attempted to show that liberal Protestantism, Catholic modernism, and communism are outgrowths of Adam Weishaupt's Illuminati-Freemason plot. In all three systems, God-revealed truth is considered subordinate to man-made agendas for modernizing society, Kelly wrote. The deism of Weishaupt and the Masons led to communism, Kelly believes, by deemphasizing the value of the individual—people, like birds and trees, were considered nothing more than manifestations of a pantheistic world soul. Extend that concept to a politics in which people are manifestations of the state, Kelly believes, and you have the doctrines of Karl Marx.

Kelly graduated magna cum laude in philosophy from Catholic University in Washington, D.C. But he makes it clear that he believes Illuminism is not merely a current in the history of modern thought but a conspiracy. The primary sources for his book are John Robison, Abbe Barruel, Nesta Webster, and popes Leo XIII and Pius XI, who made statements against what they believed were international Masonic and Communist conspiracies. "[I]f the impending doom is not averted," Kelly wrote, " . . . America and civilization will be lost . . . and there will come upon us the longest, most treacherous, and severest 'dark night of the soul' the race of man has yet known."

Kelly's book was published by the John Birch Society and dedicated to the society's founder, Robert Welch, and His Grace, Archbishop Marcel Lefebvre.

6

Bankers, Communists, and Jews

"A vast conspiracy against mankind has been organized on two continents, and it is rapidly taking possession of the world. If not met and overthrown at once it forebodes terrible social convulsions, the destruction of civilization, or the establishment of an absolute despotism."

—from the platform of the
People's Party, 1892

By the late nineteenth century, the Illuminati panic and the anti-Masonic scare were fading memories. A Vatican take-over of the United States had failed to materialize, and anti-Catholic conspiracy theories began to wane. But the paranoid tradition had developed a momentum of its own. The minds of millions of Americans had become stamped with the image of an international conspiracy, run by a secret elite that manipulated the masses with mysterious powers: an absolutely evil force that was supposedly trying to undermine U.S. sovereignty, abolish Christianity, and bring on Armageddon. If the conspirators weren't located in the Vatican, conspiracy theorists feared that perhaps they were meeting in other secret chambers.

To replace the Pope, three new devils emerged: international bankers, Communists, and Jews—particularly Zionists. Since the paranoid mind tends to see all opponents as part of a

103

single satanic spirit, the three new versions of the Illuminati legend quickly became intertwined. The result was the perplexing notion of the capitalist-Communist-Jewish plot, which has dominated political paranoia for most of the twentieth century and has been revived in recent years by a Washington, D.C., extremist organization called Liberty Lobby.

Each week, Liberty Lobby sends more than 330,000 subscribers the latest issue of the *Spotlight,* which details the developments in a conspiracy of international "megabankers" and leaders of multinational corporations, who supposedly are plotting with Communists and Zionists to weaken the United States and absorb it into a one-world empire. In their conspiracy theory, Liberty Lobby leaders include the Trilateral Commission, the Council on Foreign Relations, the Federal Reserve System, and the Anti-Defamation League of B'nai B'rith.

In recent years, *Spotlight* stories have claimed that this unlikely mix of conspirators is scheming to sap the strength of the United States by embroiling the country in a futile Vietnam-like war in El Salvador; that David Rockefeller's Chase Manhattan Bank tricked President Carter into admitting the deposed Shah of Iran to the United States, triggering the takeover of the American embassy in Tehran and damaging U.S. prestige abroad; and that the Trilateral Commission is duping the country into subjugating its needs to a new international economic community, which will include Communist countries. Liberty Lobby regularly excoriates the Anti-Defamation League as part of a plot to brainwash the United States into bankrolling Israeli war efforts. American Jews who support Israel are condemned as traitors who value Zionism above patriotism.

In their isolationist fervor, Liberty Lobby's leaders try to explain every war the United States has been involved in as part of the conspiracy. In their version of World War II, Roosevelt plotted with Churchill to provoke the German bombing of Britain and the Japanese attack on Pearl Harbor—all as an excuse to wage the war the bankers and Communists had already planned.

Over the last hundred years, this world view in which

bankers, Communists, and Jews are twisted into a single enemy has become so engrained in the minds of some right-wingers that it is difficult to unravel the threads and explain exactly how they are supposed to fit together. The connections are more emotional than rational, but the purpose of a conspiracy theory is to impose a system on inchoate hate. To Liberty Lobby, the world works something like this:

By promoting U.S. involvement in foreign wars, the bankers force the federal government into debt. To cover its mounting deficit, the country must borrow money from the Federal Reserve System—which is supposedly run by the international bankers—or tax citizens through the Internal Revenue Service, another element in the plot. The Soviets benefit because the United States is so distracted by its various foreign ventures that it has no time to oppose the Communist plan to enslave the world with a Marxist superstate.

According to the theory, Communists and capitalists only seem to be competitors, while, in truth, they are working toward the same goals: socialism and one-world government. Expensive federal social programs increase government borrowing, enriching the bankers. Taxes and government regulation oppress small-scale entrepreneurs and businessmen, keeping them from challenging the bankers' wealth. In a one-world government, this power over the people would be extended to every continent, strengthening the banker's stranglehold on the planet.

As a sign of the symbiotic relationship between capitalism and communism, the conspiracy theorists point to Karl Marx's *Communist Manifesto*, which lists the establishment of an income tax and the centralization of credit in a national bank as two of the steps necessary to bring a country to communism. One by one, countries will gradually be led from capitalism to socialism to communism; then they will be linked together into a world federation. But while the Communists continue to espouse an ideology that champions the masses, they supposedly will be serving the international financiers.

From the stories in *Spotlight,* it is difficult to tell whether the Communists are supposed to be conscious agents of the bankers or unwitting dupes. International communism and international capitalism are fused into a homogenous mix. The role international Zionism is supposed to play in the plot is even more ambiguous. But what is clear is that the people running Liberty Lobby hate bankers, Communists, taxes, big government, foreign aid, Zionists, and liberals. The organization opposes foreign aid, busing, peacetime draft, government spending, illegal immigration, and all things international, including the metric system. It is in favor of withdrawing United States troops from Europe and prohibiting welfare recipients from voting.

All these goals are supported in the name of what Liberty Lobby calls "populism" and "nationalism." Populism, as Liberty Lobby defines it, "means government by those who supply the money for the bills and the blood for the wars. It means government of, by, and for the producing and creating middle class of America, not for the predatory superrich and the shiftless poor." Nationalism is "undiluted sovereignty over our skies and shores. It means a foreign policy to advance . . . the interests of *all* the people—not just the interests of irresponsible international bankers, multinational corporations, ethnic, religious and political minorities and foreign countries."

Like the isolationist, nativist organizations that preceded it, Liberty Lobby's ideology reduces its enemies to pegs and plugs them into the holes of an immensely complicated plot, based on the extraordinary document called the *Protocols of the Elders of Zion.*

THE PROTOCOLS

The myth in which Jews are cast as both bomb-throwing Bolsheviks and international financiers was first popularized in czarist Russia in 1903, when an anti-Semitic newspaper published what purported to be the minutes of twenty-four meetings held six years earlier in Basel, Switzerland, at the time of the first international Zionist conference. Two years later, these so-called *Protocols of the Elders of Zion* were included in a book written by a Russian mystic, Sergei Nilus, who used them as documentation for the coming of the Antichrist's world empire.

The *Protocols* purported to describe a plan by the elite of international Jewry to gradually dominate the world. With their allies the Freemasons, the Jews would control the minds and the lives of "the *goyim.*" By introducing the concept of human rights—liberty, equality, fraternity—the elders supposedly had fomented revolutions and defeated benevolent aristocrats. They had invented Darwinism and Marxism to create a world view in which people were seen as little more than animals: mouths to consume the products sold by the operators of the international money system. To further this dehumanization, God was replaced by "the sovereignty of reason." The minds of the people were controlled through the press and their will diminished by making them dependent on experts. "The *goyim* have lost the habit of thinking," the writer of the *Protocols* boasted, "unless prompted by the suggestions of our specialists."

By manipulating the economy, the elders supposedly created depressions and wars that eventually would make the people clamor for an international "super-government" under the rule of the "King-Despot of the blood of Zion." Wages were raised to addict workers to luxury and consumption, but the pay increases were paid for by devaluing the currency through inflation. The people were forced to borrow, putting themselves under the control of the creditors.

In short, the *Protocols* described a world in which an elite of money managers sat atop an economic pyramid accumulating the benefits of a hedonistic society controlled by technocrats. "Surely we shall not fail with such wealth to prove that all that evil which for so many centuries we have had to commit has served . . . the cause of true well-being—the bringing of everything into order." Everyone would have a place in the system.

The *Protocols* was an outgrowth of earlier tales in which Jews were condemned by Christians as adepts of occult powers conferred by Satan. During the Middle Ages, stories circulated claiming that a secret council of rabbis was hiding in Spain, using sorcery to wage an invisible war against Christendom. This new version of the myth, in which the conspirators used the power of reason to destroy governments and Christianity, was influenced by the legend of Adam Weishaupt's Illuminati.

One of the earliest references to a Judeo-Masonic alliance appeared during the aftermath of the French Revolution in a work by Abbe Barruel, the priest who wrote *Memoirs of Jacobinism,* the multivolume book that helped launch the Illuminati scare. After *Memoirs of Jacobinism* was published in 1797, Barruel received a letter from a man in Florence congratulating him on exposing the plot but suggesting that he had overlooked an important element: Jews. The writer claimed that the Illuminati and Freemasons were the latest agents in a Jewish conspiracy that also included the Moslem Assassins and ancient Christian heretics. Furthermore, he wrote, eight hundred Italian Catholic leaders, including bishops and cardinals, were secretly Jews. Barruel shared the letter with some of his colleagues, and he described a Jewish-Templar-Masonic conspiracy in a manuscript that he destroyed two days before he died—but not before mentioning his latest theory to a fellow Jesuit.

During the next century, stories that Jews and Masons were part of a satanic plot proliferated throughout France. The myth was reinforced by the fact that French Masonic lodges admitted Jews as members. Conspiracy theorists also found it significant that Freemasons included the Star of David among the ancient symbols they revered, and that they sometimes studied the mystical Jewish cabala. A book published in 1869 claimed that the cabala was established by Lucifer at the beginning of the world and passed to Cush—builder of the Tower of Babel—and eventually to the Jews, Gnostics, Assassins, Knights Templar, and Freemasons. Currently, the author claimed, the Jews were using cabalistic powers to help bring on the kingdom of the Antichrist.

Drawing on this anti-Semitic tradition, the *Protocols* was concocted in late nineteenth-century Paris, apparently by a member of a group of Russian émigrés, which included a woman named Yuliana Glinka, the daughter of a Russian diplomat, a dabbler in the occult, and an agent of the czarist police. She delivered the *Protocols* to Russia, where it was used to justify the need for pogroms.

As believers in the supernatural, nineteenth-century occultists were likely adherents to conspiracy theories. Glinka was a follower of another Russian émigré, Madame Blavatsky, whose mystical Theosophical Society taught an occult religion whose followers included William Butler Yeats and Thomas Edison. Blavatsky herself believed in a worldwide Jesuit conspiracy. In their efforts to transcend the worldly, some Theosophists succumbed to the age-old stereotype of Jew as materialist. In 1888, the Theosophical Publishing Society republished a book called *The Hebrew Talisman,* which described a worldwide international conspiracy of Jews who wielded power through magic and money. On the frontpiece of the book was a caricature of Nathan Meyer Rothschild.

Before delivering a copy of the *Protocols* to the Russian police, Glinka had given them a book called *The Secret of the Jews,* which told of arcana passed from Hermes Trismegistus through a chain consisting of the Eleusinian mystery cult, the Knights Templar, and the Freemasons. As in the *Protocols,* capitalism, secularism, and a revolution of peasants were considered part of an elitist conspiracy. While the Jews in the *Protocols* used their rational expertise to rule the masses, those in *The Secret of the Jews* used occult powers.

In early twentieth-century Russia, the *Protocols* provided supporters of the czar with a way to blame the Bolshevik Revolution on a world Jewish-Masonic conspiracy. Like the aristocratic foes of the French Revolution, the Russian monarchists believed that only conspirators with evil powers could rouse the masses to oppose the divine rule of the czar. Members of the Russian aristocracy, fleeing the revolution, brought the *Protocols* to Germany, where the work became a best-seller. By 1920, 120,000 copies of a German edition of the *Protocols* had been sold. When early Nazi theoreticians such as Alfred Rosenberg worked the *Protocols* myth into their racist ideology, they found a ready audience.

The German people were demoralized after losing World War I. Moreover, they were feeling the effects of the Great Depression and feared that the Bolsheviks would exploit the situation by spreading their revolution to Germany. Nazism offered the Germans the fantasy that they were members of a superior Aryan race destined to rule Europe. The German peasant was romanticized both as the product of holy German soil and as the victim of Communists, who opposed their traditional way of life, and financiers, who produced nothing yet prospered through usury.

In the Nazi conspiracy theory, these forces represented "the evil principle," as described by an associate of Adolf Eichmann after the war. "Against this world of evil the race-mystics set the world of good, of light, incarnated in blond, blue-eyed people."

According to the Nazis, the flowering of German spirituality was being blocked by the Jews. The *Protocols* provided the Nazis with a way to roll the seeming opposites of the Jewish capitalist and Communist into one. In a 1937 lecture, Heinrich Himmler described the Nazis' "natural opponent" as "international Bolshevism run by the Jews and Freemasons." In 1939, Josef Goebbels blamed Germany's problems on "the circles of international Jewry, international Freemasonry and international Marxism." In *Mein Kampf,* Hitler wrote that the fact that the Jews said the *Protocols* was a forgery was "the best proof that they are authentic."

By lending their excess wealth and charging interest, Hitler wrote, the Jews learned to produce something from nothing, eventually controlling governments through the power of credit. In Hitler's conspiracy theory, Jews were using the press to mold public opinion. By allying with Freemasons and Marxists, Jews promoted internationalism to destroy nation-states and increase their own influence over the world economy. Hitler tried to rationalize his view of the Jew as capitalist and Communist: as financiers and industrialists, he wrote, Jews were responsible for exploiting workers; but by pretending to sympathize with their victims, Jews encouraged the revolutions that destroyed nations.

"In resisting the Jew, I am fighting the Lord's battle," Hitler wrote. He foresaw the day when "another power stands up against him [the Jew] and in a mighty struggle casts him, the heaven-stormer, back to Lucifer." Although Hitler believed that Jesus was an Aryan, he claimed Christianity was invented by Jewish conspirators to weaken the will of the purebloods by teaching pacifism and egalitarianism.

HENRY FORD

In the United States, the *Protocols* was also used to blame a Jewish conspiracy for social and economic uncertainty. Between 1920 and 1927, automaker Henry Ford's 600,000-circulation *Dearborn Independent* printed a number of articles based on the *Protocols,* claiming that Jews were using communism, banking, labor unions, alcohol, gambling, jazz music, the newspapers, and the cinema to weaken American culture and absorb the United States into a world government, called "All-Judan." One story declared that the Jews were behind plots that had been unfairly blamed on the Masons and Weishaupt's Illuminati. Many of the articles were reprinted as a book, *The International Jew: The World's Foremost Problem,* which sold more than 500,000 copies in the United States and was translated into sixteen languages. Hitler admired the book and praised "Heinrich Ford as the leader of the growing Fascist movement in America."

In 1923, Ford was endorsed as candidate for president of the United States by the populist People's Progressive Party. In a poll by *Collier's* magazine, he led all other candidates.

Ford's following had grown from a populist tradition that blamed financiers for the economic problems of American farmers. In the United States, antibanker conspiracy theories first became widespread during the 1890s, when a tight money supply was making it hard for farmers to get the loans they needed for planting. Leaders of the Populist movement blamed the problem on international bankers, who were often stereotyped as Jews.

The myth of the evil Jewish banker dates from medieval times, when banking was one of the few trades open to Jews. Because of the biblical ban on usury, Christians weren't supposed to loan money at interest. To accommodate the expanding European economy, a few wealthy Jews were allowed, and in some cases compelled, to become bankers. With their consciences eased, the Christians borrowed money, while hypo-critically condemning Jews as usurers.

By the late nineteenth century, Anglo-Saxon financiers such as the Morgans were at least as powerful as the Roth-schilds, but the myth persisted that all powerful financiers were Jewish. Stories about the Rothschilds still circulated in the United States, and soon the populists were blaming Jewish bankers for skillfully engineering conflicts throughout Ameri-can history, including the Civil War. In 1913, when the bank-ing community succeeded in convincing Congress of the need to establish the Federal Reserve System, the action further in-flamed populist paranoia. Since the authors of the Federal Re-serve Act included banker Paul Warburg and Senator Nelson Aldrich (John D. Rockefeller, Jr.'s father-in-law), Jews and Wall Street capitalists were woven into the conspiracy theory.

When news of the Bolshevik Revolution reached the United States, the Jewish Communist vied with the Jewish banker as villain in the fantasies of the right. In 1919, the Com-munist International was founded, espousing the cause of world revolution. The Justice Department took such idealistic notions at face value. Invoking the specter of an international conspiracy, Attorney General A. Mitchell Palmer ordered the arrest of thousands of aliens and attempted to deport them as Communists. Employers used fears of a Red conspiracy to arouse opposition to the developing labor-union movement. White Protestant organizations like the Ku Klux Klan spread stories that Jewish immigrants were soldiers in a Communist plot.

It was true that some of the 2 million Jews who came to the United States between 1881 and 1914 favored liberal poli-tics and socialism. They were fleeing countries where the estab-lished powers exploited laborers and Jews. In the United States, many Jews looked to Socialist political groups and the labor-union movement to protect them from employers eager to take advantage of newcomers who desperately needed jobs. A few of the more radical American Jews became Commu-nists. But while the majority of the 15,000 members of the small American Communist party were Jews, they represented a fraction of the Jewish population.

In retrospect, it seems that what the nativists really feared was less a Communist-Jewish takeover than the influx of new ideas. They were looking to blame a visible group of foreigners for the cosmopolitanism, secularism, and pluralism that were becoming part of modern life. Discoveries in science were challenging religious truth. Better transportation and communication were exposing citizens to other cultures. World War I shattered the comfortable but stultifying notion that the United States could exist in isolation from the world community. The white Protestant way of life was becoming one of a number of cultures commingling in the United States. Instead of welcoming this cultural plurality, the nativists rallied behind a strict monistic view. They defined their beliefs as "one hundred percent Americanism"—a force for absolute good challenged by evil.

The *Protocols* was used as a way to explain away society's rapid changes. In 1920, an article appeared in the *Chicago Tribune* arguing that communism was part of the Jewish plot for world domination. On the same day, *The Christian Science Monitor* printed a lead editorial, "The Jewish Peril," that noted how much the *Protocols* resembled the doctrines of Adam Weishaupt's Illuminati.

Nesta Webster cited the *Protocols* in her 1924 book *Secret Societies and Subversive Movements,* ensuring that occultism would continue to be seen as a force in the Jewish plot. In her books, including *World Revolution* and *The Socialist Network,* she described communism and socialism as evil philosophies that were an outgrowth of an esoteric tradition including the Knights Templar, Assassins, Freemasons, Rosicrucians, Illuminati, and even Blavatsky's Theosophists. The Templars, Webster noted, accumulated so many riches during the Crusades that they became lenders to kings—the first international bankers. Webster, a member of the British Fascist movement, apparently developed a personal interest in conspiratorial causes of subversion when she had a mystical experience that convinced her that she was possessed by the spirit of a countess who had suffered during the French Revolution at the hands of the commoners.

In 1927, after a libel suit was filed against him by a prominent Jewish attorney, Henry Ford retracted the anti-Semitic statements made in his newspaper, claiming they were published without his knowledge. Following his apology, the suit was dropped. But the image of the Communist-capitalist-Jewish conspirator had become firmly established in right-wing minds. During the Depression, the conspiracy theory was promoted by Father Coughlin and Gerald Winrod, who both cited the *Protocols* and worked Adam Weishaupt's Illuminati into the plot. Coughlin blamed international bankers for the Depression. While he denounced the New Deal for enriching bankers, Elizabeth Dilling, another conspiracy theorist of the time, believed it was a Communist scheme.

In the 1970s, almost a century after it was first forged, the *Protocols* continued to circulate. Gamal Abdel Nasser used them in his propaganda against Israel. Nazi immigrants popularized the work in South America. In 1976, the *Protocols* was cited by New Zealand's Minister of Labor in a denunciation of Communists. A Malaysian magazine quoted from the *Protocols* in condemning a Zionist-Freemason plot against Islamic thought.

WILLIS A. CARTO

After the Holocaust of World War II, anti-Semitic conspiracy theories became repugnant to all but the fringe of the American right. Populist fears of the power of the rich became focused instead on organizations that promote international capitalism, such as the Trilateral Commission, the Council on Foreign Relations, and the Bilderbergers, a group of world leaders and businesspeople who held one of their early conferences on international relations at the Bilderberg Hotel in the Netherlands.

In the 1980s, neo-Nazi groups and the various organizations that claim to be descendants of the Ku Klux Klan still distribute the *Protocols*. But there are only about 8000 to 9000 Klan followers and about one-fourth that many American Nazis. It has been largely through the work of Liberty Lobby's founder, Willis A. Carto, that the vision of a conspiracy of bankers, Communists, and Jews has been revived and preserved as a force in right-wing politics.

Carto, who founded Liberty Lobby in 1958, after soliciting $15,000 from fellow right-wingers, has described integration as "racial mongrelization" and the "niggerfication of America," and decried "the power of organized Jewry." He has written that in allying itself with the Soviet Union against Germany's Third Reich, the United States fought on the wrong side of World War II. In 1969, journalist Drew Pearson published a memo Carto had written to a colleague. "There are 600 million Chinese and about 200 million Russians," the memo stated.

> All are united in a determination to destroy the West. . . . Hitler's defeat was the defeat of Europe. And America. How could we have been so blind? The blame, it seems, must be laid at the door of the international Jews. It was their propaganda, lies and demands which blinded the West as to what Germany was doing.

Carto denied writing the memo, but the sentiments it expressed are consistent with the philosophy of the man he considers his mentor, Francis Parker Yockey, author of a book called *Imperium*, dedicated to "the hero of the Second World War," whom he considered to be Adolf Hitler.

In June 1960, with Liberty Lobby in its infancy, Carto went to the San Francisco jail to visit Yockey, who had been arrested after it was discovered that he owned three passports made out in different names. It wasn't clear what Yockey was doing in his travels about the world, but he had a past that aroused suspicion. Yockey, the San Francisco newspapers reported, had been discharged from the Army after he was diagnosed as a paranoid schizophrenic. After graduating with honors from Notre Dame law school, he served in 1945 as a lawyer for the War Crimes Tribunal, but quit because he felt the Nazis were getting an unfair trial. He believed the Holocaust atrocities had been fabricated by the Jews and that the Nazis were persecuted martyrs, whom he compared to Galileo, Henry David Thoreau, and Joan of Arc. Yockey went to Ireland, where he spent six months writing *Imperium: The Philosophy of History and Politics*. In the book, he wrote that he hoped for a day when religion and authority would triumph over rationalism and money, as they had begun to under the Third Reich, and the forces of nationalism would be subjugated into an international Imperium, in which all power possessed by individuals would be surrendered to the state. What prevented the coming of this state of spiritual fascism was, Yockey wrote, the "culture distorter," or Jew.

"I knew that I was in the presence of a great force," Carto wrote after meeting Yockey, "and I could feel History standing aside me." About a week later, Yockey ingested potassium cyanide and died in jail. But Carto kept alive his legend, republishing *Imperium* in 1962.

Inspired by the memory of Yockey, Carto expanded his movement. In 1962, Liberty Lobby opened a Washington, D.C., office. During the 1964 presidential campaign of Barry Goldwater, the group raised $346,000 by selling right-wing tracts. Two years later, Carto bought H. L. Mencken's magazine *American Mercury*, using it to print excerpts from *Imperium* and articles promoting Aryan supremacy. Carto insisted that the root of superiority was genetic. He published articles such as "Genetic Diseases Disprove Racial Equality Lies," which argued that white genes should be kept isolated from those of blacks and Jews. While the *Mercury*'s writers concentrated on anti-Jewish conspiracy theories, they occasionally explored the conspiratorial evils of mystical cults, witchcraft, and the Illuminati.

Carto also started his own publishing company, Noontide Press, to distribute *Imperium*, the *Protocols*, *Mein Kampf*, and such works as *Anne Frank's Diary—A Hoax*, *Debunking the Genocide Myth*, and *The Makers of Civilization in Race and History*, which was billed in an advertisement as a story of the "Rise of the Aryan . . . an exciting factual account of Mankind's greatest race."

In 1979, another Carto organization, the Institute for Historical Review, held its first conference purporting to expose what its leaders call the "Holocaust hoax." The institute offers a $50,000 reward to anyone who can prove to its satisfaction that Hitler really killed 6 million Jews. (In 1981, an Auschwitz survivor sued the organization after it refused to give him the reward.)

This so-called Holocaust revisionism has become so com-

mon a form of anti-Semitism that some West German legisla-
tors are trying to pass a law that would make it a crime. In
England, historical revisionism is espoused by the right-wing
National Front, which also subscribes to a conspiracy theory
including Zionists, Communists, international bankers, the
Trilateral Commission, and the Council on Foreign Relations.
In the United States, the movement has been promoted largely
by Carto, who spoke at the Institute for Historical Review's
conventions at Northrop University in 1979 and at Pomona
College in 1980.

At the conferences, researchers presented papers such as
"Fake Atrocity Photographs" and "The Mechanics of Gas-
sing." Since the revisionists believe the Holocaust was invented
as part of a Communist-Zionist plot, it is no surprise that they
resort to the same techniques of pseudoscholarship used by
conspiracy theorists. They deluge their audiences with a preponderance of "facts," chosen to document a conclusion arrived at in advance. Calculations are used to show, for example, that after burning 6 million Jews, the Nazis would be faced
with the difficult task of disposing of 15,000 to 27,000 tons of
ash. The gas chambers and canisters of cyanide gas found in the
concentration camps were actually used for delousing clothes
and prisoners, the revisionists say, and the crematories for disposing of victims of a typhoid epidemic. By "final solution"
Hitler supposedly meant exporting Jews, not killing them.
Through distorted demographics, the revisionists claim to
show that the number of missing Jews can be accounted for by
relocation and absorption into the populations of other countries.

The articles in the institute's *Journal of Historical Review*
discuss such issues in the calm tones of academia. Its format
resembles that of a scholarly journal. Included on its editorial
advisory committee are several college professors from the
University of Buenos Aires, California State University,
Northwestern University, the University of Lyon in France,
the University of Kentucky, Concordia University in Montreal, and the University of Tulsa. Also on the board is Dr.
Martin A. Larson, a columnist for Liberty Lobby's newspaper,
Spotlight.

Carto and his cohorts deny they use "international banker" and "Zionist" as synonyms for "Jew." The editors of *Spotlight* distinguish between anti-Semitism, which they say they do not embrace, and anti-Zionism, which they promote wholeheartedly. They argue that they are not against Jews as people but against those they believe dominate banking and the media.

Critics argue that Liberty Lobby uses anti-Zionism as a cover to promote anti-Semitism. A report by the Anti-Defamation League described Carto as "probably the most important and powerful professional anti-Semite in the United States."

Carto denies the Anti-Defamation League's contention that the Institute for Historical Review, Noontide Press, and the *Mercury* are parts of an anti-Semitic network he controls. Liberty Lobby modestly lists him as its treasurer. But the same names keep appearing on the staffs of publications and organizations that all advertise and praise one another and espouse the same philosophy, while denying that they are anti-Semitic. A business license on file in Torrance, California, where Carto lives, was submitted by a group called the Legion for the Survival of Freedom, Inc., doing business as "the Noontide Press/Institute for Historical Review." It was signed by Carto's wife and listed a post office box that had been used by the *Mercury*.

Spotlight regularly reports the institute's activities, but in a tone more shrill than that of the journal. The paper sells a reprint—100 copies for $16—called *The Great Holocaust Debate*. Headlines include: "Famous 'Gas Chamber Victims' Living Well," "Patriot Smeared in Phony 'Nazi' Hunt," "Torture Used to Make Germans 'Confess'," and "Need $50,000? Find a Holocaust Victim."

By the early 1980s, Liberty Lobby was taking in $4 million a year in membership fees and proceeds from *Spotlight*. The organization boasted that its daily radio show, "Spotlight on the News," was being broadcast on more than four hundred radio stations. In 1981, when *Spotlight*'s circulation reached the one-third of a million mark, fifteen hundred guests, including United States representatives George Hansen of Idaho and

Gene Chappie of California, gathered at the National Press
Club to celebrate. Other congressmen, such as William L.
Dickinson of Alabama, James Collins of Texas, and Gene Tay-
lor of Missouri, praised Liberty Lobby in statements quoted in
the organization's promotional literature. One Liberty Lobby
pamphlet quotes Watergate hero Sam J. Ervin, Jr., former
senator from North Carolina: "I want to commend the Liberty
Lobby as I have observed it in the twenty years I was in Congress. It has been faithful to the concept of the Constitution."

In the same year as its celebration, the organization made
national headlines when President Reagan tried to appoint a
former Liberty Lobby official to the post of assistant secretary
of health and human services. The nominee, Warren Richardson, seemed to have impeccable New Right credentials. He
was recommended to Reagan by Senator Paul Laxalt of Neva-
da, a prominent leader of the New Right. For several years,
Richardson had been a member of the Kingston Group, a con-
clave of about forty conservatives who regularly met in the
office of New Right organizer Paul Weyrich.

Richardson was forced to withdraw his name from nomination after it was revealed that from 1969 to 1973 he had
served as the general counsel for Liberty Lobby. Richardson
said he realized after joining Liberty Lobby that it was "anti-
Jewish" and guilty of "vicious racist and ethnic stings" and that
he would have resigned immediately if he hadn't needed the
job. But former employees told the *Washington Post* that Richardson was in charge when Carto was absent. Reporters noted
that in 1970, *True* magazine published a story in which Richardson and another Liberty Lobby official, Colonel Curtis Dall,
were interviewed about the organization. As Richardson lis-
tened, Dall described Liberty Lobby's theory that Zionism was
dedicated to "political and financial world domination" and the
Rothschilds headed a "one-world large-monied group" that fi-
nanced communism and socialism. In the interview, Richardson implied that sex education and the environmental movement were part of the plot.

After the controversy, a Liberty Lobby staffer complained
that the *Washington Post* had made the group look like Nazis. "I
ought to be wearing a swastika around my neck as far as

they're concerned," he said. "We're a populist organization, very pro-America. This of course is in direct conflict with many citizens who have loyalties to other countries such as Israel." He singled out *Washington Post* publisher Katharine Graham, who is Jewish. "She's of *that* persuasion, so naturally we're in direct conflict with her," he said.

THE SEAMY SIDE OF CHRISTIANITY

According to a disclaimer published in each issue, *Spotlight* reserves the right "to edit, revise or reject" any advertising. Among the advertisements that are regularly accepted are those for an Inner City Survival Defense Pencil, with a spring-activated pop-out needle; a 4000-volt electric-shock rod; and a board game called Public Assistance ("You'll howl with laughter every time you receive a welfare check . . . or have an illegitimate baby . . . while your opponent in the 'working person's rut' is drowning in mortgage payments"). Also available is a game called Capital Punishment. In the classified ad section (billed as "the world's most interesting classifieds") are published such appeals as: "WHITE PEOPLE!!! Stand up for your rights!! Send for your FREE copy." By responding to these offers, readers can descend another tier into right-wing paranoia.

Compared with some of *Spotlight*'s advertisers, such as the New Christian Crusade Church of Metairie, Louisiana, and the Christian Defense League of Baton Rouge, Liberty Lobby seems relatively tame. Liberty Lobby takes a nonreligious approach in its conspiracy theory. The kind of fervor that often results in unbridled anti-Semitism seems to be fueled by the fundamentalism of such periodicals as *Christian Vanguard,* published by the New Christian Crusade Church, and *The CDL Report,* published by the Christian Defense League. Both organizations are headed by James K. Warner, who has been an officer of the American Nazi Party and the Knights of the Ku Klux Klan. In Warner's conspiracy theory, Jews, Communists, and the Trilateral Commission are in league with the Antichrist.

Readers of Warner's publications need not ponder distinctions between anti-Zionism and anti-Semitism. *Christian Vanguard* publishes caricatures that make its opinions of Jews obvious. A drawing of a Jewish racketeer lighting a cigar with a burning dollar is captioned "Federal Reserve a Private Jewish Mafia." Beneath a grotesque cartoon of a Hasidic Jew is a statement denouncing "greedy, usurious, scheming Christ killers."

Sons of Liberty, a mail-order book company run by Warner, is a prime source of conspiracy-theory material. The company's catalogue offers some five hundred titles on secret societies, international banking, Nazism, historial revisionism, and white supremacy. The books range in tone from the relatively subdued *Who's Who In the World Zionist Conspiracy* ("A must for your reference library") to *Jewish Ritual Murder,* which revives the medieval myth that Jews sacrificed Christians to celebrate holy days. About one-fourth of the works are about various aspects of the conspiracy, including a series of about fifty pamphlets on the Illuminati, also available on cassette tapes.

Sons of Liberty also sells racist books, such as *Proof of Negro Inferiority* and *Great Achievements of the Negro Race*— "with numbered blank pages." The racism promoted by Warner's organizations is rationalized in the same way as is their anti-Semitism: like Jews, blacks are linked to the conspiracy. In their efforts to impose one-world government, the liberal Jews are said to encourage civil rights and integration. Not only will blacks be used as revolutionaries to overthrow white governments, but also their weaker chromosomes will pollute the Aryan gene pool and make white Christians easier to dominate. A Sons of Liberty book called *Who Brought the Slaves to America?* proves "without a doubt that the Jews were responsible."

James Combs, who writes for *Christian Vanguard,* argued in the paper's April 1981 edition that Adolf Hitler was a true Christian, but evangelist Billy Graham, a supporter of Israel, is not. In the article, Combs, who admitted that Hitler made moral mistakes such as allying with the non-Aryan Japanese, was clearly perplexed that a man who did so much to combat the conspiracy was allowed by God to lose World War II. Combs has written that Moral Majority leader Jerry Falwell is a traitor for teaching that Jews are God's "chosen people."

Warner's publications promote what has come to be called the "Identity movement." According to this idiosyncratic interpretation of the Bible, only white people are descended from the Garden of Eden. The "pre-Adamic" people, the brown people of the earth, supposedly were created on the sixth day. On the seventh day, while he was resting, God saw that they had failed to progress and produce civilization, so he made Adam and Eve to carry on his plans. While Abel was the son of Adam, Cain was the son of Satan, who seduced Eve in the Garden of Eden. When Cain killed Abel and was banished from Eden, he married an Asian and produced the first mongrel race. The Israelites are descended from the Asians, so they are Satan's children. Whites—the descendants of Adam—are the chosen people, and America, not Israel, is the Promised Land.

Identity fundamentalism is a common theme in other publications, such as the *Torch,* published by the White People's Committee to Restore God's Laws (of Bass, Arkansas), and the *Thunderbolt,* published by the National States Rights Party (of Marietta, Georgia). Pastor Sheldon Emry of the Lord's Covenant Church of Phoenix spreads Identity fundamentalism through broadcasts on thirty radio stations in all parts of the United States.

The most extreme perpetrator of anti-Semitic conspiracy theories published an advertisement in *Spotlight* that began, "WHITE group seeks information-plans-ideas for improvised-clandestine weapons. . . ." Inquirers receive a booklet from the Church of the Holy Brotherhood in San Francisco, which declares that "God's holy WHITE people are commanded to arm themselves and to resist, fight, and kill the anti-christ, and those who serve the anti-christ, in the last great war called AR-MAGEDDON," when, the Bible teaches, the kingdom of Satan will be defeated by Jesus. The Holy Brotherhood teaches that the Antichrist will triumph because of the intrigues of Jews, blacks, and Communists. Where the group parts ways with its competitors is in advocating murder: "God commands his people . . . to kill all non-whites and WHITE traitors," the Holy Brotherhood booklet states. It includes advice to the "novice warrior of God," including instructions for killing with knives. "When it comes time for you to kill, you might

hesitate because of your previous teachings. . . . When that nig-
ger dog starts to cry, beg, and plead to you to spare him . . .
REMEMBER that you are God's people and that now GOD
COMMANDS YOU TO KILL."

Although it is unclear whether the Holy Brotherhood's
membership includes anyone besides the director, enough fundamentalist Christian groups, survivalist organizations, and
weapons sellers bought space in the booklet's classified ad section to fill five pages.

POSTSCRIPT

Illuminati conspiracy theories come in pairs: the Illuminati
are bankers and Communists, rationalists and occultists, Catholics and Freemasons. In 1974, the Macmillan company published *The Occult and the Third Reich,* a translation of a book by
two French authors who used the joint pseudonym Jean-Michel
Angebert. The writers condemned Nazism as a manifestation
of an occult tradition that they traced back to the Freemasons,
Theosophists, Rosicrucians, Knights Templar, Cathars, and
Gnostics. Included in the chain were Adam Weishaupt's Illuminati. According to the authors, the Nazis considered themselves heirs to ancient secret knowledge. They believed their
evil was justified as the means to an end: the rule of a superior,
illuminated elite.

Other books, such as *Gods and Beasts—The Nazis and the
Occult,* by Dusty Sklar, expound the same theme. In an article
in the encyclopedia, *Man, Myth & Magic,* Ellic Howe, a historian of the occult, suggested how a conspiracy theorist might
"prove" that Hitler was an Illuminatus—or at least that he
thought he was. Nazism grew partly out of a German folk
movement whose reverence for German soil and blood was
almost mystical. Some of the followers of the various German
folk groups rejected Christianity and embraced a form of
neopaganism based on the worship of ancient Nordic gods
such as Odin and Thor. Although Hitler later rejected the folk
movement as politically ineffective, the Nazis' ambivalent attitude toward Christianity might lead one to conjecture that they
took mysticism seriously.

At the time of the birth of Nazism, there was also a strong
German interest in the occult. Nazis such as Rudolf Hess,

Heinrich Himmler, and Alfred Rosenberg believed some occult teachings. Rosenberg's *The Myth of the 20th Century,* which sold more than a million copies, traced the origins of the Aryan race to Atlantis. But the overwhelming evidence is that any occult influence on Nazism was slight. Once the Nazis came to power, they opposed the various occult groups as possible enemies. Organizations such as the Theosophists were suppressed. Occult bookstores were raided by the Gestapo, and hundreds of occultists were arrested and forced to renounce their beliefs.

Still, Hitler's men weren't above exploiting the public interest in matters esoteric. Josef Goebbels briefly employed an astrologer to write propaganda pamphlets justifying Nazi aspirations as fulfillments of the prophecies of Nostradamus. Although Goebbels did this out of a cynical desire to deceive the citizenry, British intelligence agents learned of the project and hired their own astrologer. They wanted to know what kind of advice Hitler might be receiving. The Germans also suspected the British of dabbling in magic. When a Nazi naval captain suspected the British might be using occult means to track German U-boats, he directed a project to discover whether it was possible to locate British ships by swinging a pendulum over a map of the ocean.

There is at least one version of the Illuminati conspiracy theory invented by a Jew. In 1974, Rabbi Marvin S. Antelman published *To Eliminate the Opiate,* "the frightening inside story of communist and conspiratorial group efforts to destroy Jews, Judaism, and Israel." In Antelman's scenario, the Illuminati not only plotted the French Revolution, invented communism and women's liberation, and put the eye in the pyramid on the back of the one-dollar bill, but also launched the Reform movement to fight true, orthodox Judaism. Among the traitors were the Warburgs and Rothschilds. Antelman's sources included John Robison's *Proofs of a Conspiracy.* "Perhaps the most distressing aspect of this study," Antelman wrote, "is that there may have been a grain of truth in . . . the *Protocols of the Elders of Zion.*" It was not a Jewish conspiracy, he wrote, but a conspiracy against Jews.

7

The Insiders

"Communism is not a political party, nor a military organization, nor an ideological crusade. . . . Communism, in its unmistakable present reality, is wholly a conspiracy, a gigantic conspiracy to enslave mankind."
—Robert Welch,
founder of the John Birch Society, 1958

In 1959, when he was in the midst of organizing Liberty Lobby, Willis A. Carto worked for several months in the national office of the newly founded John Birch Society, in Belmont, Massachusetts, and contributed two articles to the group's magazine, *American Opinion*. In "The Hundred-Year Hoax," Carto argued that Karl Marx invented the word "capitalism" as a brainwashing device: by reducing the only "true" economic system to a label, Marx brought it down to the level of communism, making it that much easier to destroy. In "What's *Right* in America?" Carto described various categories of right-wing groups, defending the followers of "eugenic" organizations, who believed that the problem with equal rights was that only a dictatorship could "enforce equality among men when there is no equality."

Shortly after the second article was published, Carto was involved in a dispute with the John Birch Society's leader, Robert Welch, and left the organization. While Carto's analysis of communism was compatible with John Birch Society philosophy, his allusion to a genetically superior race was not. Welch, a wealthy New England candy manufacturer, was trying to promote a sanitized version of the Communist conspiracy theory that was not anti-Semitic. At the time he started the John Birch Society in 1958, anti-Semitic conspiracy theories were moving away from the mainstream of right-wing ideology. But anti-Communist paranoia remained at center stage, as did the tradition of blaming conspirators for the increasing secularization of American society.

In the 1790s, the Federalists and Congregationalists had condemned French rationalism and cosmopolitanism for eroding the morals of the United States and setting the stage for an Illuminati takeover. In a similar manner, later conspiracy theorists blamed Communist agents for disseminating corrupting ideas to prepare the way for a psychological takeover from within. In 1949, Congressman George A. Dondero of Michigan told the House of Representatives that Communists were undermining America's cultural tradition by promoting modern art, or what he called "the isms": cubism, expressionism, futurism, abstractionism, dadaism, surrealism. At stake was true American art, based, of course, on realism.

In 1953, J. B. Matthews, director of research for the House Committee on Un-American Activities, complained that Charles Darwin's theory of evolution and John Dewey's pragmatic approach to education were causing America's educators to "reject the concept of any timeless truths." Because they were being brainwashed to accept that all value systems were relative, Americans were becoming powerless "to combat the activities which are plotted in the dark cellars of the Communist conspiracy," wrote Matthews.

It was Senator Joseph McCarthy who most emulated Jedediah Morse, perpetrator of the 1790s Illuminati scare, when, in his now-famous speech in Wheeling, West Virginia, in 1950, McCarthy declared: "I have here in my hand a list of two hundred and five . . . members of the Communist party" who supposedly had infiltrated the State Department. McCarthy didn't single out Jews, bankers, or Illuminati in his conspiracy theory, preferring instead to condemn the federal government for letting China go Communist and for not winning the Korean War. But in a 1951 speech to the Senate, McCarthy made it clear that he considered the conspirators to be satanic.

"How can we account for our present situation unless we believe that men high in this government are concerting to deliver us to disaster?" McCarthy asked.

> This must be the product of a great conspiracy, a conspiracy on a scale so immense as to dwarf any previous such venture in the history of man. A conspiracy of infamy so black that, when it is finally exposed, its principles shall be forever deserving of the maledictions of all honest men.

Like Morse, McCarthy was unable to prove the existence of a single conspirator. By late 1954, when he was censured by the Senate, he had been thoroughly discredited. But Welch and the John Birch Society revived McCarthy's memory, republishing his book, *America's Retreat From Victory.*

Eventually, the John Birch Society acquired a membership of between 60,000 and 100,000, a level it has maintained for the last two decades. By the 1980s, its annual budget reached $8 million. By developing a version of the Illuminati conspiracy theory that concentrated on condemning Communists and not ethnic groups, the Birchers sought to make political paranoia respectable and ensure that the spirit of McCarthyism outlived its inventor.

INVASION FROM WITHIN

Welch's investigations of communism began in the 1950s when he was a board member and chairman of the Educational Advisory Committee of the conservative National Association of Manufacturers. By 1958, when he retired to start the John Birch Society, he had been studying communism for nine years; for the past three years he had made it a full-time effort. To familiarize himself with his enemy's ideology, he subscribed to the *Daily Worker* and the *National Guardian.* He visited England twice to study the effects of socialism, and traveled throughout Europe, Asia, North America, and South America. In Formosa he met with Chiang Kai-shek.

Welch had studied at the University of North Carolina, the United States Naval Academy, and Harvard Law School, but his education hadn't prepared him to understand the way an idea seemed to be transforming the planet. One by one, countries in Eastern Europe and Asia were adopting a political and economic system antithetical to the values of capitalism. In the past, the great empires of Britain and Rome had expanded by openly waging war. Welch thought there was something mysterious about this force called communism and the devices through which it spread. In 1848, Karl Marx and Frederick Engels had written the *Communist Manifesto,* outlining ten prerequisites to communism, including a progressive income tax, free federal education, abolition of private property, and a government-controlled economy with its own central bank. To Welch, that one book seemed to have touched off a chain reaction. He was unable to believe that there was anything natural or spontaneous about the spread of communism. The manifesto of Marx and Engels seemed less like a philosophical statement than a master plan, the blueprint of a conspiracy.

On December 8 and 9 of 1958, Welch called together eleven "influential," "patriotic and public-spirited" men to a meeting in Indianapolis to hear him speak of what he had come to believe was a Communist plot for world domination. By infiltrating agents into governments and fomenting civil wars, the "International Communist Conspiracy," as he called it, had first taken Eastern Europe, then most of Asia. Now it was concentrating on the Western Hemisphere. "[T]he truth I bring you is simple, incontrovertible, and deadly," Welch told his guests.

> [U]nless we can reverse forces which now seem inexorable in their movement, you have only a few more years before the country in which you live will become four separate provinces in a worldwide Communist dominion ruled by police-state methods from the Kremlin. The map for their division and administration is already drawn.

Country by country, Welch described a Communist empire that was spreading to cover two-thirds of the earth. *Russia,*

Poland, Albania, Yugoslavia, Romania, Bulgaria, East Germany, China, North Korea, Czechoslovakia. . . .
Political scientists might quarrel with Welch's criteria for what constituted membership in the new federation. (Welch considered Eisenhower and Truman to be knowing agents of the conspiracy because of their relatively moderate approaches to the cold war.) Wherever there was a government exhibiting leftist sympathies, Welch believed, it was part of the plan. *Indonesia, Burma, India, Ceylon, Syria, Iraq, Lebanon, Egypt, Libya, Tunisia, Algeria, Morocco. . . .* Western Europe was being squeezed in from the east and south. There were enough Communists in Norway, Iceland, and Finland to complete the circle. The United States was being encroached upon from the south by Communist movements in Latin America. Even Hawaii was going Communist, Welch believed. But worst of all, he said, there were Communists within our borders:

> [T]he unions which control our shipping and many vital parts of our economy are Communist ruled or Communist dominated. . . . The best-informed authorities say that there are at least thirty huge Communist espionage rings operating in this country today. . . . Communist sympathies and even actual Communist subversion are daily made more respectable by the actions of our government, our great universities, much of our press, and by the complacency of the people.

Communism, Welch said, would be injected into the psychology of America so gradually and in such small doses that the public would never know what had happened. By the time it had completely taken hold, communism would be so basic to our assumptions that it would seem as natural as capitalism once had. With a Communist-dominated United Nations trying to seduce America into subjugating its sovereignty to "internationalism," and Communist agitators fomenting a civil war under the rubric of civil rights, Welch was certain the United States was ready for the fall.

Soon after Welch's speech, the guests at the Indianapolis meeting agreed to help start the John Birch Society, named for a U.S. intelligence officer killed by Chinese Communists ten days after the end of World War II. Welch considered Captain John Birch to be a victim of the conspiracy. "With his death ... the battle lines were drawn," Welch wrote, "in a struggle from which either Communism or Christian-style civilization must emerge with one completely triumphant and the other completely destroyed."

By this time, Welch had already founded his magazine, *American Opinion*. In 1958, he published his first annual Scoreboard, a list of countries indicating by percentage the degree to which they supposedly had fallen to the Communists. His figure for the United States was 20 to 40 percent. With federally funded mental-health clinics indoctrinating the masses, and taxes and interest rates stifling free enterprise, the threat increased. In 1962, Welch predicted that in ten years the United States would be occupied by Chinese troops. There would be "concentration camps, tortures, terror, and all that is required to enable 3 percent of a population to rule the other 97 percent as complete slaves." The Scoreboard for 1962 conceded 50 to 70 percent of the country to Communist influence. In 1982, Welch declared that his researchers had determined that 40 to 60 percent of the country was under the control of the conspiracy, which had come to include not only Communists, but the Council on Foreign Relations, the Bilderbergers, the Trilateral Commission, and "assorted Insiders of international finance."

INVISIBLE EMPIRE

An early sign that the Birchers' conspiracy theory wasn't limited to Communists came in 1962, when *American Opinion* began carrying advertisements for *America's Unelected Rulers*, by Kent and Phoebe Courtney, and *The Invisible Government*, by Dan Smoot, a former FBI agent who denounced the conspiracy in regular radio and television broadcasts. Both books advanced the theory that the Communist conspiracy had found an ally in the Council on Foreign Relations, a group of influential financial, academic, and political leaders who were attempting to fight isolationist fears similar to those that had kept the United States out of the League of Nations. Council members believed that stronger international relations would lead to peace and understanding—and to a healthier world economy.

Thus, much of the council's support came from international financiers such as the Rockefellers.

In the minds of the Birchers, the word *international* ignited the old paranoia about one-world government. Since the Council on Foreign Relations had a membership list that included international bankers, government officials, journalists, and Ivy League academics, many right-wingers believed it was headquarters for an East Coast liberal plot.

Later in 1962, *American Opinion* published an article, "To See the Invisible," which described a branch of the Communist conspiracy that supposedly consisted of the Council on Foreign Relations and such seeming bastions of American capitalism as the Committee for Economic Development, the Business Advisory Council, the Advertising Council, and the Ford Foundation. Also included were the *New York Times*, the *Washington Post*, *Time*, *Newsweek*, *Life*, the Rockefeller Foundation, and the Bilderbergers.

In the eyes of the Birchers, these groups represented the same East Coast financial elite that had been condemned by the agrarian populists of the 1890s. Even though the John Birch Society was founded by capitalists, not farmers, it represented the small-town, conservative side of American business. The charter members of Welch's national council included a former president of the Missouri Chamber of Commerce, a president of a Wichita oil refinery, presidents of a carpet manufacturing company, a lumber company, and a refrigerator company, and two former presidents of the National Association of Manufacturers, the conservative group to which Welch had belonged. The organizations the Birchers opposed tended to support welfare programs, centralized economic planning, and international cooperation—even with Communists—as means of enhancing business. The National Association of Manufacturers promoted a more isolationist, laissez-faire view. Its members saw big government as an enemy of business. They could see nothing logical about trading with countries they believed were trying to destroy capitalism, which they were certain was the foundation of democracy.

At about the same time the Birchers began to weave capitalists into their conspiracy theory, they discovered the works of Nesta Webster, who expounded on the occult aspects of the one-world plot. As a result, the world view of the John Birch Society took on a supernatural air.

In 1962, Revilo P. Oliver, a founding member of the John Birch Society and an associate editor of *American Opinion,* wrote an article denouncing plans to build a $5 million Temple of Understanding in Washington, D.C. With six wings to represent each of the world's major religions—Christianity, Judaism, Buddhism, Islam, Hinduism, and Confucianism—the temple was described by its supporters as a "spiritual United Nations." Many members of the establishment considered the project eminently respectable. Its benefactors included Rober McNamara, John D. Rockefeller IV, Eleanor Roosevelt, several hundred government officials, and religious, academic, and corporate leaders from more than fifty countries.

To America's right-wingers, the effort toward international religious understanding sounded like preparation for the Antichrist's one-world church. A nationally syndicated newspaper columnist charged that the temple was a step toward establishing a humanistic world religion that would oppose Christianity. Within the temple, she wrote, would be a meditation room called the Hall of Illumination, where "the Illuminati, Masters of Wisdom . . . will train the public in the new humanistic cult."

A controversy already had arisen over the internationalist implications of the meditation room in the United Nations. Robert Keith Spenser, author of *The Cult of the All-Seeing Eye,* believed he could discern in the room's cubist painting symbols of the cabala and Weishaupt's Illuminati.

In his article in *American Opinion,* Oliver claimed that the temple represented an internationalism that was part of a pagan force including Gnostics, hermetic-cabalistic philosophers, alchemists, witches, the Alumbrados, and such "Enlightenment mystics" as Cagliostro, Mesmer, Mirabeau, and Adam Weishaupt, a "vicious degenerate." But Oliver took a relatively cautious approach to the Illuminati legend. He wrote that he didn't believe there was proof that Weishaupt's organization had survived its banishment by the Bavarian government and gone on to plot the French Revolution. He defined Illuminati as "masterminds that have been pumped full of esoteric wisdom by some magical process." Among the superstitions they embraced, he wrote, were eighteenth-century Enlightenment beliefs in noble savages, the equality of man, and world federations.

In the March 1964 issue of *American Opinion,* Oliver speculated on which group was at the top of the conspiratorial pyramid: Illuminati, satanists, Bilderbergers, Zionists, Pharisees, international bankers, Rockefellers, Rothschilds, or a group called Force X, which the publication *Intelligence Digest* claimed was controlling the world's illegal drug trade. "It is entirely possible," Oliver wrote, "that we may never be able to identify the head of the octopus, but that will matter little if we can lop off enough of its tentacles."

Robert Welch picked up the Illuminati theme in a 1964 speech in which he named Weishaupt's group as a likely source of the Communist-capitalist plot. Because the Illuminati had successfully pulled "the veil of secrecy over themselves almost completely and permanently," Welch said, "we do not know to what extent Weishaupt's group became the central core . . . of a continuing organizaton with increasing reach and control over all collectivist activities." But, he said, the "strong probability [was] that Weishaupt's Illuminati has been the dominating factor in this development" and that it was an "inevitable" conclusion "that the present worldwide Communist conspiracy has evolved out of some such earlier organization."

Welch suggested that the link between the Illuminati and twentieth-century communism was the League of the Just, which had engaged Marx and Engels to write the *Communist Manifesto.*

By 1966, the Illuminati conspiracy theory had become part of the official John Birch Society line. In that year, *American Opinion* published an article in which Welch laid out the entire plot, citing as his sources such Illuminati conspiracy theorists as John Robison, Abbe Barruel, and Nesta Webster. Beginning with the Bavarian Illuminati, he described how the "Insiders" had established the Federal Reserve System, plotted World Wars I and II, and invented the graduated income tax to rob the middle class. Meanwhile, the Insiders sheltered their own wealth with tax-exempt organizations such as the Ford and Rockefeller foundations, which were also used to fund social programs to mollify the masses. Welch told how the Insiders started the United Nations as a forerunner to one-world government. In the 1960s, he wrote, they engineered the Vietnam War and the civil rights movement, which strengthened the power of the federal government over citizens' private lives.

"Communism," Welch wrote, "is not at all the movement which it pretends to be, of downtrodden masses rising up against a ruling class which exploits them. It is exactly the opposite." Members of the social, educational, economic, and political elite were using communism "to impose their rule ever more rigidly and tyrannically, *from the top down,* on the total population. . . . The Communist *Party,* with its considerable percentage of idealistic dupes and misguided fools, has been simply a tool of these power-hungry conspirators."

In 1967, the John Birch Society reprinted Robison's *Proofs of a Conspiracy.* In an introduction to the book, modern American Freemasons, many of whom are staunch anti-Communists, were absolved of complicity in the plot. In 1968, Welch wrote that the Poor People's March on Washington that year was— like the siege of the Bastille, which began the French Revolution—an operation of the Insiders.

> It took a tremendous effort and expense, and a lot of cunning and planning, on the part of these Insiders, to foment the march of a huge mob on the Bastille, and make its capture look like the spontaneous action of an outraged people. . . .
> Nor is there any doubt that the planning and organization behind this *Poor March* was tremendously more extensive and expensive.

This disbelief in chance and spontaneity is a common theme in *American Opinion.* In "Marxmanship in Dallas," Revilo Oliver speculated that Lee Harvey Oswald was a Communist agent, employed to shoot John F. Kennedy and ignite a ghetto riot. "The numerous vermin that have been living for years in ill-conceived anticipation of the glorious day when they will be able to hack Americans to pieces and drag bodies through the streets could have 'spontaneously' started looting, burning, and murdering."

During the next decade, the society's conspiracy theory continued to develop. An *American Opinion* writer named Gary Allen blamed the Rockefellers for bankrolling the Bolshevik Revolution and postulated that the Students for a Democratic Society, the Black Panthers, and the Yippies were funded by the Rockefeller and Ford foundations to wage a socialist revolution in the United States. Allen described Weishaupt's Illuminati as the forerunner of the Council on Foreign Relations —both groups, he wrote, were secret elites conspiring to rule the world.

Allen's theories were described in his book *None Dare Call It Conspiracy*. With 5 million copies in print, it has become the Bible of the paranoid right. As late as 1983, it was still being touted in *American Opinion*. In the book, Allen complained that those "who believe that major world events result from planning are laughed at for believing in the 'conspiracy theory of history.' . . . Politicians and 'intellectuals' are attracted to the concept that events are propelled by some mysterious tide of history or happen by accident." This "accidental theory" is used by the conspirators "to escape the blame when things go wrong."

By 1980, the Birchers were also condemning the Trilateral Commission, the group David Rockefeller founded in 1973 to improve relations among North America, Western Europe, and Japan. The Birchers believed that, like the United Nations, the commission was encouraging détente with enemies who wanted to dominate the United States. The Trilateralist conspiracy theory made national news during the 1980 presidential campaigns, when the Birchers, Liberty Lobby, and other right-wing organizations charged that the commission, with the help of the Council on Foreign Relations, had hand-picked Carter in the early 1970s to become president. The rumors became so widespread that both organizations were deluged with mail. The Trilateral Commission printed a pamphlet denying that it was part of a one-world conspiracy. Magazines such as *U.S. News and World Report* and *Forbes* ran articles trying to debunk the myth. George Bush, a former Trilateral Commission member who challenged Reagan for the Republican nomination, and Independent candidate John Anderson were also accused of being part of the plot.

After he was nominated, Reagan selected Bush as his running mate, won the presidency, and appointed members of the Trilateral Commission and the Council on Foreign Relations to top posts: Alexander Haig, George Shultz, Casper Weinberger, William Casey, Malcolm Baldridge, and Jeane Kirkpatrick. America's foreign policy establishment is as replete with members of these groups as it is with Ivy Leaguers. Although the Carter and Reagan administrations both were top-heavy with Trilateralists and council members (it seems difficult to find experienced bureaucrats who are not), that did not dissuade the Birchers from fearing a conspiracy. Indeed, to them it was evidence that the two-party political system was an illusion: both sides were controlled by the puppet-masters.

As the John Birch Society's conspiracy theory grew more engulfing, it became harder to separate it from anti-Semitic versions. In *None Dare Call It Conspiracy,* Gary Allen included banking families such as the Rothschilds, Warburgs, Kuhns, Loebs, and Schiffs in the plot, along with the Rockefellers and Morgans. In a disclaimer, Allen wrote that it was irrelevant that many of the bankers he named were Jewish and that it was "unreasonable and immoral to blame all Jews for the crimes of the Rothschilds." He accused the Warburgs of contributing to the slaughter of Jews by financing Hitler. The Anti-Defamation League, he wrote, serves as an agent of the plot by condemning legitimate conspiracy researchers like the Birchers as anti-Semites.

Welch blamed "agents provocateurs" hired by the Insiders for infiltrating his society and sowing anti-Semitism to convince the public that the Birchers hated Jews. Welch tried to keep the interlopers out. In the mid-1960s, Robert DePugh, leader of a paramilitary right-wing organization called the Minutemen, and journalist Westbrook Pegler were dropped from the society because they were considered by the public to be anti-Semites. Revilo Oliver was eased out in 1966 after he said, in a speech at the society's New England Rally for God, Family, and Country: "If only by some miracle all the Bolsheviks or all the Illuminati or all the Jews were vaporized at dawn tomorrow, we should have nothing to worry about." Oliver became an ally of Willis Carto and joined the board of the Institute for Historical Review to promote Holocaust revisionism.

Welch's efforts to purify his organization seem to have been sincere. For a right-winger, he was unusually liberal in his religious beliefs. He attended a Unitarian church and believed in evolution. In *The Blue Book of the John Birch Society*, he described his beliefs in a way that sounded very much like deism. The "Divine Being" made man "by creating Milky Ways and astronomical universes, with laws and purposes which caused planets like our Earth to develop; and by creating evolutionary forces." He wrote of communism as a threat to believers of "every great religion of the world": Catholics, Jews, Moslems, and Buddhists as well as Protestants. Right-wingers are often assumed to be fundamentalist Protestants, but, like Father Coughlin in the 1930s and Senator McCarthy in the 1950s, Welch also attracted a Catholic following. Despite Welch's characterization of the civil rights movement as part of the Communist plot, the society officially supports racial equality, though it opposes using the federal government to guarantee equal opportunity. Welch has claimed that there are a thousand black members in the society, including six speakers in the Birchers' American Opinion Speaker's Bureau.

POSTSCRIPT

Communists can be as paranoid as Birchers. In 1974, in a party-sponsored lecture delivered in Moscow, a Soviet academic named Valery Nikolaevich Emelyanov told of a conspiracy by Zionists and Freemasons to take over the world. As part of the plot, the "baptised Spanish Jew," Ignatius Loyola, invented the Inquisition to destroy "the best *goyish* minds." Now the "Judaic-Masonic pyramid" controlled "80 percent of the economy in the capitalist countries and 90 to 95 percent of the information media." The year 2000 was the date the conspirators supposedly had set to take complete control.

Three years after his lecture, Emelyanov wrote a memorandum to Soviet officials, including in his conspiracy theory the Anti-Defamation League of B'nai B'rith, the Carter administration, Eurocommunism, Amnesty International, the Helsinki human rights monitoring groups, and dissidents Alexander Solzhenitsyn, Andre Sakharov, Roy Medvedev—and Leon Trotsky. Emelyanov called on the Soviet government to fight the conspiracy by establishing an institute to study Zionism and Freemasonry and to implement conspiracy awareness programs in the schools, universities, and military, as well as on television. He even made a veiled reference to an obscure passage in the *Protocols of the Elders of Zion* that claimed the conspirators planned to use the subway systems to blow up the cities of Europe: "[T]he dissidents, led by Zionists and the Masons, have gone over to acts of bloody terror against the civilian population in metro passages, a terror planned by them exactly eighty years ago," Emelyanov warned.

In a 1978 article appearing in a mass-circulation newspaper for Soviet youth, another writer included "big business" and the Bilderbergers in the Zionist-Masonic conspiracy.

It sounded as though the Soviet conspiracy theorists had been reading *Spotlight*.

8

The Doomsday Plot

"I believe the Trilateralist movement is unwittingly setting the stage for the political-economic one-world system the Bible predicts for the last days. . . . What the Trilateralists are trying to establish will soon be controlled by the coming world leader—the anti-Christ himself."

—Hal Lindsey,
The 1980s: Countdown to Armageddon, 1981

It was August 6, 1981, and Bill Maupin was ready. By the next morning, he and the fifty members of his Lighthouse Gospel Tract Foundation in Tucson expected to rise like angels and meet Jesus in the Arizona sky. August 7, Maupin had predicted, would be the day of the Rapture, when the Lord—true to his word in First Thessalonians—would beam his people to heaven. "[A]t the sound of the archangel's voice and God's trumpet-call . . . the Christian dead will rise, then we who are left alive shall join them, caught up in clouds to meet the Lord in the air."

While the living and the dead of Christendom would make the ascent, Maupin believed, nonbelievers would be left to endure the seven years of punishment that fundamentalist Protestants call the Tribulation. "I'd like to see you go with us," Maupin told a news reporter. "It will be the worst trouble the world will ever know."

The details of the suffering are described in the Book of Revelation: death by sword, famine, pestilence, and wild beasts; earthquakes so strong that every mountain and island will be moved from its place. The sun will turn black, the moon blood red. A third of the earth will be burned and swarms of locusts with the stingers of scorpions will torment nonbelievers. But in the end, Christ will make his Second Coming, defeat the forces of evil, and begin the Millennium, a thousand-year reign of peace on earth.

Maupin based his prediction on passages in the Old Testament that fundamentalists interpret to mean that the generation that sees the Jews returned to their homeland will be the last before Jesus "raptures" his believers to heaven and begins the Tribulation. On May 15, 1948, the United Nations recognized Israel as a nation. By adding forty years—the length many fundamentalists assign to a biblical generation—the day of the Second Coming comes out to be May 14, 1988. Subtract seven years for the Tribulation and the result is May 14, 1981, a day some fundamentalists expected to leave the planet.

Using the ancient Jewish calendar, which consisted of 360-day years, Maupin first calculated that the Rapture would occur June 28. Two of his followers sold their houses in preparation. When the day passed uneventfully, Maupin reopened his Bible and attempted to fine-tune his prediction. To be consistent, it seems he should have used 360-day years to calculate the length of the forty-year generation, but that would have put the Rapture back in December. After rereading Matthew, Maupin thought he discovered where he had gone wrong. Jesus said the "end times," as fundamentalists call them, would be "as things were in Noah's days." From the rest of the passage, it sounds as though Jesus simply meant that the Tribulation would take the world by surprise, as had the Great Flood. But Maupin decided Jesus was hinting that the first day of the Rapture would correspond to the beginning of the Flood. Just as Noah had saved the animals in his ark, so would the Lord rescue his people from the destruction. The Flood lasted forty days and forty nights before depositing Noah on Mount Ararat. And so, Maupin believed, it would take forty days from the beginning of the Rapture until the spirit of God floated his followers to heaven. Add forty days to June 28, and the result is August 7.

That morning, Maupin and his flock were still waiting in Tucson, answering telephone calls from newspaper reporters. Because of the time difference between Arizona and Jerusalem, he decided God actually had until the morning of August 8 to begin rapturing Christians. But, as history will record, August 8th was followed by the 9th, and Maupin joined a centuries-long tradition of false prophets who were convinced they had divined a system to prove the world was drawing to an end.

In the last century, William Miller, a Baptist pastor from Vermont, used biblical prophecy to predict the world would end on March 21, 1843. After mankind awakened as usual the next day, Miller changed the prediction to October 22, 1844, a date the 50,000 or so Millerites came to call the Great Disappointment when it too passed them by. In fact, historians say that the disciples believed Jesus promised to return within their own lifetimes. Disappointed Christians have been postponing the date ever since.

While most fundamentalists don't try to calculate the exact day of the Rapture (in Matthew, Jesus said not even the angels will know the hour and day of his return), Maupin's followers are among millions of Americans who believe that biblical prophecies are being fulfilled in the 1980s at so accelerated a pace that we are being sucked inexorably toward doomsday. They are sure that events described in the newspapers match the predictions in the Bible so exactly that there is little question that the forces of evil are conspiring to bring on the Tribulation. They are convinced they are members of the terminal generation, living in the last century before the end times.

Evangelist Hal Lindsey's book, *The Late Great Planet Earth*—which details how biblical prophecies are supposedly coming to pass—has sold more than 15 million copies. When another Lindsey book, *The 1980s: Countdown to Armageddon,* was published in 1981, it was on the *New York Times* best-seller list for weeks.

There are numerous indications that biblical prophecies

were meant for ancient generations, not modern man. At the end of Revelation, Jesus said, "Yes, I am coming soon." The book begins with the promise that "the hour of fulfillment is near." In Matthew, it seems clear that Jesus was promising an imminent return: "I tell you this: the present generation will live to see it all." But fundamentalists believe that by "present generation" Jesus did not mean the disciples who were listening to his words, but the generation that is alive when the prophecies are fulfilled.

In Matthew 24, Jesus warned his disciples that the end times would be heralded by earthquakes, famines, and wars—all of which fundamentalists believe are on the rise. In Revelation, the prophet John wrote that the Tribulation would be preceded by the rise of a leader called the Antichrist, who would establish a world empire. Lindsey believes John was talking about the European Common Market, the Trilateral Commission, the Council on Foreign Relations, and the international bankers. Some fundamentalists add Adam Weishaupt's Illuminati to the list of satanic one-worlders.

"The Illuminati," Maupin wrote in his book, *The Key to the Book of Daniel,* "is the behind-the-scenes organization of this one-world system. . . . This is a secret organization that has been in existence for many centuries. They had a plan for a one-world government over two hundred years ago. They have been working toward their goal since that time."

Most fundamentalists don't specifically mention Illuminati in their end-time scenarios, but the assumptions of the Illuminati conspiracy theory are implicit in fundamentalist prophecy. The evils the conspiracy theorists attribute to the Illuminati—secularism, rationalism, cosmopolitanism, and occultism—are claimed by fundamentalists to be the devices that Satan is using to enslave the world with the international empire described in Revelation. Lindsey claims the end times are being foreshadowed by welfare programs, drug use, rationalist skepticism, and a growing interest in religious cults and witchcraft—signs that Satan's influence is spreading and the world is becoming so evil that the day is nearing when God will take revenge.

Like the conspiracy theorists, the fundamentalists see the

world as a battleground for good and evil. In a world in which
modern thought challenges the truths of the Bible, they seek to
comfort themselves with the belief that the chaos they see
around them can be explained. They do not believe in accidents. Just as the conspiracy theorists construct elaborate systems to explain the past, students of biblical prophecy cross-
reference Bible passages and draft complex charts in an attempt
to systemize the future.

In Lindsey's scenario, the final cataclysm begins when
Russia (which he believes is described in Ezekiel 38 as the land
of Magog, "in the far recesses of the north") allies with the
Arab nations against Israel. But the head of the ten-nation
European Common Market (the ten-horned monster in Revelation 13) brings peace to the Middle East by signing a pact
with Israel, as described in the Book of Daniel. Then the seven-
year Tribulation begins. The leader of this new international
empire, the Antichrist, is a respected figure whose success at
removing the threat to world peace enhances his popularity.

With the help of the Trilateral Commission and the
Council on Foreign Relations, the Antichrist persuades the
people of the western nations, including the United States, to
unite under the flag of his one-world government, tempting
them with the promise of everlasting world peace. The international government is accompanied by an occult international
religion (the "whore of Babylon" in Revelation 17) and an international economic system. Both are run by an ally of the
Antichrist called the Beast or False Prophet.

As the story goes, the Antichrist's peace is a false one.
Egypt (the king of the south in Daniel 11) leads the Arab
confederation in an attack on Israel and its Western allies.
Russia takes this as an excuse to invade the Middle East. In his
books, Lindsey details the troop movements with charts based
on Bible verses. The battles result in World War III, the Battle
of Armageddon. Russia is destroyed by fire and brimstone,
leaving China (the army of 200 million described in Revelation
9) to fight the Western nations, allied under the Antichrist.

This war to end all wars is described in Revelation 9,
which tells of a plague of locusts with breastplates of iron and
wings as loud as "horses and chariots rushing to battle." The

locusts, Lindsey believes, are helicopters. In Revelation 8, "a great star [shoots] from the sky, flaming like a torch," poisoning a third of the water on the earth." Thus, Lindsey predicts, Armageddon will be fought with nuclear weapons. But just as it looks as though the inhabitants of earth are about to destroy themselves, Jesus will make his Second Coming. He will kill the Antichrist and the Beast, demonstrating the futility of pledging allegiance to godless kingdoms—whether in the form of international communism or the Antichrist's one-world government, religion, and economic system. With Jesus in control, the thousand-year reign of peace will begin.

Other fundamentalist doomsday predictions differ from Lindsey's in detail, but they all include the idea of an evil one-world system in which international capitalists and Communists are cohorts of Satan. One contemporary scenario resembles a high-technology version of the international banker plot with undertones of the occult. The interpretation is based on one of the most mysterious passages in Revelation, describing the Beast's one-world economic system.

> [The Beast] worked great miracles, even making fire come down from heaven to earth before men's eyes. By the miracles it was allowed to perform . . . it deluded the inhabitants of the earth. . . . Moreoever, it caused everyone, great and small, rich and poor, slave and free, to be branded with a mark on his right hand or forehead, and no one was allowed to buy or sell unless he bore this beast's mark, either name or number.

The number, the Bible cryptically says, is 666.

Modern biblical scholars believe 666 is a code, derived through numerology, for Emperor Nero, and that Revelation was written to comfort Christians persecuted under his reign. But for centuries, Christians have tried to show that the name of some current despot such as Hitler or Mussolini could be somehow transformed into this number.

At the same time, believers in biblical prophecy have awaited the day when only those in possession of the "mark of the Beast" will be allowed to participate in the economy. In the days of czarist Russia, Sergei Nilus, the mystic who believed the *Protocols of the Elders of Zion* heralded the coming of the Antichrist, devised a system to detect the mark of the Beast in commercial trademarks. In the United States, fundamentalists thought Franklin Roosevelt's National Recovery Administration emblem was the mark of the Beast.

In the 1980s, a Montgomery, Alabama, businesswoman named Mary Stewart Relfe has popularized the theory that the mark is the zebra-striped universal product codes, which now appear on most products. Relfe's book, *When Your Money Fails . . . the '666' System Is Here,* describes a future in which similar symbols will be invisibly tattooed by laser on our foreheads and hands like permanent credit cards. Just as computerized cash registers now read the marks on merchandise to determine prices, in the future, Relfe believes, they will read the marks on our bodies to debit our bank accounts.

Six months after the publication of Relfe's book in 1981, there were 600,000 copies in print. It became the best-selling Christian paperback in the country. Conspiracy theorists traditionally have found the abstract nature of paper money discomforting, but when money becomes nothing but electronic pulses in wires, the conspiracy seems to ascend to a new plane of evil. Banking becomes occult in a new, technocratic sort of way. As computer networks around the world continue to link together, the electronic economy will become dominant, Relfe believes. The marks will be required, and those who refuse them will starve.

As in the *Protocols of the Elders of Zion,* technocrats will have ultimate control over our lives. Like the conspiracy theorists of the French Revolution—who confused Illuminati (believers in Enlightenment philosophy) and *illuminés* (practitioners of the occult)—Relfe believes rationalism (in the form of technology) has joined with black magic to bring on the one-world system. In Relfe's version of the conspiracy, we will be slaves to a computer that will be powered and programmed by Satan. The access code that will be prefixed to our credit card numbers to allow them to function in the international system will be 666, she predicts, followed by a three-digit national code, the owner's telephone area code, and a nine-digit

Social Security number. The eighteen-digit identification number will be arranged in three groups of six numbers each. She believes this coming new world order is symbolized by the eye in the pyramid on the back of the one-dollar bill.

As documentation for the rise of the 666 system, Relfe illustrated her book with photographs of a J. C. Penney credit card that has the prefix 666, a shirt made in China with 666 in the collar, and a label for a Lear Siegler computer bearing the number 666. She listed dozens of other examples, including reports of Christians who returned their credit cards to the companies that issued them because the numbers contained the digits 666. When Anwar Sadat reopened the Suez Canal in 1975, he was aboard a warship with 666 printed on its bow, Relfe wrote. She predicted that Sadat would become the Antichrist. In a sequel, *The New Money System,* Relfe noted that Sadat was killed on October 6, by six assassins, six years after riding on the 666 ship.

To help readers do their own research, Relfe described how to convert names in Latin, Greek, and Hebrew into numbers. According to the system, Nimrod, as well as Nero, comes out 666. Nebuchadnezzar, she noted, commanded his people to worship an idol 66 cubits high and 6 cubits wide. To convert English names, Relfe suggested a base-six system: A = 6, B = 12, C = 18, and so on. Add up the letters in "Kissinger," "computer," or "mark of Beast," and the sum is 666.

Relfe believes the Rapture will occur midway through the Tribulation, so she advocated buying land outside the city and planting gardens. Because inflation is part of the plot to enslave us, she advised readers to invest in gold, silver, real estate, and food. When the Antichrist comes, she predicted, all the world will be made to worship his image, projected on their television screens, which will be hooked to the computer network, enabling the Beast to monitor the frequency of our prayers.

PREMILLENNIALISM

Since the beginning of Christianity, religious leaders have preached that civilization will be destroyed by heaven-sent fire and brimstone. But the practice of inventing complex biblical scenarios to make detailed predictions of the end times has its roots in the late nineteenth century, when conservative Protestants—known as evangelicals, from the Greek word for message bearer—were trying to shore up their beliefs to meet the challenge of liberal theology. The evangelicals were disturbed by the rising interest in biblical criticism and Charles Darwin's theory of evolution, which contradicted the account of creation in Genesis. They opposed the humanistic notion that men could use their rational faculties to question the Bible or discover universal laws not based on the word of God. By showing that the Bible contained a system to explain everything that transpired on earth, the evangelicals hoped to combat the rise of secular thought, which they felt was elevating mankind's importance at the expense of God's.

By the 1870s, this controversy between liberals and conservatives had resulted in a split in American Christendom. Liberal theologians favored modernizing Protestantism by discarding the notion of the infallibility of the Bible, interpreting it instead as a message written by men to the generations of their time. As early Christianity had met the need of ancient peoples, the liberals believed, now it should conform to the demands of a new era; religion must serve humanity, not vice versa. Instead of worshiping the Bible, its lessons should be updated and, with the help of science and the arts, used to inspire humankind. The liberals believed evolution was part of God's plan that life evolve from the simple creatures of the seas to amphibians, reptiles, birds, mammals, and men. Now, they theorized, this progression would continue as mankind improved the quality of life through scientific discovery, social reform, and a more liberal religion. Humanity would use Christian ideals to create its own heaven on earth. When this man-made Millennium was established, the world would be ready for the Second Coming. People would have made the earth good enough for Jesus.

Many evangelicals thought the liberals had turned reality inside out. If man's science conflicted with God's word, then it must be man who was wrong, they believed. And what was against God was satanic. To the conservatives, there was no such thing as progress. Man didn't rise out of the animal world; he fell from his perfect state in the Garden of Eden because a snake convinced him to eat from the Tree of Knowledge. Ever after, mankind was tainted with this Original Sin. No amount of social welfare would help inherently depraved creatures. The only salvation was through unquestioning belief. Modern civilization was as evil and misguided as that of the Babylonians, who were punished for trying to build the Tower of Babel. The world could not ascend toward the Millennium because of man's efforts, the conservatives believed. Christendom was disintegrating as planned. Jesus would step in and punctuate the decline with a cataclysm.

While the liberals reacted to modernism by adapting, the conservatives dug further into the foundation of their faith, the literal truth of the Bible. They became known as premillennialists, because they thought Jesus would return to earth before the Millennium; their liberal opponents were postmillennialists, who thought the Lord would arrive—figuratively, if not literally—when the good works of man had been completed.

Shortly before World War I, the conservative movement gained momentum with the appearance of twelve paperback books called *The Fundamentals,* which opposed modernist theology with premillennialism and the doctrine of biblical inerrancy. Two southern California oil millionaries, Lyman and Milton Stewart, paid to have more than 250,000 copies of each approximately 125-page volume of *The Fundamentals* distributed free to every "pastor, evangelist, missionary, theological professor, theological student, Sunday school superintendent, YMCA and YWCA secretary in the English-speaking world whose address could be obtained," religious historian C. Allyn Russell wrote. With the publication of *The Fundamentals,* the most conservative of the evangelicals began to cohere into a movement. Not all premillennialists adopted the name fundamentalist. Those who preferred a less rigid theology continued to call themselves evangelicals. Both groups favored a conservative approach to Christianity and a literal interpretation of the Bible, but the fundamentalists were more extreme. They prided themselves as militants against modernism.

The fundamentalists even adopted their own version of the Bible. The *Scofield Reference Bible,* first published in 1909, is a version of the King James edition that was footnoted and cross-referenced by fundamentalist scholar C. I. Scofield for use by students of premillennialist prophecy. The scenario in which earthquakes, wars, famines, and a one-world government are followed by the Rapture, Tribulation, and Battle of Armageddon was not laid out in any one place in the King James Bible. The end-time sequence was developed from a complex interweaving of passages. The system was described in Scofield's notes, which occupy as much space as the Scriptures themselves. Since its publication, the Scofield Bible has become so widely accepted among fundamentalists that many pastors and laymen take its commentaries as literally as the text. The most recent edition (1967) has sold more than 2 million copies.

To challenge the liberals' claim that rationality proved the Bible was not literally true, fundamentalists such as Scofield tried to show that biblical inerrancy was based not only on faith but on reason. Like conspiracy theorists, the premillennialists started with what they believed was true, then constructed elaborate systems to rationalize it. Fundamentalism is often stereotyped as a movement of country preachers with minds insufficient to understand the deeper, allegorical meanings of the Bible. But the early theoreticians of premillennialism considered themselves intellectuals who used the scientific method to prove the Bible contained the blueprint for the history and future of the earth. They wanted to show that the secularists had no monopoly on reason, that rationality could be used in the service of God.

Reuben A. Torrey, Scofield's colleague, was aptly described by historian George Marsden as "one of the principal *architects* of fundamentalist thought. . . . [F]ar from rejecting intellect, [he] assigned vast importance to ideas. . . . A sympathetic biographer described him as almost immune to emotional persuasion: 'rather was he swayed by the logical element of cold reason.' "

Since the days of colonial America, there has been a tension between the emotional and intellectual sides of Christianity. While the early Puritans analyzed and systematized the doctrines of God, later denominations, such as the Methodists, were more interested in salvation through the emotions of revivalism. Preachers such as Dwight Moody and Billy Sunday preferred this direct approach. "It makes no difference how you get a man to God, provided you get him there," Moody said.

But Scofield and Torrey believed the path to salvation came through arranging the verses of the Bible into complex, interlocking networks. They believed in the empirical method of science, but the object of their observation was not the ephemeral world of sensory impressions but what they believed to be the rock-solid words of God. They were not rejecting the powers of the mind; they simply had different rules for ordering reality. They shared a strong belief that everything transpired in a precise, mechanical style. They admired Isaac Newton's efforts to describe the heavenly clockwork mathematically. As the handbook for God's machine, the fundamentalists believed the Bible was the last word, not only on morality but also on history, sociology, psychology, biology, anthropology, economics, geology—and evolution.

This passion for order is demonstrated in the chains of references in the Scofield Bible and in complicated premillennial charts that attempt to explain all history, leaving nothing to chance. In the center of a typical chart is the statuesque figure of a ruler who appeared to King Nebuchadnezzar in a dream that was interpreted by the prophet Daniel. The head is of gold, the torso of silver, the belly of bronze, and the legs of iron. Each section, Daniel said, represented a kingdom that would follow the golden one of Nebuchadnezzar. Premillennialists are especially interested in the description of the fourth, final kingdom. "[A]s iron shatters and destroys all things, it shall break and shatter the whole earth." Later in the book, Daniel has a dream in which four beasts represent the four kingdoms. The first three are described as a lion with eagle wings, a bear, and a leopard. The beast of the final kingdom has ten horns, just like the Beast of Revelation.

A skeptic might assume that the author of Revelation was familiar with the Book of Daniel when he wrote his end-time vision, but to the fundamentalists the parallels are proof of the internal consistency of the system. In the premillennial charts, metals are correlated with beasts; cross sections of the statue in

Daniel are linked to a historical time line. To the premillennialists, everything in the Bible fits together.

Secular historians believe Daniel's "prophecies" were
written to provide solace for Jews persecuted during a Syrian
occupation of Palestine during the last two centuries B.C.—just
as Revelation was written some three hundred years later to
reassure Christians being persecuted by the Roman empire. By
showing that the future could be foretold, the writers of Daniel
and Revelation were imposing order on chaos. In a similar
manner, the fundamentalists have developed the Scofield Bible,
The Late Great Planet Earth, and the Illuminati conspiracy
theory to rationalize the modern sufferings of Christians under
the reign of the secularists.

FUNDAMENTALIST POLITICS

With a system designed to provide an answer to every
question, fundamentalism might have become a fortress of
faith isolated from the political realm. With history predetermined and Jesus destined to win, fundamentalists might have
retreated into their own finely crafted universe to pray, read
Scripture, and wait for the end. But the fundamentalists believed that, as custodians of the one true faith, it was their
Christian duty to recruit as many brethren as possible. According to Matthew 24, the end won't come until "this gospel of
the kingdom [is] proclaimed throughout the earth." Jesus
warned his followers that the infidels "will hate you for your
allegiance to me. . . . But the man who holds out to the end
will be saved."

Instead of withdrawing from the modern-day Babylon
that seemed to surround them, the fundamentalists believed the
Bible told them to fight back. Naturally, some conservative
Protestants believed religion and politics should not mix. But
to the more militant fundamentalists, there could be no distinction. Politics was a projection of the spiritual war described in
the pages between Genesis and Revelation. Some fundamentalists applied their belief in absolute good and evil and their
mechanistic world view to politics, developing the conspiracy
theory in which Communists and intellectuals were working to
bring on the Antichrist's rule.

One of the first political preachers was Billy Sunday, who warned of a great conspiracy of Bolsheviks, evolutionists, theological liberals, and followers of the kaiser to bring about the Devil's kingdom on earth. In 1919, Sunday and other evangelists, including Gerald Winrod, who later wrote *Adam Weishaupt, a Human Devil,* formed the World Christian Fundamentalist Association. Whether or not Sunday knew the details of the Illuminati legend, his sermons show that he believed that capitalist moguls, intellectual elitists, and Communists all were agents of Lucifer. "The church in America would die of dry rot and sink forty-nine fathoms in hell if all members were multimillionaires and college graduates," he said. "When the word of God says one thing and scholarship says another, scholarship can go to hell!"

Another famous fundamentalist leader, William Jennings Bryan, epitomized this reaction against intellectuals in a remark he made while representing antievolutionists in the Scopes "monkey trial" of 1924, when a Tennessee teacher was tried for teaching Darwin's theory of evolution. "It would be better to destroy every other book ever written, and save just the first three verses of Genesis," Bryan said.

After Sunday and Bryan, fundamentalist politics passed to a new generation, led by a New Jersey preacher named Carl McIntire, who in the 1940s founded the fundamentalist American Council of Christian Churches and the International Council of Christian Churches. He denounced the second group's liberal counterpart, the World Council of Churches, as a tool of Moscow, a "modern Tower of Babel."

McIntire speculated that other international networks—the Communist conspiracy and the "Roman Catholic terror"—were also part of the Antichrist's plot. He wrote of "a master plan and a master mind" behind what he saw as anti-Christian, anti-American intrigues. When the liberal National Council of Churches of Christ was formed in 1950, McIntire was certain that scriptural prophecy had been fulfilled. The "superchurch" was the Whore of Babylon in Revelation, he said, the Beast's one-world religion.

In 1946, McIntire called upon the United States to over-

come the timidity caused by "pacifist propaganda" and to use
nuclear weapons in a showdown with the Soviet Union:
"America used the atomic bomb at Hiroshima as an instrument
for freedom. It worked. For just the same reason, America
should now use the atomic power. . . . If she does not, she is
failing her stewardship before God."

To McIntire, a war against the conspirators was inevitable. In Matthew 24, Jesus said there would be wars and rumors of wars until the end times. Fundamentalists assume that
the future is out of mankind's control.

McIntire's organizations worked with Senator Joseph
McCarthy in an attempt to blame Communist conspirators and
liberal intellectuals for inventing modern theology and the Revised Standard Version of the Bible to corrupt the word of
God. During the resurgence of right-wing political paranoia in
the 1960s, McIntire provided fundamentalist interpretations of
the conspiracy theories of groups such as the John Birch Society. While Robert Welch opposed the United Nations for supposedly encouraging obeisance to the one-world conspiracy,
McIntire's fundamentalists saw it as a "house of red Babel."

By 1960, McIntire's fund-raising ministry, the Twentieth
Century Reformation, had built its annual income to more than
$380,000—almost double that of the John Birch Society. McIn-
tire raised the money through donations solicited on his religious broadcasts and through his magazine, *Christian Beacon*.
By the middle of that decade, both organizations were collect-
ing more than $3 million a year.

Until 1961, only one other fundamentalist political organization surpassed McIntire's in earnings—the Christian Crusade of Tulsa, Oklahoma, run by radio evangelist Billy James
Hargis. He had become famous among fundamentalists by su-
pervising McIntire's Bible Balloon Project: an effort to float
Bibles across the Iron Curtain with helium balloons. Hargis
said he believed he had been "called of God to launch a mass
movement of resistance to . . . world government, apostate
religion, and appeasement of satanic 'isms' such as communism." He belonged to the John Birch Society and Liberty Lobby and dismissed the Kennedy administration as "a group of

Harvard radicals who have long ago been 'hooked' by the insidious dope of socialism and [who] view human life from an international standpoint."

As the machinations of the end-time conspiracy seemed to become more involved, some fundamentalists felt a need to monitor the enemy. Conspiracy theorists share a passion for gathering and collating data matched only by professional intelligence agencies. In 1937, the fundamentalist Church League of America, in Wheaton, Illinois, began to compile dossiers on the enemies of Christ. By the late 1960s, the group claimed to have seven million index cards on subversives, a collection they said was second only to that of the FBI. An associate of McIntire, Major Edgar C. Bundy, assumed control of the Church League of America in 1956. Using his experience as a former Air Force intelligence officer, Bundy built up a data bank the organization had inherited from J. B. Matthews, a former investigator for Senator McCarthy.

For more than two decades, the Church League of America has prepared intelligence reports for anti-Communist clergymen, who believe that the conspirators are infiltrating their churches. It has distributed filmstrips such as *Communism on the Map* and *The Truth About Communism,* narrated by Ronald Reagan. The league uses undercover agents to infiltrate organizations believed to be involved in the conspiracy. The group's promotional literature boasts that Church League agents obtained "sound film footage showing H. Rap Brown and Stokely Carmichael urging people doing housework in private homes to poison the food when the signal is given, and to drop cyanide in police coffee urns."

In the 1980s, the Church League still publishes its newsletter, *News and Views.* The lead story in the June 1982 issue, "A Syncretistic One-World Religion in the Making?" revived the anti-Illuminist legend of the Temple of Understanding (the "spiritual U.N." that the John Birch Society denounced in the 1960s), linking it to the World Council of Churches, the World Congress of Faiths, the U.S. Inter-Religious Conference on Peace, the World Alliance for International Friendship through Religion, the Council on Foreign Relations, the "Communist-controlled Russian Orthodox Church," the Jesuits, the Vatican, the United Nations, and the Rockefellers.

By the late 1970s, McIntire and Hargis had slipped from the public eye. News stories on McIntire mostly concerned the financial problems he had incurred by trying to support multimillion-dollar religious centers in Cape May, New Jersey, and Cape Canaveral, Florida. Hargis resigned the presidency of his American Christian College in Tulsa after five students—four of them men—accused him of having sexual relations with them. But he continues to send out Christian Crusade fundraising letters asking for $1000 donations to fight the "darkness and conspiracies all about us." One letter asked, "Will 1983 Be The Year America Is Destroyed By The Soviets? Another warned that herpes and AIDS (Acquired Immune Deficiency Syndrome, a fatal immunological disorder that afflicts mostly male homosexuals) are plagues sent by God as punishment for the sexual revolution. Hargis asked his followers to send money to buy full-page ads in the *National Enquirer* warning of the Communist conspiracy. He promised those who made large donations that "God [will] bless you as you have never been blessed in your life."

In the 1980s, doomsday politics has been revived by the Moral Majority and the New Right. In 1981, Secretary of the Interior James Watt told a House subcommittee that, because Christ's return was imminent, he wasn't sure how many more generations there would be to enjoy our natural resources. He later denied that his fundamentalist religious views would influence his policies as guardian of the national lands, but the remark has led some political observers to speculate on what effect biblical prophecy might have on government leaders who are either conservative Christians or are catering to voters who belong to the Moral Majority.

Most fundamentalists believe that before the end times begin, Israel must regain the borders it had in Old Testament days. Although Lindsey and broadcaster Pat Robertson believe that fundamental Protestantism is the one true religion, they also consider themselves Zionists. In 1982, when Israel invaded

Lebanon, Robertson told "700 Club" viewers that the war was a fulfillment of biblical prophecy.

President Reagan did not quote Scripture to justify the sale of jet fighters to Israel, but he campaigned for president as a born-again Christian and enjoyed unprecedented support from an evangelical voting block mobilized through such organizations as Jerry Falwell's Moral Majority. Falwell told *Christianity Today* that "God has raised up America in these last days for the cause of world evangelism and for the protection of his people, the Jews. I don't think America has any other right or reason for existence than those two purposes."

According to fundamentalist reasoning, after the Second Coming, Jews who do not acknowledge their two-thousand-year-old error and accept Jesus will be punished. But Israel's leaders find it convenient to take advantage of the fundamentalists' support. According to an issue of *Moral Majority Report,* three days after Israel's 1981 bombing of an Iraqi nuclear reactor, Prime Minister Menachem Begin called Falwell to thank him for his support and ask that he explain to America the necessity of the attack. Falwell obliged in a televised sermon. If Israel was destined to regain its biblical borders, he believed, then Begin's bombing was not only sanctioned but predetermined by God.

THE SURVIVALISTS

While premillennial politicians encourage their followers to oppose Satan's machinations, most of them believe that before life on earth becomes unbearable, Christians will be raptured away. But biblical references to the Rapture (the word itself does not appear in the Scriptures) are obscure enough that fundamentalists debate whether it will occur before or after the Tribulation. In the early 1980s, the so-called pretribulationists are being challenged by posttribulationists, who believe that Christians, like atheists, Jews, Buddhists, Hindus, and Moslems, will also have to suffer the seven years of torment God unleashes. And so they had better be prepared.

In the early 1980s, wire services and television networks carried stories about the survivalist movement. Families and groups fearing disaster were moving to the countryside and stockpiling food and weapons to defend their caches against less prudent neighbors. Few of the reports recognized the degree to which posttribulationism contributed to the phenomenon. Some posttribulationists believe Jesus advocated survivalism in his parable of the ten virgins who await the bridegroom (a symbol for Christ). Five of the virgins take no oil with them for their lamps. Night comes, the bridegroom is late, and they are left in the dark. But the other five virgins planned ahead and brought reserve fuel supplies. Their less prudent sisters are forced to return home for more oil and miss Jesus' arrival.

To help Christians be better prepared, a survivalist mail-order firm in Oregon offers seven-year supplies of freeze-dried food, to last for the duration of the Tribulation. In his book *Christians Will Go Through the Tribulation—And How to Prepare for It,* fundamentalist Jim McKeever shows how to build shelters to survive earthquakes and radiation. Included are charts displaying fallout decay rates, the kilotonnage of bombs, and the likelihood that various American cities will be Soviet targets. In his *End-Time News Digest,* McKeever quotes Scripture, offers survivalist advice, and monitors the occurrence of earthquakes, volcanic eruptions, wars, famines, the rise of the occult, communism, secular humanism—all the signs that are supposed to herald the end. To help readers during the interim, McKeever also publishes the *McKeever Strategy Letter,* which, like Robert White's *Duck Book,* gives advice on how to survive the conspirators' planned economic collapse by investing in gold, silver, and money-market funds.

Some posttribulationist organizations take a more active role than publishing books and newsletters. In June 1981, 3000 people attended a conference of the Christian-Patriots Defense League of Flora, Illinois, an organization that teaches Identity fundamentalism—the belief that white Americans are God's chosen people. During the five-day Freedom Festival, held on the fifty-five-acre estate of an allied organization called the Christian Conservative Church, attendees learned survival techniques ranging from tree and plant identification to knife fighting, demolition and camouflage, guard-dog training, and family defense. Also included were seminars on butchering and preserving meat, operating a chain saw, health foods, "Women's Responsibility to God and Country," and the "Federal Reserve Hoax."

"You can't make a mess of the earth and expect the Lord to come down in a chariot and take us all out of it," said John Harrell, founder of both the Christian-Patriots Defense League and the Christian Conservative Church. "The stage is set. It could happen any time. I'd say most of our people are thinking in terms of two to three years." At the time of the 1981 Freedom Festival, Harrell claimed that each month his 25,000-member organization was gaining 1000 to 2000 new adherents to his theory that a Communist conspiracy and racial mixing are about to trigger America's collapse.

When the end comes, Harrell and his members plan to use their weapons and survival skills to establish a new, smaller America in the Midwest. The map has already been drawn, a parallelogram in which the corners are formed by Pittsburgh; Atlanta; Lubbock, Texas; and Scottsbluff, Nebraska. The new country will be a white, Christian nation. "We're being Negroized, Orientalized, and Mexicanized," Harrell said. "What our forefathers gave us, we're losing."

Harrell said he believes in the doctrine of "separate but equal." Only whites are allowed to attend the annual Freedom Festivals (applicants must state their name, age, and race), but Harrell said smaller, unpublicized gatherings are conducted for the organization's few black members. Put blacks and whites together and they'll fight each other for survival, he said. "This is natural. It's Mother Nature's way of trying to preserve the species."

Another survivalist group, Posse Comitatus, is even more extreme than the Christian-Patriots Defense League. The national vigilante group espouses Identity fundamentalism and a Jewish-Communist conspiracy theory that includes the Federal Reserve System and the Internal Revenue Service. *Posse comitatus* means "power of the county." The group's members believe that the only legitimate law is that of the county sheriff. If he doesn't do his job—protecting the citizens from the encroachments of the federal and state governments and the international conspiracy—the self-appointed posse members believe they are justified in taking the law into their own hands.

Posse Comitatus was founded in Oregon in the late 1960s and now claims to have thousands of members throughout the country. The group is most visible in Wisconsin, where members have attempted to form their own township, Tigerton Dells, a conglomeration of mobile homes that posse leaders claim is immune to outside law. In the township, members operate what they call the Life Science Church and the Christian Liberty Academy. Some members try to avoid paying taxes by donating their property, including guns and mobile homes, to the church, and by claiming to be ministers.

James Wickstrom, the posse's National Director of Counter-Insurgency, ran for the Senate in 1980, receiving 16,000 votes of the 2 million cast in Wisconsin. Wickstrom regularly distributes his *Posse Noose Report*. Issues published in 1982 refer to "anti-Christ Jews" and call the Holocaust "another Jew Lie." As part of the conspiracy, Jews engage in occult magic and ritual murder, Wickstrom claimed. Citing the *Protocols of the Elders of Zion*, Wickstrom described a plot in which Wall Street Jews, the Federal Reserve, Council on Foreign Relations, Anti-Defamation League, CIA, FBI, and IRS are scheming to "financially and morally rape this Christian Republic" and absorb it into the Antichrist's one-world empire.

In February 1983, a posse member and convicted income-tax dodger named Gordon Kahl was involved in a shoot-out in rural Medina, North Dakota, when the state's federal marshal tried to arrest him for violating parole. Kahl was confronted as he was leaving a tax-resistance meeting accompanied by his wife, son, and several colleagues who had been discussing the Federal Reserve–Internal Revenue Service plot. The marshal and one of his deputies were killed in the resulting gunfight. Kahl escaped but his son and an accomplice were later arrested and convicted of second-degree murder. Several weeks after the incident, Wickstrom received a letter signed by Kahl claiming the gunfight was a fulfillment of biblical prophecies of "a great shaking in the Land of Israel," which Identity fundamentalists believe is the United States. The result, he wrote, would be the destruction of Jews and Communists, who have "conquered and occupied" the United States. Kahl urged Americans to refuse to pay their income taxes, which, he said, went to fund the conspiracy:

If you've been paying tithes to the Synagogue of Satan, under the 2nd plank of the *Communist Manifesto* to finance your own destruction, stop right now, and tell Satan's tithing collectors, as I did many years ago, "Never again will I give aid and comfort to the enemies of Christ."

He urged all Christians to rise up against the conspiracy. "Let each of you who says that the Lord Jesus Christ is your personal Savior sell his garment and buy a sword, if you don't already have one, and bring his enemies before him and slay them."

Kahl, his mind steeped in fundamentalist prophecy and conspiracy theory, was certain he was on the side of God, fighting an inevitable war against absolutely evil conspirators. In the battle of Armageddon, all rules were off, including the Fifth Commandment: Thou shalt not kill.

On June 3, 1983, almost four months after the incident in North Dakota, Kahl was discovered hiding in the northern Arkansas farmhouse of a fellow tax protester. In a second shootout with police, Kahl and a sheriff who tried to arrest him shot each other to death. Wickstrom, the Posse Comitatus leader, hailed Kahl as "a legend and a martyr. His death will stand for righteousness and the real truth."

POSTSCRIPT

American fundamentalists are not the first true believers to see their nation as the focus of biblically prophesied schemes. In the early part of this century, the Anglo-Israel movement attracted some 2 million adherents to its theory that Britain was the new Israel and that biblical prophecies would be fulfilled on British soil. The British-Israelites believed that some of the tribes of Israel migrated to the British Isles after they were driven from Palestine. The British royal family was said to be descended, through a Judean princess, from King David. The Anglo-Israelites noted that according to Leviticus 26, Israel would be punished seven times for forsaking the creator. Then the Millennium would begin. "Time" was taken to mean a period of 360 years. Seven times 360 yields 2520. Add that to 720 B.C., when the punishments began with the fall of Samaria, and the result is 1800. Correcting for the difference between the astronomical and Jewish calendars, the British-Israelites calculated that the punishments ended in 1802, when Great Britain and Ireland joined to form the United Kingdom.

In 1919, these beliefs were incarnated by the establishment of the British-Israel World Federation, with branches in Great Britain, Canada, Newfoundland, Australia, New Zealand, Tasmania, South Africa, and the United States—all believed to be homes of the scattered tribes of Israel. In the 1980s, the London office of the federation still keeps the small movement alive, with the help of its ally, the Anglo-Saxon Federation of America, of Merrimac, Massachusetts. The American branch of the movement teaches that the United States is the lost thirteenth tribe of Israel, partly because of the predominance of the number thirteen in American iconography: thirteen colonies, thirteen stripes on the flag, thirteen stars above the head of the eagle on the great seal of the United States, thirteen arrows in the eagle's left talon, thirteen leaves on the olive branch in its right talon, thirteen levels to the pyramid with the eye on top. The great pyramid of Egypt is believed to be a biblical oracle (Isaiah 19 speaks of "an altar to the Lord in the heart of Egypt"), and calculations based on the dimensions of the pyramid are used by British-Israelites in end-time computations.

This interest in the eye in the pyramid has led some believers in the Illuminati conspiracy to conjecture that the British-Israelites are themselves part of the plot. Some conspiracy theorists accuse the British-Israelites of plotting to establish a British-run, one-world government by faking the Second Coming after manipulating world events to make it appear that prophecies are being fulfilled.

It is not unusual for rival conspiracy theorists to work each other into their systems. The Identity fundamentalists believe that the pro-Zionist premillennialists are part of the one-world plot. Perhaps the more mystical-minded of the anti-Semites would find significance in the fact that the zebra-striped International Standard Book Number code appears on the back of *The Late Great Planet Earth*. It was published by Bantam Books Inc., whose address is 666 Fifth Avenue in New York City.

All the modern-day Christian seers might want to consider the words of the prophet John. Near the end of Revelation, he writes: "I give this warning to everyone who is listening to the words of prophecy in this book: should anyone add to them, God will add to him the plagues described in [Revelation]."

If the 1980s draw to a close without evidence of a Rapture, someone no doubt will recalculate the dimensions of the doomsday plot. Perhaps the last generation began with the 1967 war, when Israel took over all of Jerusalem. Add forty years, subtract seven for the Tribulation, and the result is 2000 A.D., a seemingly perfect year to begin a millennium.

9

The New Right

*"It is a vast conspiracy, indeed, that thwarts the will of
the people, so the New Right rationale goes, so vast, in
fact, that everyone is a member except the tiny minority
of New Right ideologues and their constituents. The
society, indeed, the age, is the conspiracy."*
—Alan Crawford,
Thunder on the Right, 1980

In July 1980, Thomas P. O'Neill, speaker of the U.S. House of
Representatives, complained at his daily meeting with reporters
that the "John Birchers" were gaining power in Congress.
"There are more of them on the floor today than in any of the
[other] years I've been in the House," he said. If O'Neill was
talking about card-carrying members of the John Birch Society, he was exaggerating. But perhaps he had decided there was
so much overlap between the philosophies of the Birchers and
a recently formed coalition of right-wingers and fundamentalists called the New Right that they should be considered parts
of the same phenomenon.

Since the early 1970s, New Right leaders have been building a well-organized political force whose members are motivated by the conviction that their beliefs are rooted in the absolute truth of the Bible or in an old-fashioned American
morality based on individualism and laissez-faire capitalism. In

163

general, New Right supporters oppose gun control, foreign aid, the Equal Rights Amendment, abortion rights, labor unions, and federally funded social programs; they support increased defense spending to fight communism, and legislation that would allow voluntary prayer and the teaching of the Genesis account of creation in public schools. While they believe in using federal legislation or a constitutional amendment to protect the unborn from abortion, they find racial hiring quotas and busing to achieve integration "culturally destructive government policies," as New Right organizer Paul Weyrich has written. While the New Right groups each concentrate on different issues, most of them share the belief that liberalism, modernism, socialism, communism, and secular humanism are destroying America.

Sounding this theme, New Right organizers such as Weyrich, Howard Phillips, and Richard Viguerie helped raise more than $20 million for the 1980 elections and claimed to have played a significant role in defeating four liberal senators and electing President Ronald Reagan. The effort was coordinated by several large organizations, such as Weyrich's Committee for the Survival of a Free Congress, Phillips's Conservative Caucus, the National Conservative Political Action Committee, and the Heritage Foundation, a right-wing think tank started by Weyrich and millionaire brewer Joseph Coors. Much of the money came from direct-mail solicitations by the Richard A. Viguerie Company, whose computerized data banks contain the names of 25 million Americans, about 4.5 million of whom are believed to be likely supporters of right-wing causes. With his computers, Viguerie believes, he can bypass the establishment media, which is "controlled by our adversaries." The movement's grass-roots support came from an assortment of single-issue groups, such as the Gun Owners of America, Phyllis Schlafly's Eagle Forum and STOP ERA, Jerry Falwell's Moral Majority, and Christian Voice, whose promotional literature boasts that "Christ is our chairman."

While not all New Right leaders are fundamentalists (Weyrich and Schlafly are Catholics, Phillips is a Jew), many of their followers are born-again Christians—Protestants who believe they have been "saved" through a personal religious experience with Christ and who seek to spread their faith through evangelism. It has been estimated that there are about 50 million adult Americans who consider themselves Evangelicals, many of whom are politically conservative. More than half of them are fundamentalists, believing in a literal interpretation of the Bible. While membership in more liberal churches has been declining, among evangelical denominations it is on the rise. To harness this potential voting power, Weyrich and Phillips helped fundamentalist preachers organize Moral Majority and Christian Voice. Members were recruited largely through appeals on the Christian Broadcasting Network, a $60-million-a-year operation that includes more than 150 local stations and 2500 cable-television systems.

"It is basic to my philosophy that God's truth ought to be manifest politically," Weyrich has written. "I believe with truth on our side we have great cause for hope."

It is debatable how much of the conservative swing in the 1980 elections was due to the efforts of the New Right. Several of the senators whom the New Right claimed to have helped elect later denounced their supposed benefactors as zealots. Reagan's term in office had barely begun when New Right theoreticians began complaining that the president was ignoring them in favor of traditional establishment conservatives.

But the Reagan administration considered the New Right formidable enough that several of the movement's ideologues were appointed to government posts. James Watt became Secretary of the Interior. Robert Billings, former executive director of Moral Majority, became Reagan's religious liaison during the campaign and was awarded a post in the Department of Education. Reagan appointed as surgeon general the antiabortionist C. Everett Koop, whose book *Whatever Happened to the Human Race?* is a classic among works attacking the influence of secular humanism. Koop and the book's coauthor, Francis Shaeffer, conducted an antiabortionist road show in the late 1970s, presenting a film version of their book, which warned that secular humanists were devaluing human life with plans to control society technologically through abortion and euthanasia.

Through Morton Blackwell, Reagan's special assistant for public liaison, the White House maintains ties with the Council for National Policy, a New Right group founded to oppose the prointernationalist efforts of the Council on Foreign Relations. The group's leaders include Phillips, Weyrich, Viguerie, Coors, Schlafly, and Texas oil millionaire Nelson Bunker Hunt. The group's president is Tim LaHaye, a fundamentalist preacher who is one of the national leaders of Moral Majority. Reagan appointed LaHaye's wife to the White House's Family Policy Advisory Board.

With so many links between New Right groups and the White House, it would be easy for a liberal to become paranoid contemplating the existence of a conspiracy of right-wingers. A few of the New Right's opponents have constructed conspiratorial charts almost as intricate as those of the Illuminati conspiracy theorists. But as with all conspiracy theories, the most that is proved is that people who share an ideology are working together, and in a few cases have gained positions of influence.

The New Right's power comes not from a few men and women plotting in dark chambers, but from the ability of its leaders to apply professional organizing and fund-raising skills to right-wing politics. As a result, they have created a movement with a more respectable image than groups such as the John Birch Society have ever been able to achieve. But once the slick facade is penetrated, the same old conspiracy theories are found writhing underneath.

Christian Voice's promotional literature states: "We believe that America, the last stronghold of faith on this planet, has come under increasing attack from Satanist forces in recent years . . . launched by the 'rulers of darkness of this world' and insidiously sustained under the ever more liberal ethic." Moral Majority leader Falwell warned his followers that "the bleeding heart liberals in this society [are trying] to pass their socialistic and godless legislation. . . . We must band together . . . and wage open warfare against the forces of Satan. . . . We must put the devil on the run."

Pat Robertson, host of the "700 Club," condemned "the humanistic/atheistic/hedonistic influence on American government" caused by the Trilateral Commission and the Council on Foreign Relations.

Reagan revealed his own penchant for absolutist thinking in 1983, when he told the National Association of Evangelicals that since communism is "the focus of evil in the modern world," the arms race is not a "giant misunderstanding" but the "struggle between right and wrong, good and evil." Communism, Reagan said, is a faith based on man instead of God and was "first proclaimed in the Garden of Eden with the words of temptation: 'Ye shall be as Gods.' " In the form of "modern-day secularism," Reagan warned, this godless faith is eroding America's spiritual strength from within. Reagan's belief that the United States is imperiled by dark conspiracies dates back to the Hollywood red scare of the 1950s when he presided over the Screen Actors Guild, which denounced "the international Communist Party conspiracy against our nation." In his autobiography, *Where's the Rest of Me?*, Reagan wrote of a "master scheme" to take over the American film industry, not "only for its profits . . . but also for a grand worldwide propaganda base."

The rhetoric of Reagan and his New Right allies is similar to that of fundamentalist politicians like Carl McIntire and Billy James Hargis. By using populist rhetoric to motivate followers to fight plots of evil elitists, the New Right leaders are engaging in the paranoid style of American politics.

Weyrich has written that "a debt to Senator Joseph McCarthy must be acknowledged for his role in [the] political awakening" of the "working-class anti-Communism" that has developed into the New Right. "Many of the Catholic New Right activists have a further element in common," Weyrich wrote. "Their parents were often faithful listeners to the radio broadcasts . . . of Father Charles Coughlin, the noted political commentator." In his list of those who have influenced the New Right, Weyrich might also have listed Robert Welch and the John Birch Society. In 1983, Larry McDonald, a U.S. representative from Georgia and a leader of the New Right, succeeded Welch as national chairman of the organization. Weyrich has a regular column in a weekly John Birch Society publication called *Review of the News*. In an article in the society's magazine *American Opinion,* he joined the chorus of Birchers complaining about the corrupting influence exerted on the Reagan White House by the Trilateral Commission and Council on Foreign Relations.

New Right leaders are also found on the rosters of such extremist organizations as the Church League of America—the anti-Communist group that compiles dossiers on supposed conspirators and infiltrates left-wing organizations. The group's National Committee of Sponsors includes such New Right leaders as Representative John Ashbrook, Senator Jesse Helms, and Howard Phillips, head of the Conservative Caucus.

Alan Crawford, former editor of the Young Americans for Freedom's magazine, *New Guard,* and former assistant editor of the New Right's *Conservative Digest,* believes groups like the John Birch Society are using the New Right to increase their political influence. "The New Right leaders seem to welcome them," Crawford wrote. "The New Rightists may indeed feel more comfortable with the primitive Birchers than they do with *National Review* types, whom they regard as effete Easterners."

William F. Buckley's *National Review,* which represents the conservative establishment's viewpoint, denounced the John Birch Society in 1965 in a special issue that included condemnations from conservatives Russell Kirk and senators John Tower and Barry Goldwater. In the 1980s, many traditional conservatives are denouncing the New Right in the same terms Buckley's magazine used against the Birchers. Conservatives, they say, want to *conserve* the established order. Because of their attempts to overturn the status quo, members of the New Right are seen as radicals

New Right conspiracy theorists denounce the old-line conservatives as part of the one-world plot. In Schlafly's 1964 book, *A Choice Not an Echo,* she claimed that for the past two decades the Republican presidential nominees had been chosen by "a small group of secret kingmakers using hidden persuaders and psychological warfare techniques." The conspirators supposedly included the Rockefeller establishment, bankers such as Thomas Lamont of J. P. Morgan, Ivy League intellectuals, the media, and the Bilderbergers. By pretending to be

Republicans, the "kingmakers" saw that the GOP nominated weak candidates—Wendell Willkie and Thomas Dewey—ensuring that the liberal, internationalist Democrats would win. "Can it really be possible that a little clique of powerful men meet secretly and plan events that appear to 'just happen'?" she wrote. "Most of what is ascribed to 'accident' or 'coincidence' is really the result of human plans." The book sold 3 million copies and was distributed to every delegate to the 1964 Republican national convention to aid the nomination of Goldwater, the man Schlafly believed would oppose the conspiracy.

In her next book, *The Gravediggers,* Schlafly and coauthor Chester Ward charged that one-worlders in the federal government were plotting to unilaterally disarm the United States. The book sold 2 million copies during two months in 1964. It was followed by several other books that continued to piece together the conspiracy theory, which has come to include Robert McNamara, Harold Brown, Cyrus Vance, and Henry Kissinger. The "gravediggers'" meeting place, Schlafly claimed, was the Council on Foreign Relations.

New Right leaders are not only recycling the conspiracy theories of the Birchers and the apocalyptic imagery of the fundamentalists but also constructing their own visions of grand satanic schemes. While their predecessors blamed the ever-increasing tides of modernism and cosmopolitanism on Freemasons, Jews, Communists, and internationalists, the conspiracy theorists of the New Right have concentrated on a new foe: the secular humanists.

ATHEISTIC SECULAR HUMANISM

To those who believe in absolute truth, secular humanism is the ultimate threat. Instead of accepting a single religion as the arbiter of truth and morality, secular humanists believe mankind should decide itself what is right and wrong. Just as right-wingers and fundamentalists assume a world in which there is one correct religion and a definable right and wrong, secular humanists assume pluralism and situational ethics; they believe there are multiple ways to understand reality.

Dostoevsky wrote that without a God everything is possible. While many secularists find that a positive notion, the absolutists recoil at the idea of such a rootless, epistemological void. They want solid foundations and exact definitions—fundamentals. They don't trust man to make his own decisions, case by case. Faced with troubling problems in medical ethics—who shall live and who shall die—antiabortionists want life defined as beginning at the moment of conception. Fearing that the fluctuating value of the dollar will result in economic disaster, survivalists invest in gold and call for a return to the gold standard. Fundamentalists reject the ever-changing theories of science for a static system codified thousands of years ago in the Bible.

Because they don't believe in chance, many members of these right-wing groups assume ethical, economic, and scientific changes are being orchestrated. As people who pride themselves as rugged individualists, they believe all things happen because of specific actions by identifiable men, working under the influence of either God or Satan. And so they see secular humanists as agents of a sinister system that claims to be philosophically neutral and objective while pursuing a hidden agenda: the apotheosis of rationalism and the establishment of a tyranny of experts; the undermining of religion and patriotism with secularism and cosmopolitanism. The conspiracy believers' nightmare is that mankind will use godless reason to turn the world into an anthill: individualism will be suppressed and there will be no religion. Everyone will have a defined place in an international order ruled by the priests of reason, the technocrats.

These are the same charges Robison, Barruel, and Jedediah Morse made against the Enlightenment philosophers, the Freemasons, and the Illuminati. The same sins were ascribed to the Learned Elders of Zion. Secular humanism is Illuminism. And, as in the days of the French Revolution, its modern opponents see it as the energizing force of a conspiracy.

In 1977, the John Birch Society published a 500-page book called *The SIECUS Circle, A Humanist Revolution,* by Claire Chambers. SIECUS, the Sex Information and Education Council of the United States, was condemned in the late 1960s by conservatives for advocating public sex education. The organization's more extreme opponents, including Billy James

Hargis and the John Birch Society, denounced SIECUS as part of a Communist, one-world plot to undermine Christian-American morality.

After several years of research, Chambers believed she had exposed a "well-concealed humanist underground," consisting of an "interlocking and overlapping" network of "humanist organizations." She had discovered that there was in the United States a culture of liberals (some were self-avowed humanists) who shared a belief in the use of reason and technology to shape society and fulfill the needs of mankind. Many of the humanists favored federally funded programs to teach modernist ethics. They talked about the need for world federation and international cooperation. They believed in sex education and population control. They believed in abortion rights and the equal value of cultures and religions that were not Christian. Those who shared these beliefs tended to belong to the same organizations. And so, Chambers concluded, they were conspiring.

As she explored the connections, she discovered that the "humanist underground" included not only SIECUS but Zero Population Growth, the Planned Parenthood Federation of America, the National Association for the Repeal of Abortion Laws, the American Humanist Association, *Humanist* magazine, and UNESCO, which was working to promote world population control. She even included the YWCA and YMCA, which she described as "two more cogs in the socialist-Humanist wheel."

Because SIECUS used the Taoist yin/yang symbol (to represent male and female sexuality), Chambers believed occult forces were involved in the plot. She traced the peace symbol, used by anti–Vietnam War demonstrators, to the first century A.D. when, she wrote, it was used to signify Nero, the Antichrist. Since the days before Jesus, occultists had joined with rationalists—she named Democritus, Lucretius, Spinoza, Diderot, Voltaire, Darwin, and Bertrand Russell—to conspire against the heavens by promoting rationality over religion, cosmopolitanism over patriotism.

Chambers also condemned philosopher John Dewey, whose writings set off an educational revolution earlier this century. Dewey and his followers believed the purpose of schools was not to teach students religious and moral laws that were supposed to be timeless, but to help them adapt to the changes of modern, secular society. To Chambers, Dewey's ideas did not represent a philosophical advance but were part of "an international subversive movement whose aim is no less than world domination by way of destruction of Christianity, traditional morality, and the whole fabric of society.

> Judging by the evidence at hand, it seems reasonably certain that among the major components of this worldwide conspiracy are Humanism, Socialism, Communism, the Council on Foreign Relations, the tax-exempt foundations, and occultism. . . . Humanism is now engaged in a militant religious war, its Godless army having by now reached into almost every phase of our national existence. . . . Little known to the public is their most cunning tactic: the art of labeling and quoting each other as "experts."

As proof of the conspiracy, Chambers revealed its master plan. In 1933 and again in 1973, "Humanist Manifestos" had been signed by Dewey, writer Isaac Asimov, poet John Ciardi, Planned Parenthood president Alan Guttmacher, and dozens of other professors, ministers, and intellectuals. The declarations called for a world where religion served man, and belief in the supernatural gave way to science and technology. The writers of the manifestos envisioned a day when the world would be united by an international economic and political order that guaranteed rights for all.

Chambers's efforts at making "secular humanism" a household word among members of New Right organizations was furthered by the publication of Tim LaHaye's *The Battle for the Mind* in 1980. Before helping Falwell and Weyrich start Moral Majority, LaHaye, a fundamentalist Baptist preacher, founded San Diego's Christian Heritage College. During the past two decades, he and his wife, Beverly, have written seventeen books, which have sold more than 5 million copies; subjects include premillennial biblical prophecy and creationism. In *The Battle for the Mind* LaHaye warned: "An invisible enemy threatens our society. Its name? Humanism. Its target? Your mind." By trying to solve the nation's problems through federal intervention and the world's problems through internationalism, the humanists are plotting a godless planetary society, LaHaye wrote. It will be ruled by an intellectual elite that believes in evolution, one-world government, atheism, and amorality—and that rejects the biblical doctrine of Original Sin for an unrealistic humanist belief in the inherent goodness of man.

"Humanism," LaHaye wrote, "is a man-centered philosophy that attempts to solve the problems of man and the world independently of God." He condemned Darwin for removing God from science; Dewey for banishing Him from education. "Almost every major magazine, newspaper, TV network, secular book publisher, and movie producer is a committed humanist," LaHaye wrote. Humanists founded the United Nations out of a technocratic hubris, a belief that they could use reason instead of religion to stop war.

> Humanism seems so credible and logical to the man who does not understand God's wisdom that it is adopted readily by the masses—much to their own peril. Today's wave of crime and violence in our streets, promiscuity, divorce, shattered dreams, and broken hearts can be laid at the door of secular humanism. As the Scriptures teach, "Professing themselves to be wise, they became fools (Romans 1:22)."

In his book, LaHaye used drawings of two bookshelves to symbolize the good and evil forces battling for our minds. On one shelf were the books of the Bible, Genesis through Revelation. On the other shelf were the works written by the men LaHaye considered enemies: Aristotle, Socrates, Plato, Voltaire, Rousseau, Hegel, Russell, Thomas Paine, and Adam Weishaupt.

CREATIONISM

In his fight against secular humanism, LaHaye has been a primary supporter of the creation science movement, which is an attempt to prove that an almighty God created the world in seven days, as described in Genesis. The creationists' goal is to have their doctrine taught in public schools alongside Darwin's theory of evolution. LaHaye believes that by refusing to include God in their theories, scientists are promoting the secular-humanist conspiracy. LaHaye's Christian Heritage College is the home of the Institute for Creation Research, headquarters for this effort to exorcise evolution—and all theories based on randomness and relativism—from the realm of science.

Creationists contend that when the generations of the Bible are added together, the age of the earth comes to less than 10,000 years, but geologists teach that the planet is billions of years old. The book of Genesis says all life was created during the week in which God made the universe, but Darwin's theory claims the earth's myriad species evolved through chance mutation and natural selection over millions of years.

Perhaps, the creationists say, the geologic layers were not deposited over millions of years but during the great biblical flood. Mountains were raised, the Grand Canyon carved, and the menagerie of men and dinosaurs, crustaceans and bears, all drowned together and became fossils, except those rescued by the ark. The more advanced animals climbed to higher ground, the simpler ones sank. Thus the geologic column was formed, in days, not eons. There was no randomness in the process. Men were not here by chance interactions of blind physical forces, but according to a plan.

Like the premillennialists and the conspiracy theorists, the creationists do not believe in accidents. The randomness of evolution is as unthinkable to them as the "accidental theory of history" is to the conspiracy theorists. While conspiracy theorists fight the uncertainties of our modern age by rewriting history as a perfectly defined plot, the creationists are attempting to recast science into one of the clockwork systems that are the hallmark of the fundamentalist mind. Just as fundamentalists use premillennialism and Illuminati conspiracy theories to explain how the world's troubles are plotted by Satan, they use creationism to show how God crafted the universe.

· Conservative Protestants have not always been at odds with science. Since the days of the Reformation, when Protestants rebelled against the power of the Catholic church, Protestantism has been based on the notion that the common man could discern God's rules for himself without the intercession of saints or the help of ecclesiastic authorities. Kepler, Galileo, and Newton were revered by Protestants for using reason to oppose the unscientific view of the cosmos promoted by the Catholic church. In the Catholic system, known as the Great Chain of Being, God sat at the top of a celestial ladder with mankind at the bottom. On the rungs in between were the various grades of angels. God ruled by fiat, passing his decrees down the chain, angel by angel, until they arrived on earth. The church used this image to deify its own chain of command —pope to cardinal to archbishop to bishop to priest to man. The reality of the church reflected that of Ptolemaic astronomy: earth at the center, with planets, each moved by an angel, extending heavenward in concentric spheres.

The universe of the Church was challenged when Copernicus—and, later, Galileo and Kepler—demonstrated that astronomical observations could be explained more neatly if the sun were at the center of the system. Then Newton showed that the planets moved according to simply defined mathematical laws. The rules of the universe were not promulgated continuously by decree, they had been wired-in at the beginning. The Catholic God, who ruled arbitrarily, was challenged by a Protestant God, who ruled through law and order. Creation was a great machine, with the Almighty as engineer.

For centuries, science and Protestantism worked hand in hand to delineate the complexities of creation and better understand the genius of God. The idea of the universe as heavenly machinery meshed perfectly with the Calvinist view that everything was predetermined. The pieces of creation seemed to fit together exactly. The rules were not mystical or arcane but simple. They made common sense. In nineteenth-century America, the academic community was pervaded with what was known as common-sense realism. "Two premises were absolutely fundamental," wrote historian George Marsden.

> God's truth was a single unified order and . . . all persons of common sense were capable of knowing the truth. . . . This philosophy was above all democratic or anti-elitist. . . . Evan-

gelical Christians and liberal Enlightenment figures alike assumed that the universe was governed by a rational system of laws guaranteed by an all-wise and benevolent creator.

The philosophy seemed more Christian than that of British philosophers such as Bishop Berkeley who argued that reality might exist only in the mind. And it seemed more American. All men were free to gather data and use their God-given intellects to discover the world's order. Rocks, animals, stars, and flowers were classified and arranged into charts not unlike the diagrams of the premillennialists.

But as scientific thought developed, it parted ways with theology. Scientific empiricism led to skepticism, and scholars began to use their rational faculties not to prove the consistency of the Bible but to question it. First came Darwin's theory of evolution. Then in the twentieth century, Einstein and the quantum physicists developed a world view that departed so drastically from common sense that it could only be understood in terms of abstractions such as multidimensional space, partial differential equations, and Eigenvalues: man-made conceptions that grew in complexity as scientists sought to explain a world that seemed to work independently of a god. To conservative Protestants, the scientists were guilty of the sins of the builders of the Tower of Babel: they were elevating their powers above the Almighty's. Science was no longer a simple system that the common man could fathom. Like Freemasons and Illuminati, scientists seemed to be possessors of secret knowledge.

While Newton had a place in his cosmos for God, by the twentieth century scientists had completely ruled the supernatural out of the ken of science. Privately, scientists might worship a Creator, but according to the rules they have agreed to for the pursuit of science, all explanations must rely on what they call natural forces. The idea of a perfectly planned universe has been challenged by one in which chance and relativity seem to be the rule. In quantum theory, scientific observations are said to be dependent in part on the observer. The suggestion is that reality might be more a construct of the mind than the product of a Creator.

Many contemporary conservative Protestants long for a return to the universe of eighteenth- and nineteenth-century science, when reality was seen as a tightly woven net of causal links, with none of the slack caused by chance and relativity; when science seemed to glorify the Creator instead of seeking man-made replacements for God. They wish to preserve the old system, carrying it like a fossil into the twentieth century.

In the 1980s, creationists still refuse to concede to the secular world the power to decide what is science. In their attempts to get equal time in public schools for the fundamentalist view of creation, they not only cite Bible verses but also talk in the language of thermodynamics and statistical theory. They build wave tunnels to test the Flood theory of geology and send expeditions to seek Noah's ark. They attempt to devise systems to explain subatomic physics without the randomness of quantum theory, and try to account for astronomy without Einstein's relativity.

The essence of this strange mix of science and fundamentalism is captured in a creationist study guide called *In the Beginning*. On the cover are pictures of Noah's ark and a double-helical strand of DNA. One might think that DNA, the molecule that carries genetic information, would be more likely used as a symbol of evolution: the discovery of its self-replicating structure and ability to preserve inheritable information has done much to explain life as chemistry. But creationists argue that the elegantly arranged shape of the molecule demonstrates against the idea that life could have arisen by chance:

> The genetic information contained in *each cell* of the human body is roughly equivalent to a library of 4000 volumes. For chance mutations and natural selection to produce this amount of information . . . [they] would have to produce the equivalent of far more than 10^{3000} animal offspring. (To just begin to understand how large 10^{3000} is, realize that the visible universe has less than 10^{80} *atoms* in it.

Other creationist calculations show that a barge 450 feet long, 75 feet wide, and 45 feet high would not only be stable in rough waters but could, with eight human passengers, support for one year the thousands of animals Noah supposedly saved from the Flood. Allowances are made for providing food and water, ventilation, waste disposal, and exercise space.

This fascination with calculating the size of Noah's ark is similar to the attempts of the historical revisionists to disprove the Holocaust with computations of the capacity of gas chambers. Like the revisionists, the creationists engage in pseudo-scholarship. By gathering thousands of facts and numbers and paying painstaking attention to details, they create the illusion that what they are doing is science. Their approach is quite different from that of scientists and historians, who consider the scenarios they construct to be temporary models, to be replaced when better ones are found. They assume that nothing is ever ultimately proved, and that there is more than one plausible system for arranging facts. When enough observations are found that do not fit their models, they take that as a sign that a new system is necessary. But when a model is taken on faith to be absolutely true, contradictory data can only be accommodated by making the system increasingly complex and unwieldy, until—like a conspiracy theory—it becomes an end in itself, a fragile cathedral of thought that bears little resemblance to reality.

When astronomical observations did not fit the Catholic church's model of the universe (with the earth at the center and the planets and stars revolving around it in perfectly circular orbits), astronomers tried to explain away the discrepancies by constructing systems in which the orbit of each planet consisted of epicycles: circles within a circle. When observation of the planets' motions still did not fit the model, the orbits were made even more complex: there were circles within circles within circles. Given enough ingenuity, it is always possible to construct an elaborate model to explain what is already assumed.

The creationists use their most complex calculations to challenge nuclear dating techniques, which indicate that life began millions of years ago. Radioactive dating is done by determining the rate at which uranium decays to lead, or ribidium to strontium. By measuring a rock's ratio of so-called mother and daughter elements, scientists can calculate how old it is. But, the creationists ask, how do we know that radioactive decay rates have always been the same? If, in the past, uranium changed into lead at a faster pace, then the earth's great antiquity would be an illusion. If one assumes decay rates have slowed by just the right amount, it is possible to reinterpret the data and show the earth is, as the Bible indicates, only several thousand years old.

Research is also under way to develop a model of the atom that would explain the orbits of the electrons as mechanistically as Newton did the motions of the planets. Creationists write papers that argue that the second law of thermodynamics proves that life cannot evolve from chaos, as the scientists suppose when they say we are descended from molecules combining randomly in the primordial soup, the most stable ones surviving. The second law, which says that systems move irreversibly from a state of order to disorder, is taken by creationists as a mathematical description of the biblical fall from grace, mankind's punishment for tasting the fruits of knowledge. Like most fundamentalists, creationists believe progress is impossible for a people cursed for believing they could be smarter than their creator.

In fact, the need to believe in a biblically consistent young universe has led creationists to reject almost all of modern astronomy. Quasars, for example, appear to be so distant that their light would take billions of years to reach earth. That would seem to indicate that these starlike bodies are billions of years old. Creationists believe that not just the earth but also the heavens were created during the seven days of Genesis. In the past, they had to rely on the argument that God created the celestial objects with light beams already attached. Now they are trying to disprove Hubble's law and the red shift, on which stellar measurements are based. They are trying to show that Einstein was wrong and that there is no upper limit to the speed of light. If the velocity of light exceeds 186,000 miles per second, the quasars would not be so distant after all.

A few creationists are trying to prove that the earth is at the center of the solar system. To some fundamentalists, Bible verses such as Ecclesiastes 1:5 ("The sun rises and the sun goes down . . .") seem to assume a geocentric universe. In *A New*

Interest in Geocentricity, creationist James Hanson recently argued that the Michelson-Morley experiment, which heralded Einstein's special theory of relativity, supports geocentricity instead. In the 1881 experiment, the two scientists attempted to measure the motion of the earth against the ether (the invisible substance that was then believed to fill the universe) by using an apparatus that sent out two beams of light: one moving with the earth, the other at a right angle. They presumed the first light beam would cover an equal distance faster than the second beam because it was, in effect, given a boost by the earth's velocity.

Instead, Michelson and Morley discovered that the two beams moved at the same speed. The motion of the earth seemed to have no effect on the speed of light. Other physicists, Fitzgerald and Lorentz, suggested an explanation: if objects shrink in the direction of their motion, then the light beam moving with the earth would traverse a slightly smaller distance than the beam moving perpendicularly. Eventually, Einstein developed his theory in which moving objects shrink and their time slows—always by the exact amount necessary to preserve the speed of light as constant. Time and space became relative.

As Hanson sees it, relativity was invented as an abstruse means of denying the obvious: the light beams moved at the same velocity because the earth is standing still, at the center of creation. Which makes more common sense, he asked: to accept a world in which the sun rises in the east, traverses a motionless sky and sets in the west, or to retreat into a universe that can only be explained mathematically? "To the person who accepts heliocentricity, earth is no special place," he wrote.

> But when we read the Bible, we find that earth has a very special place and a very special relationship to God's throne. . . . Because the Bible stresses absolutes, and because geocentricity is associated with absolutes more than are relativity or heliocentricity, I believe geocentricity to be the cosmology of the Bible.

Creationists debate whether a literal interpretation of the Bible requires believing in geocentricity, but at the root of creationist thinking is the notion that mankind is at the focus of the creator's eye. Can it be chance, they ask, that the earth exists at just the right distance from the sun so it is not too hot or too cold to sustain life?

Like the premillennial charts and honeycomb diagrams of Illuminati conspiracies, the creationists' theories parody reason. All three systems are built with the same ingrained assumptions: a distrust of intellectuals, a rejection of humanism, a literal interpretation of the Bible, a disbelief in chance, and a world view in which history is a struggle between absolute good and evil. Premillennialism, creationism, and anti-Illuminism all assume a precision universe. Like the verses of the Bible, every object and event is interlinked. To the fundamentalists, mankind was born and will die in a world with a history that is divinely engineered. Reality is as exacting as circuitry.

POSTSCRIPT

While there is no evidence that secular humanists have their own Illuminati conspiracy theory, during the 1960s a group of sophisticated practical jokers caused a wave of Illuminati legends to appear in the revolutionary press of the left-wing counterculture.

On June 4, 1969, the *East Village Other,* an underground newspaper in New York City, printed a chart titled "Current Structure of the Bavarian Illuminati Conspiracy and the Law of Fives." The interconnected boxes were labeled with the usual targets of the conspiracy theory—the Elders of Zion, the House of Rothschild, the Federal Reserve System, the Freemasons, the Rosicrucians, and the Jesuits. Also included were leftist groups then at the height of their fame: the Black Muslims, the Students for a Democratic Society, the Black Panther Society, and the Yippies. And there were some new additions: the Combine (the evil manipulators in Ken Kesey's novel *One Flew Over the Cuckoo's Nest,* who control reality by speeding and slowing the clocks), Mark Lane (a prominent Kennedy-assassination conspiracy theorist), and Saint Yossarian, named for the hero of Joseph Heller's *Catch-22.* In the center of the chart were five circles representing the main divisions of the conspiracy: the Sphere of Discord, the Sphere of Chaos, the Sphere of

Aftermath, the Sphere of Bureaucracy, and the Sphere of Confusion. The circles surrounded a pentagon, the symbol of the conspiracy.

The chart had been prepared with the help of an aspiring writer named Robert Anton Wilson, an acquaintance of such countercultural figures as Timothy Leary and Alan Watts. Wilson had become fascinated by the Illuminati legend in the 1960s as an editor at *Playboy* magazine, where he was in charge of answering letters submitted to an advice column. Right-wingers would write to ask about the Illuminati. Left-wingers, he noticed, had their own conspiratorial obsessions.

At the time, the Kennedy assassination conspiracy theories of New Orleans district attorney Jim Garrison were creating a sensation in the underground press. One of Garrison's aides believed the Illuminati were part of the plot. Wilson was annoyed that the left accepted Garrison's revelations as blindly as the establishment press believed the Warren Commission's "lone-assassin" theory. The left, he wrote, was as "robotic" as the right.

To challenge these entrenched beliefs, Wilson and his accomplices started planting Illuminati stories. "We accused everybody of being in the Illuminati—Nixon, Johnson, William Buckley, Jr., ourselves, Martian invaders, all the conspiracy buffs, *everybody*," Wilson wrote.

Wilson and his friends were members of an anarchist group called the Discordians. The first law of Discordianism was "convictions cause convicts," or, as Wilson explained it: "Whatever you believe imprisons you." The Discordians worshiped Eris, the goddess of chaos. They rejected the belief that events occur according to a plan, calling it the Aneristic Illusion. But they considered their own belief in chaos, the Eristic Illusion, to be just as dubious. The Discordian bible, *Principia Discordia,* explained this seeming paradox with what was called the Law of Fives, illustrated with a picture of five pebbles:

Do these 5 pebbles *really* form a pentagon? Those biased by
the Aneristic Illusion would say yes. Those biased by the Eristic Illusion would say no. Criss-cross them and it is a star.

An Illuminated Mind can see all of these, yet he does not
insist that any one is really true, or that none at all is true.
Stars, and pentagons, and disorder are all his own creations
and he may do with them as he wishes. . . . Conceptualiza-
tion is art, and YOU ARE THE ARTIST.

"You have achieved Discordian enlightenment," Wilson
wrote, "when you realize that, while . . . the Law of Fives [is]
not literally true, *neither is anything else.* Out of the hundred
million buzzing, bright, busy signals received every minute,
the human brain ignores most and organizes the rest in con-
formity with whatever belief system it currently holds." By
"introducing so many alternative paranoias . . . everybody
could pick a favorite, if they were inclined that way. I also
hoped that some less gullible souls, overwhelmed by this em-
barrassment of riches, might see through the whole paranoia
game."

Wilson continued his parody of conspiracy theories by
writing, with Robert Shea, a three-volume science fiction novel
called *Illuminatus!,* published in 1975. In the books, the Discordians fight the Illuminati, "a secret society seemingly dedicated to rationality, science, law 'n' order, and Total Control of
Everybody," for dominion over the earth. The Discordians'
allies include:

● ELF, the Erisian Liberation Front, headed by the mystical Dealy Lama, who lives in the sewers below Dealy Plaza in
Dallas, where John F. Kennedy was assassinated, and "seemingly plots irrationality, mysticism, anarchy, and Total Liberation
of Everybody."

● the JAMS, or the Justified Ancients of Mummu, a secret
society founded in the days of Babylon, which worships its own
goddess of chaos and has been at war with the Illuminati for
fifty-nine centuries. The head of the JAMS is John Dillinger,
who, it turns out, was not really killed in 1934 by FBI gunmen.
(As a thirty-third-degree Mason and Illuminatus Primus, FBI
director J. Edgar Hoover is, of course, an enemy of the JAMS.)

● the Legion of Dynamic Discord, headed by a libertarian

genius named Hagbard Celine, who owes allegiance to no nation and travels the anarchic world beneath the seas in his own submarine.

● Markoff Chaney, a midget who "is carrying on a one-man war against the standardization (he is very substandard) and mechanization (he is very alive) of modern society." Chaney rewires traffic signals so the "Walk" and "Don't Walk" signs come on at the wrong times and performs other guerrilla acts to introduce the random factor into the well-ordered world of the Illuminati. In mathematics, a Markov chain is used in calculations of probability.

The first book of the trilogy, *The Eye in the Pyramid*, begins with a scene on East Sixty-eighth Street in New York (near the Council on Foreign Relations), where the office of a left-wing magazine called *Confrontation* has just been bombed. Police department detectives find among the wreckage a box of interoffice memos describing the magazine's investigation of the Illuminati. Like most students of conspiracy theory, the *Confrontation* researcher mixes reputable sources with disreputable ones, slowly piecing together a fantastic mosaic in which the Illuminati seem to be related to a chain of secret societies. According to the more fantastic sources, George Washington and Adam Weishaupt were the same person, and the pyramid design for the Great Seal of the United States was given to Thomas Jefferson by a mysterious black-cloaked visitor, possibly from outer space.

While researchers comb the library for information on the Illuminati, *Confrontation*'s editor sends reporter George Dorn to Mad Dog, Texas, reputed to be the home of a right-wing organization responsible for the assassinations of the Kennedys, Martin Luther King, George Lincoln Rockwell, and Spiro Agnew. Dorn is arrested for possession of marijuana and held in the Mad Dog jail until he is rescued by a squad of Discordians led by a beautiful woman named Mavis, who is armed with a machine gun. During the escape, George sees a pyramid-shaped altar in the jail, which, Mavis tells him, is the secret chapel of the Illuminati. She takes him aboard Hagbard Celine's submarine and administers the sexual rites of initiation into the Legion of Dynamic Discord. The submarine's destina-

tion is the underwater ruins of Atlantis. There, Celine fights
Illuminati spider ships for Atlantean art treasures, which will be
given to the Mafia to convince them to sever their relationship
with the worshipers of imposed order and to join the Discordians in an attempt to prevent an Illuminati-engineered World
War III.

The secret war between the conspiracy of chaos and the
conspiracy of order continues in the next two installments of
the trilogy, *The Golden Apple* and *Leviathan*. The story's climax
occurs at a rock festival at Ingolstadt, Bavaria, held on the two-
hundredth anniversary of the founding of Weishaupt's secret
order. By the time the reader comes to the last few chapters,
nuclear war seems imminent and a strain of a CIA-produced
virus threatens to kill off civilization. The United States is
rocked by riots instigated when the president (who is being
manipulated by the Illuminati) imposes authoritarian laws,
which cause more rioting and result in still more laws. But that
is just as the Discordian laws predict: escalation of order equals
escalation of chaos.

"The history of the world is the history of the warfare
between secret societies," Ishmael Reed wrote in his novel
Mumbo-Jumbo. The quote is used as an epigraph for *Illuminatus!*
But as the trilogy draws to a close, it becomes increasingly
difficult to tell who belongs to which conspiracy. From the
beginning, George Dorn has wondered why Hagbard Celine's
sidekick, Mavis, has the eye in the pyramid tattooed on her
body. Eventually, the editor of *Confrontation* admits he bombed
his own office. There are five John Dillingers. And, strangest
of all, Celine admits he is an Illuminati leader. Weishaupt, Hitler, J. Edgar Hoover, and all those who thought they were
Illuminati were wrong, he says. They were imposters. The true
Illuminati are the good guys. Since the beginning of history,
these descendants of the supermen of Atlantis have protected
the ancient secrets and fought *against* arbitrary power and hierarchy.

The countercultural version of the Illuminati legend was
intended as a parody. Although Wilson and his friends shared
with the conspiracy theorists a suspicion of rationalist elites,

they mocked the absolutist thinking that leads to political paranoia. Still, some readers took *Illuminatus!* seriously. They began writing to Wilson, accusing him of helping the Illuminati
by making the conspiracy theory seem foolish. When Wilson
appeared on a radio talk show in San Francisco, a woman called
and said that since he knew so much about the Illuminati, he
must be one of them.

"Maybe," Wilson replied, "the secret of the Illuminati is
that you don't know you're a member until it's too late to get
out."

10

The "New Dark Ages" Conspiracy

*"We've got to use our minds as a boxer uses his fists. I
don't think everybody has a right to his own opinion—
not if it's stupid and endangering the human race."*
—Fay Sober, press relations officer for
Lyndon H. LaRouche, Jr., 1981

As he sat in his suite at the Hotel Navarro on Central Park
South in New York City, Lyndon LaRouche talked like a patri-
ot. "The people have lost power on the national level. We must
bring the little shots of the nation into public policy." He
stared, squinted, lifted his furry brows. "The problem is that
the people are not running the country.... We fought the
American Revolution to free us from that kind of nonsense. It's
been a real fight keeping the country dedicated to what the
founding fathers intended."

It was January 1981, several months after LaRouche's latest bid for the presidency of the United States. With $526,000
in federal matching funds, the fifty-eight-year-old former
Marxist and his young devotees had campaigned against what
they believed was a conspiracy of British aristocrats to depopu-
late the world with wars, famines, and birth control, reducing
the number of people clamoring for a share of the riches. According to LaRouche's scenario, citizens who were allowed to
live were drugged into passivity with narcotics, television, and

187

rock 'n' roll, kept in feudal servitude and deprived of the benefits of technology.

The aim of the plot, LaRouche believed, was to enslave the world with a "new Dark Ages." Then the oligarchs—London bankers and descendants of centuries-old royal families—would sit atop the economic pyramid, reaping the benefits of having reduced the people to mindless, manipulated consumers.

If elected president, LaRouche had vowed, he would see that the United States helped raise the standard of living of the "little people" of the world. By developing nuclear power, chemical fertilizers, and other high-technology solutions, the nation would help the masses rise above their animal state and challenge the oligarchs' wealth.

"Sure, people are born little hedonistic pieces of flesh," he said, "but they can be developed into citizens."

Over the years, LaRouche has packaged his strange theories to appeal to a bewildering assortment of leftist intellectuals, right-wingers, ethnic groups, farmers, laborers, and even Baptist preachers. Since 1968, when he recruited his first followers among leftist radicals at Columbia University, LaRouche has formed a number of organizations devoted to fighting the Dark Ages plot: the National Caucus of Labor Committees, the International Caucus of Labor Committees, the U.S. Labor Party, and, more recently, the Fusion Energy Foundation, the National Anti-Drug Coalition, the Club of Life, and the National Democratic Policy Committee, which his followers immodestly refer to as "the LaRouche wing of the Democratic party."

While LaRouche's earlier organizations had had a leftwing orientation, lately he had been cultivating a conservative image. In his nationally televised campaign advertisements, he spoke surrounded by American flags; in one commercial he posed in front of the Alamo.

But the statesmanlike manner was a difficult charade. In his attempt to secure the Democratic nomination, LaRouche accused President Carter of plotting mass murder on the scale of the Holocaust because his administration supported world population control. He condemned nuclear power opponents as Neanderthals; solar power supporters as heirs of pagan sun-worshiping cults. Because of Senator Edward Kennedy's sympathy for environmentalists, he was denounced in bumper stickers and signs that read "More People Have Died in Ted Kennedy's Car Than in Nuclear Power Plants" and "Chappaquiddick 1, Three Mile Island 0."

Because he had uncovered his enemies' plot, LaRouche believed they would do anything to stop him. But he wasn't afraid. He leaned back, smiled, and in the same measured tones a politician might use to tell campaign-trail anecdotes, he described the night a team of professional assassins appeared at his door.

"And, through a comedy of errors, another assassin showed up. . . ." They scared each other off, and LaRouche was saved. But, later, he said, they tried to kill him again. Altogether, he claimed, there were three assassination attempts during his campaign. As he spoke, a bodyguard stood outside the door.

During the past two decades, LaRouche has developed his exaggerated sense of fear and grandeur into a conspiracy theory that his believers find so compelling that they dedicate their lives to help him play out his fantasies. At their headquarters in Manhattan, the reception area is monitored by a closed-circuit television camera; the receptionist sits behind a sheet of bulletproof glass. Each of the three doors leading from the lobby to the inner offices is secured with an electronic lock with a constantly changing push-button code. Inside, LaRouche's followers sit at desks, telephoning government and corporate officials, gathering bits of information to be woven into the Dark Ages plot. Sometimes information is solicited by posing as newspaper reporters. "We're an intelligence operation," says Paul Goldstein, LaRouche's chief of counterintelligence. "Sometimes you have to be shrewd."

A Telex line links the Manhattan office to Wiesbaden, Germany, headquarters for LaRouche's European branch, which is run by his wife, Helga Zepp-LaRouche. LaRouche claims to have fourteen domestic offices, located in most major cities of the United States, and foreign offices in Montreal, Mexico City, Bogotá, Caracas, Paris, Brussels, Copenhagen,

Milan, and Dusseldorf. Every day, members plan demonstrations, campaign in local elections, and file reports on the activities of the conspirators. Because of their cultlike devotion—reminiscent of the followers of Reverend Sun Myung Moon's Unification Church—they have come to be known as LaRouchies. Every day they hawk their papers on the street and confront passengers in most of the big-city airports, helping to raise the $200,000 a week it purportedly costs to help LaRouche maintain the illusion that he is an important world leader, the one man who can defeat the conspiracy.

In 1979, *The New York Times* reported claims that five members had each given LaRouche $100,000 and that a computer firm (now bankrupt) run by several of his followers might have helped supplement the organization's budget. But most of the money comes from selling periodicals: the twice-weekly newspaper *New Solidarity* and the magazines *Fusion, War on Drugs, Campaigner, Investigative Leads,* and *Executive Intelligence Review.* The publications vary in tone, depending on whether they are written for members or aimed at attracting outside support. In *New Solidarity,* members read articles that warn, for example, that former Secretary of State Alexander Haig and John Birch Society leader Representative Larry McDonald are plotting to assassinate President Reagan and Pope John Paul II, and that Swiss bankers, neo-Nazis, the CIA, FBI, KGB, and the Anti-Defamation League are included in the plot, which is supposedly coordinated by a twentieth-century extension of the medieval Hospitalers, a rival of the Knights Templar. In *Fusion,* accounts of the conspiracy are more subdued, and they are accompanied by competently researched articles on nuclear energy.

Some readers are deceived by *Fusion*'s respectable image. The National Science Teachers Association and the National Aeronautics and Space Administration both have run full-page advertisements in it. In an interview in the August 1981 issue, space-shuttle astronaut Robert Crippen, who was apparently unaware of the controversial nature of the organization, praised the Fusion Energy Foundation for supporting American science. Advertisements for the magazine boast that "50 percent of the first Columbia shuttle crew subscribes to *Fusion.*"

It has been estimated that LaRouche has only about 500 to 1000 close followers. But by emphasizing antidrug, protechnology issues and populist rhetoric, the Fusion Energy Foundation and National Democratic Policy Committee have attracted some 20,000 members and more than 300,000 magazine subscribers, almost all of whom are unaware that they are supposed to be soldiers in LaRouche's private war against the conspiracy.

Many of these peripheral supporters are first approached in airports. In summer 1981, actor Peter Fonda flew into a rage at Denver's Stapleton International Airport when he saw Fusion Energy Foundation members ridiculing his sister, Jane, for her environmentalist activities. He drew a pocketknife and attacked their sign, which read "Feed Jane Fonda to the Whales."

A year later, LaRouche was in the news again when Nancy Kissinger, wife of former Secretary of State Henry Kissinger, was accused of attempting to choke a Fusion Energy Foundation demonstrator at Newark International Airport. The young woman had asked Henry, whom LaRouche considers to be a British agent, if it were true that he slept with young boys. Nancy, who was escorting her husband to Boston for a triple-bypass heart operation, was not amused. "I took her by the neck and pinched her," Nancy admitted at her trial in Newark Municipal Court. She asked the woman, "Do you want to get slugged?" The judge ruled that Nancy had engaged in "a spontaneous, somewhat human reaction." Since there was no injury, he acquitted her of assault.

In August 1982, LaRouche followers held a Washington press briefing to denounce Kissinger as a homosexual and release information claiming to link him, through an Italian Masonic lodge, with the murder of Aldo Moro. At about the same time, members of a LaRouche front called the Committee Against Genocide picketed in New York, denouncing Averell Harriman, a leading liberal in the Democratic party, as a Nazi because his aristocratic family supposedly supported eugenics research.

The LaRouchies refer to their slanders as "psywar techniques." In a world in which the conspirators supposedly saturate us with their books, music, newspapers, and television shows, LaRouche's followers fight back with words that stick in one's mind like shards of glass.

"We're not very nice, so we're hated," said Paul Goldstein. "Why be nice? It's a cruel world. We're in a war and the human race is up for grabs."

THE PHILOSOPHY WAR

LaRouche counts among his enemies the usual foes of right-wing conspiracy theorists: Rockefellers, Trilateralists, international bankers, Zionists, Jesuits, Freemasons, the American Civil Liberties Union, Eastern establishment liberals, the Anti-Defamation League, the Socialist International. All, he believes, are run by the British. But he also includes among the conspirators people and groups many right-wingers admire: Adam Smith, the father of capitalism; the right-wing Heritage Foundation; and Larry McDonald of the John Birch Society. While he opposes the KGB, he believes they are in league with the CIA and the FBI and that all three organizations work for British intelligence. He denounces the oligarchs for trying to enslave the people with one-world government—that favorite devil of the radical right—but, like a leftist, he supports a "New World Economic Order" in which Third World countries would fight the international banking establishment.

In the world of LaRouche, the standard left-right political scale has been twisted into a Möbius strip. "Left" and "right," LaRouche says, are false distinctions, smoke screens used by the conspirators. What counts is whether you are on the side of Plato or Aristotle, whose philosophical descendants supposedly are engaged in an ongoing psychological battle to see who gets to define the way we perceive reality. While other conspiracy theorists explain all of history as a plot, LaRouche's system also includes science, philosophy, and mathematics. The result is the quintessential version of the Illuminati conspiracy theory, a vision so complex and engulfing that it appeals to his young followers, who consider themselves intellectuals. Many have attended Ivy League universities; some have Ph.D.'s. Members have included the daughter of a president of Sarah Lawrence College, the son of a deputy assistant secretary of state, and the son of a vice president of the Ford Foundation—an organization that is supposedly part of the conspiracy.

LaRouche's followers believe that, as Platonists, they are on the side of a tradition that includes Bach, Beethoven, and Shakespeare; mathematicians Gottfried Leibniz, Bernhard Riemann, and Georg Kantor; physicist Erwin Schrodinger; Franklin Delano Roosevelt; and Mohammed and Jesus. Their ideological enemies—the followers of Aristotle—supposedly include not only Harriman, Kissinger, and the Rockefellers, but Ken Kesey, the Beatles, Menachem Begin, the Ayatollah Khomeini, Aldous Huxley, H. G. Wells, Adolf Hitler, physicists Neils Bohr and Isaac Newton, and philosophers Bertrand Russell, John Locke, Bishop Berkeley, Jeremy Bentham, and Voltaire.

Since ancient times, LaRouche believes, the Aristotelians have worked to enslave the masses by opposing technology with environmentalism, encouraging drug use, controlling the world economy, and, most of all, by demoralizing everyone with a world view in which all truth is relative. LaRouche's heros, the Platonists, fight the Aristotelians by insisting that there are absolutes. Like the philosopher-kings described in Plato's *Republic,* the members of LaRouche's elite claim to be rightful rulers because they are possessers of unquestionable wisdom.

LaRouche's conspiracy theory is a distortion of a real philosophical distinction. Plato and Aristotle proposed different answers to one of the most basic philosophical problems. The world we perceive is constantly changing, so how can we be sure anything abides? Roses bloom, reach the full of their glory, then wilt and die. Each one is slightly different. How can we call them all by the same name? What constitutes "roseness"? What are the standards by which we judge it?

Plato proposed that such ideas as roseness exist in a state of purity in a metaphysical realm. Each rose in the material world is just a poor copy of the ideal Rose. In fact, the entire material world is a shadow land, consisting of ephemeral, imperfect projections of the perfect, eternal Platonic Ideas. Just as there is a perfect Rose, so there are Truth and Goodness. If one could learn to recognize these absolutes, he would rule sternly, confident that his decisions were not whims, fiats, or opinions, but truths. He would be a philosopher-king.

Aristotle rejected the existence of Plato's invisible world. There are not Roses, he believed, just roses. Roseness is a pattern, contained in each flower, as an acorn contains the blueprint to become an oak. While Plato preferred to contemplate absolutes, Aristotle concentrated on gathering specimens and classifying them, to see what rules he could discern. While Plato mused on what would make a utopia, Aristotle collected the constitutions of the Greek city-states and studied them to see what was the best practical form of government.

In the Golden Age of Greece, the distinction between the methods of Plato and Aristotle was subtle. But over the centuries, Platonism has become a label for those who exalt the world of ideas over the world of facts. In their search for truth, Platonists look beyond the evanescent world of the senses for metaphysical absolutes. Those who instead emphasize the empirical approach have come to be called Aristotelians.

The difference between these two ways of perceiving reality is demonstrated in the approach a Platonist and an Aristotelian might take toward mathematics. When we examine the world around us, we find no such things as perfect circles or triangles, just approximations. So how do we know about circularity and triangularity? A Platonist would say that the ideas Circle and Triangle actually exist in the metaphysical realm. Because we know about these absolutes instinctively, we can recognize the poor imitations when we encounter them in nature.

An Aristotelian would say we know about circles and triangles because we see many objects in the world around us that approximate those shapes. With this knowledge, gained through our senses, we abstract the mathematical concepts of circularity and triangularity—mental constructs that are more or less artificial. What matters is not whether there really are metaphysical Circles and Triangles, but how useful such concepts are in ordering the material world.

Aristotelianism has become the essence of science. Data is

studied, then arranged into constellations that seem to explain it most simply. In theory, an Aristotelian believes there are many possible orders from which to choose. Science is concerned with description, not with seeking unshakable truth. What works is right—until it is overthrown by a more attractive system.

LaRouche believes that by emphasizing the empirical over the metaphysical, society has lost its moral moorings. Apply Aristotelianism to ethics, he says, and the result is moral relativism; in anthropology, cultural relativism; in religion, the idea that one system of belief is as valid as another—whatever works for the believer.

With Platonism defined as good and Aristotelianism as evil, LaRouche has squeezed the history of philosophy into a conspiracy theory in which everyone is on one side or the other. He sees Aristotelianism as a tool the British have honed into a weapon to demoralize mankind with a world view in which a snail darter has as much right to live as a human; where aborigines are not inferior, just different. And, LaRouche points out, it was such British empiricists as John Locke, Bishop Berkeley, and David Hume who developed Aristotle's emphasis on the observable to the extent that they believed only the world discerned by the senses is real. As LaRouche sees it, British philosopher Jeremy Bentham's utilitarian morality is based entirely on the senses: good is what maximizes pleasure for the most people. British economist Adam Smith's capitalism is also rooted in the senses, LaRouche says: it is based on hedonism, the pleasure-pain principle. The capitalists brainwash the people into believing the purpose of life is to consume all they can. Then they maximize profits by ensuring that supply never quite matches demand.

And the oligarchs—the wealthy British families—are schooled in this philosophical tradition. They use it, LaRouche says, in a psychological war to keep the masses helpless. When the idea that there are no absolutes is championed, progress becomes impossible—there is nothing by which to measure it —and without progress, nations cannot develop and challenge the oligarchs' wealth. Without progress, the "little people" are relegated to hopelessness. They retreat into sensualism, numb

their minds with drugs and rock music. Why not? If everything
is relative, then one lifestyle is as good as another. An LSD
reality is as good as a drugless one. Beethoven is no better than
the Clash. We retreat to a new Dark Ages and the oligarchs sit
back secure.

The Platonic ideal that LaRouche proposes as a beacon in
the epistemological wilderness is Progress. Our science, technology, and economics must be arranged to promote progress.
How does he define this elusive term? The ultimate value,
LaRouche believes, is human life. If we can use the earth's resources to support an increasing density of human beings, then
we are progressing. If we look at dwindling fossil-fuel reserves,
recoil in fear, and call for limits to population growth, then we
are reverting to the Dark Ages—just as the conspirators have
planned. Instead, we should seek new technologies to release
more energy: nuclear fission and fusion. With the people's
material needs taken care of through LaRouchean progress,
their minds can be enriched with Beethoven, Shakespeare,
Leibniz—whichever artists and thinkers LaRouche deems to be
Platonists. The works of those LaRouche brands as Aristotelians would not be taught. As in Plato's ideal Republic, art must
serve what the rulers say is the common good.

An article in *Campaigner,* LaRouche's theoretical journal,
describes a sixteenth-century fight by musician Gioseffe Zar-
lino to preserve the orderly structure of the well-tempered
musical scale from attacks by Claudio Monteverdi, whose any-
thing-goes approach is blamed for spawning the dissonances of
modern music and the anarchy of jazz and rock 'n' roll. Another article argues that twentieth-century physics can be rein-
terpreted to contradict quantum theorists who claim that events
occur randomly in atoms. Both articles illustrate a recurrent
theme: the idea of a world where disorder reigns is one of the
enemy's psywar techniques.

While the creationists use the Bible as the bedrock of their
attempt to write randomness out of the world, LaRouche relies
on a mystical outgrowth of Platonism that developed in the
first few centuries A.D. The Neoplatonists sought a way to explain how Plato's realm of the ideal, where the Ideas existed,
was connected with the physical world. They proposed a pic-

ture of the universe in which the earth was surrounded by a series of concentric spheres. Above the earth were the planets, then the stars, then the empyrean, where the Ideas dwelled. As they descended, level by level, the Ideas became matter, roseness became roses. When people died, the process worked in reverse. By ascending through the spheres, they left their material bodies and gradually became pure soul.

In Christian Neoplatonism, God lived in the highest realm. The Platonic Ideas were the thoughts of God. Thus Neoplatonism influenced the Catholic church's Great Chain of Being. The image of concentric Neoplatonic spheres also is reflected in the world views of the cabalists and hermeticists.

Early astronomers used Neoplatonism as the basis of their theories of the universe. When Kepler designed his model, with the sun in the center, he turned the Neoplatonic pattern inside out, though the basic idea remained the same. He identified the sun with God "the most excellent of all." The sphere of the stars was associated with Jesus, the planets with the Holy Ghost. Kepler tried to show that the distances between the spheres could be derived from calculations based on the "Platonic solids"—the cube, tetrahedron, dodecahedron, icosahedron, and octohedron—all of which interested Plato because they could be inscribed in a sphere. "They imitate the sphere— which is an image of God—as much as a rectilinear figure can," Kepler wrote.

In the twentieth century, scientists believe that Kepler's discovery of the planetary laws was made despite his preoccupation with Neoplatonic mysticism. Kepler's interest in the whys as well as the hows of the universe is now considered unscientific. But the Neoplatonist strain has been preserved in the works of other scientists such as Leibniz. In the twentieth century, the Platonic solids appear in various occult works.

LaRouche and his followers have used Neoplatonism to contruct an economic model rooted in their belief in the absolute necessity of progress. In their complex system, economies evolve, step by step, to higher stages each time a new technology is introduced. These steps by which mankind ascends toward perfection can be thought of as Neoplatonic spheres. In fact, in calculating the distances between these economic states,

LaRouche has employed the Platonic solids Kepler used to order the solar system. In a similar manner, LaRouche's followers have constructed a new atomic model in which the electron orbits are Neoplatonic spheres. They have tried to demonstrate that the musical scales are constructed according to this principle and that evolution proceeds according to the same sort of system, not by chance.

For LaRouche's followers, the crowning touch of their conspiracy theory is that it offers an epistemology that seeks to justify paranoid thinking. Privately, the LaRouchies admit that what they are describing is not a conspiracy in the normal sense of the word. "From their standpoint, [the conspirators] are proceeding by instinct," LaRouche said. "If you're asking how their policy is developed—if there is an inside group sitting down and making plans—no, it doesn't work that way. . . . History doesn't function quite that consciously."

"It's done through ideas, not mechanistic control," Paul Goldstein explained. In LaRouchean Neoplatonism, causal links are unnecessary. Because ideas are more real than facts, influencing another's thinking is, by their definition, conspiracy. According to this logic, some of the weird juxtapositions in LaRouche's world view make their own kind of sense:

Nazism may have been influenced somewhat by occultism and German pagan traditions. And so there is a connection. The back-to-nature romanticism of environmentalism is reminiscent of pagan pantheism. And so there is a connection. The ideas in British writer Aldous Huxley's book *Doors of Perception* helped inspire the psychedelic drug experimentation that was integral to the development of the counterculture. And so there is a connection. If Ken Kesey and the Beatles helped spread Huxley's ideas, then they are agents. If the Harrimans and the Nazis embraced eugenic ideas, then they are coconspirators. Solar-power enthusiasts are linked to Nazis because the swastika was an ancient solar symbol. Both environmentalists and Nazis are decendants of the ancient cult of Isis, because she was goddess of the sun. To the LaRouchies, such facile connections are second nature.

Despite the subtleties of LaRouche's system, ultimately it is little more than a glorified version of the old Illuminati conspiracy theory. LaRouche doesn't mention Adam Weishaupt or use the word "Illuminati," but all the elements of the legend are there: the world is divided between forces of good and evil; everything that has ever happened is part of a continuing plot. There are no accidents. LaRouche calls himself a rationalist, but the rationalism he champions is as rooted in absolutism as are fundamentalism and right-wing politics. What he calls Aristotelianism is much like the relativism that the conspiracy theorists of the New Right condemn as secular humanism. LaRouche even follows the anti-Illuminist tradition of twisting occultism and rationalism—the Aristotelian variety—into a common enemy.

Like most conspiracy theorists, LaRouche borrows from the folklore of political paranoia. The Aristotelians' trick of keeping the masses in darkness and exploiting their ignorance is traced not only to Egyptian cults but also to the Eleusinian mystery religions, the Gnostics, the Rosicrucians, the Freemasons—the chain of secret societies that form the root of the Illuminati conspiracy theory. (In an interesting twist, LaRouche includes the Knights Templar and Assassins among the good guys.) The British are linked into the system, because in the early part of the century, some members of the British aristocracy belonged to the occultist Society of the Golden Dawn. Just as cults have controlled their members by breeding irrationalism, LaRouche believes, so do the British promote Aristotelianism, so did Hitler promote his occultist Nazism. LaRouche claims that Protestant fundamentalism, Zionism, and Islamic fundamentalism are also based on a cultlike irrationality that the oligarchs use to control the people psychologically.

In the United States, conspiracy theories that condemn Trilateralists, Zionists, and international bankers are usually associated with right-wingers. Thus, some journalists, recalling LaRouche's days as a Columbia University radical, have characterized him as a leftist who has taken an inexplicable swing to the right. But many leftists oppose the Trilateral Commission and international banking establishment as forces of capitalist exploitation. And, the Soviet Union and some American leftist organizations are anti-Zionist, believing that Israel is a tool of U.S. imperialism. So is LaRouche a leftist or a right-winger? Again, it seems that his politics defy description.

Because LaRouche includes Zionists and Jewish bankers such as the Rothschilds and Warburgs as agents of the British plot, the Anti-Defamation League has accused him of being an anti-Semite—even though a number of his closest followers are Jewish. An article LaRouche wrote in 1978 mentions the *Protocols of the Elders of Zion,* but he gives the legend one of his typically bizarre twists. "The fallacy of the *Protocols of Zion* is that it misattributes the alleged conspiracy to Jews generally," LaRouche wrote, rather than to a few select Jewish conspirators. Actually, he explained, Oxford University invented Zionism, and "Israel is ruled from London as a zombie-nation."

LaRouche's position on the Holocaust is even more confusing. As an agent of Britain, Hitler killed 1.5 million—but not 6 million—Jews, LaRouche wrote. But now the British supposedly exaggerate the Holocaust, using it as a psywar technique to brainwash Jews into becoming Zionists. Zionism is part of the Dark Ages plot, LaRouche wrote, because the British, by signing the Balfour Declaration, helped establish Israel. LaRouche claims that neo-Nazis working with networks of Freemasons are responsible for Palestinian terrorism and that both Nazis and Zionists are British controlled. To him, the Middle East crisis is a British operation to destabilize the region, furthering the oligarchs' attempts to take over the world.

HISTORY OF A CULT

According to an article in *The New York Times,* some of LaRouche's former colleagues have described him as "a brilliant synthesizer of ideas into coherent systems." He is fascinated by physics, mathematics, and musical theory. He once wrote a paper titled "Poetry Must Begin to Supersede Mathematics in Physics." Everything, LaRouche believes, must be connected.

But sometimes there is a thin line between brilliance and madness. The feelings of persecution that led LaRouche to apply his analytical skills to conspiracy theory are described in his autobiography, *The Power of Reason,* published by his company, the New Benjamin Franklin House. It is the story of an outcast intellectual, a theoretician in search of a following.

In 1922, Lyndon Hermyle LaRouche, Jr., was born a

Quaker in Rochester, New Hampshire. It was not a very stimulating environment for a boy who would grow up to be, in his own estimation, "the leading economist of the twentieth century." Classmates called him "Big Head." He had few friends and seemed always to be in trouble in school. "The third grade was particularly hellish," LaRouche wrote.

> The teacher, for her own—undeciphered—reasons, chose to make me her special goat, and put me in the back of the class, where my myopia prevented me from seeing much of anything but blurs in the front of the room. . . . Except for my reading, adolescent life was chiefly bitterly boring and gray.

Later, in Lynn, Massachusetts, problems with an eighth-grade teacher led to "a battery of psychological and related tests," and a midyear transfer to a school on the other side of the city. "Intellectually I almost never 'felt myself' with persons of my age-group. . . . I was much more at ease with adults. . . . I survived socially by making chiefly Descartes, Leibniz, and Kant my principle [sic] peers."

At the beginning of World War II, LaRouche was a conscientious objector, later serving in the Far East as an army medic. After the war, he was a management consultant, systems designer, and computer programmer. In 1948, he joined the Socialist Workers Party, but became disillusioned when the group rejected his theories. By the time he quit in 1963, LaRouche was ready to develop his own brand of politics.

From 1967 to 1968, LaRouche taught "Elementary Marxist Economics" at the Free University in New York and began to put together a core of followers. He seemed to have had no trouble attracting admirers.

"He is one of the most personable, charming, and charismatic men I've ever met," said Gregory Rose, a former member who, in the early 1970s, spied on the group for the FBI. "It's very difficult to describe. . . . But there's something about the way he looks at people, focuses his eyes and modulates his voice that is terribly riveting—almost mesmerizing."

At Columbia University in 1968, LaRouche helped form the Labor Committee, a faction of the left-wing Students for a

Democratic Society. Early issues of *Solidarity*, the committee's newspaper, urged students to unite with workers to fight the oppressors: big business, the banks, and the military-industrial complex. The committee defended the Black Panthers and organized conferences on socialism.

But from the beginning it was clear that LaRouche's people were championing a brand of socialism very different from that of other elements of SDS. Labor Committee members alienated SDS leaders by supporting New York City teachers who were striking against a favorite leftist ideal: community control of schools. Community control was a tactic to erode the power of the unions, LaRouche's followers believed. While most of the student left favored decentralized political power and even decentralized electrical power (solar collectors on rooftops), LaRouche's people supported a strong centralized government and became promoters of nuclear power plants large enough to energize cities. They believed economic reform would come only with technological progress, and that the Small Is Beautiful sentiments of the counterculture would lead to a return to the Dark Ages, just as the oligarchs wanted. Zero population growth was branded a "blueprint for extinction." The Labor Committee ridiculed anarchists and terrorists such as the Weathermen (another SDS offshoot) as "the scum of the student movement."

In 1969, the Labor Committee split with SDS and changed its name to the National Caucus of Labor Committees, which later formed the U.S. Labor Party to run candidates in elections. Opponents say LaRouche's people were expelled from SDS. LaRouche says he infiltrated the group to undermine it and recruit its best minds. Either way, the line was drawn for what LaRouche believed was a fight for control of the American left.

First, there was Operation Mop Up, LaRouche's 1973 attempt to eliminate such rivals as the U.S. Communist Party and the Socialist Workers Party by arriving at meetings, confronting opponents, and "poking at their minds" with psywar techniques. An article in the party's newspaper, now called *New Solidarity,* described a fight that erupted when some of LaRouche's followers tried to disrupt a meeting of a Communist youth group in Buffalo. When a member of the group attempted to call the police, LaRouche's people stopped him. By the time the fight was over, the article stated, three of the enemies had to be hospitalized. An investigation of LaRouche's organization commissioned by the AFL-CIO described similar attacks: "Usually, [LaRouche's] goon squads numbered between fifteen and fifty persons, generally armed with numchukas." (A *numchuka* is an Oriental martial-arts weapon made of two clubs connected with a chain.)

Operation Mop Up was followed in 1974 and 1975 by a campaign to take over the U.S. labor union movement. The AFL-CIO has compiled a list of leaders of union locals who were denounced in leaflets distributed by LaRouche's followers as homosexuals, dope addicts, and child molestors. An FBI analysis obtained by the National Lawyers Guild, a leftist organization that opposes LaRouche, described the tactics of U.S. Labor Party followers during those years: "They disrupt meetings; shout until they get thrown out; file lawsuits apparently as an intimidation device; harass targets with obscene phone calls; get themselves arrested and occasionally get involved in physical confrontation."

As the mid-1970s approached, LaRouche's followers seemed to renounce street-fighting for psychological warfare and conspiracy theory. They denounced the idea of community control of schools as a fascist scheme created by Nelson Rockefeller, the Ford Foundation, the CIA, and the KGB. Throughout 1974, stories in *New Solidarity* told of CIA plans to brainwash the U.S. population. Articles explained how to detect brainwashing and administer psychological first aid.

In January 1974, LaRouche announced that he had uncovered a plot by KGB-CIA agents to assassinate him. Party member Christopher White supposedly had been brainwashed to set up LaRouche for a hit by a squad of terrorists. The operation started, LaRouche told a reporter, in September 1973, when White, who led the now-defunct British branch of the organization, took a teaching assignment at Sir William Collins School in London as part of the work on his doctoral dissertation. On his first day, White supposedly was approached from behind and jabbed with hypodermic needles. Then began a daily series of brainwashing and torture sessions that lasted more than three months. White was drugged and hypnotized, his mind invaded with sounds from a pair of stereo headphones connected to a remote computer. At the end of each day, LaRouche said, the conspirators superimposed a false memory in White's mind so he would go home unaware of what was happening, ready to return the next morning for another session.

LaRouche called White back from England and "deprogrammed" him. A *New York Times* reporter who heard a tape recording of LaRouche's sessions with White described sounds of weeping and vomiting, and White's voice complaining of weariness and hunger. The conspirators, LaRouche told the *Times,* had reduced White's mind to "an eight-cycle infinite loop . . . with homosexual bestiality." Among the LaRouchies, such rhetoric is common. Members are indoctrinated with a system that includes not only LaRouche's conspiracy theory but his ideas on cybernetics and psychoanalysis. A member who deviates from the party line is likely to be accused of having a mother complex or an impotency problem.

ENFORCING REALITY

To prevent members from questioning his version of reality, LaRouche keeps his followers isolated from the outside world. Members' social lives, like their thoughts, are channeled into closed systems. Gregory Rose saw firsthand how discipline was enforced. From 1973 to 1975, he was a member of the U.S. Labor Party and the National Caucus of Labor Committees, serving most of the time as LaRouche's chief of counterintelligence. "It was in the nature of my job that conversations ceased when I entered a room," he said. "My role was basically that of Lyn's Himmler." In those days, LaRouche called himself Lyn Marcus, a derivation from the names Lenin and Marx. At the same time that Rose was moving within LaRouche's inner circle, he was feeding information to the FBI.

Rose recalled the night that he led a five-man security squad to a female party member's New York apartment. She was in bed with a fellow member and the affair had not been approved by her superiors:

One of her roommates called me at the office. I called the National Executive Council member on duty that evening, and he instructed me to take a team to her apartment and work her over. . . . We kicked open the door to her bedroom and [an assistant] . . . held her down and ran the blunt end of a knife about her body. Finally, when it just got to be too much, I called an end to the operation. . . . We took the boy-friend out of the apartment. The next morning, he was transferred to the San Francisco local.

Lyn had this thing about unauthorized relationships.

Rose's double life began at the University of Cincinnati, where, in the summer of 1973, an organizer for LaRouche invited him to a meeting. Several months later, a member called and invited him to another meeting. Shortly afterward, he was recruited by the FBI.

"In four months I went from being a rank-and-file party member to secretary of the National Committee to senior member of the security staff to director of counterintelligence," Rose said. "I think Lyn saw me as the son he never had politically."

In the summer of 1974, Rose was asked to be an instructor at a party weapons-training camp on a farm near Salem, New York. He taught military history:

Imagine the worst aspects of Marine boot camp. [Party leaders] had the training of SS officers in mind. . . . Members would get up at six in the morning, shit, shine, shower, shave, military fashion. Then calisthenics, breakfast . . . an hour or so of weapons training, breaking down your gun. Close-order drill until noon, more calisthenics, lunch, then weapons practice out on the range . . . demolitions class, dinner, more drill, night classes in techniques of interrogation, scientific approaches to collating information . . . treatment of prisoners.

That was the first week. For the second week, we started two to three days of field problems. How to take this hill, that hill. How to ambush. For the rest of the week, members divided into two twenty-member squads, one at each end of the farm, and played a deadly earnest version of "capture the flag" with dummy grenades, weapons with blanks.

The camp has since been abandoned. By the early 1980s, the party was sending some members to Cobray International, a commercial "counter-terrorist" training school in Georgia that offers lessons in combat and weaponry. The teacher is Mitchell Livingston Werbell, star of *Spooks,* a book on "the haunting of America by private intelligence agencies," written by Jim Hougan, a former Washington editor for *Harper's.* Werbell has worked as an international arms dealer, free-lance secret agent, and promoter of right-wing causes. His efforts to produce and sell silenced submachine guns earned him the nickname "Wizard of Whispering Death." In the early 1980s, he was a security consultant for LaRouche. The party's explanation was that they must train members to guard LaRouche against terrorist agents of the conspiracy. Other presidential candidates, they noted, got Secret Service protection.

LaRouche dismisses Rose's stories as part of the conspiracy. But his accounts agree with those of members who have quit the organization.

"The fundamental tendency which holds the [party] together . . . is mania," according to a statement given to reporters by a group of defectors in 1979. "Since 1973, LaRouche has continuously announced a series of 'deadlines,' no more than three months in the future, by which time some horrible catastrophe will occur unless prevented by [the members]."

When the disasters failed to occur, the former members wrote, the organization was credited with successful intervention.

"The result of this continual mania is to prevent members from having any time to think or question. The leadership, and LaRouche in particular, maintain an atmosphere of psychological terror."

Many of those who finally wondered at the craziness of it all had made too great an emotional investment to leave. So, the ex-members wrote, they concentrated on long-range party goals, such as stopping drug traffic and promoting technology.

After leaving the party, Rose worked as a journalist. He spent six months in Guyana covering the aftermath of the mass suicide at Jim Jones's People's Temple. Rose believes that LaRouche and Jones have much in common.

"Ultimately, LaRouche is more dangerous and crazier than Jim Jones ever was. The similarities between the People's Temple and [the U.S. Labor Party] are extraordinary: high-level sexual repression, deification of the leader, imposition of extraordinary discipline, humiliation, physical disciplining, arms training, an all-pervasive security apparatus."

Rose said he believes speaking out against LaRouche could have bad consequences. So, in an undisclosed location somewhere in the United States, he keeps boxes of party records: financial logs, internal memoranda, recordings of National Executive Council meetings—information, he said, that party leaders would like very much kept secret. If anything happens to him, he said, the records will be made public. He considers them his "insurance policy."

STRANGE ALLIANCES

In the mid-1970s, LaRouche tried to form a marriage of convenience with the radical right. Rose said that in 1974 contacts were made with Ken Duggan, leader of a right-wing organization called the National Provisional Government and publisher of *The Illuminator,* a periodical that promoted the Illuminati conspiracy theory. Rose said Liberty Lobby's founder, Willis Carto, met regularly with an official of LaRouche's party and may have helped solicit more than $90,000 from right-wing extremists for LaRouche's 1976 presidential campaign. Former members have written that LaRouche hoped to use right-wing allies to instigate a military coup against the United States government.

But there are signs that LaRouche's overtures to the right were more practical than sincere. A 1975 party memo talks about uniting with the right to overthrow the conspirators: "Once we have won this battle, eliminating our right-wing opposition will be comparatively easy."

During his flirtations with right-wingers, LaRouche also supported the Soviet Union. In 1974, Rose said, he was asked by LaRouche to establish contact with the Soviet mission to the United States. Rose said LaRouche met with a Soviet diplomat at least twice—once at the Soviet mission in New York and once at U.S. Labor Party headquarters. In 1975, LaRouche visited Iraq at the request of the leftist Baath Party.

In the late 1970s, after failing to recruit either Soviets or right-wingers for his fight against the conspiracy, LaRouche's followers began trying for a more mainstream image. The director of the Fusion Energy Foundation attended a science conference in Moscow and addressed a class at West Point. In the fall of 1980, the organization dropped the name U.S. Labor Party and added to its titles the more sedate-sounding National Democratic Policy Committee. The July 1981 issue of *Fusion* reported that two Fusion Energy Foundation officials had a breakfast meeting with Secretary of the Interior James Watt. A children's magazine called *The Young Scientist* was begun.

To demonstrate their interest in promoting culture, a LaRouche front called the Lafayette Foundation for the Arts and Sciences began sponsoring classical music concerts. The Fusion Energy Foundation organized mathematics presentations for schoolchildren. In 1980, shortly after some ex-members described a meeting at which a senior party member supposedly endorsed selective assassination and a military coup to seize control of the United States government, the LaRouchies raised enough donations for their leader to qualify for federal matching funds to run for president of the United States.

In June 1982, LaRouche flew to Mexico City, under the auspices of his National Democratic Policy Committee, and gained an audience with Mexican president Jose Lopez Portillo, to warn him about attempts by international bankers to wreck the Mexican economy. Both the American Embassy and the Democratic party issued disclaimers. LaRouche, they said, was not an important American political figure, as the Mexican newspapers apparently assumed. He just acted as though he were one. Earlier that year, LaRouche met with India's prime minister, Indira Gandhi. LaRouche believes developing countries, such as India, are especially vulnerable to the oligarchs' plot.

With the Fusion Energy Foundation supporting nuclear power, the National Anti-Drug Coalition opposing the narcotics trade, and the National Democratic Policy Committee calling for parity for farmers, government-stimulated industrial development, and development of Third World countries, LaRouche's followers are trying to forge a coalition of engineers, scientists, farmers, minorities, and laborers. LaRouche's call for higher agricultural price supports is designed to appeal both to farmers, who want to make more money on their crops, and to leftists, who believe the proposal would increase food production and alleviate starvation in Africa. LaRouche's position that population control is a form of genocide, a view commonly held by Marxists in developing countries, is being packaged to appeal to "pro-lifers." In 1982, LaRouche candidate William Wertz attracted the support of antiabortionists in his unsuccessful primary bid for the Senate seat sought by California Governor Jerry Brown.

In elections all over the country, LaRouche candidates wage unsuccessful campaigns, bewildering voters with their rhetoric. In Chicago's 1983 mayoral race, LaRouche's organization supported a young black woman who is a leader of the National Anti-Drug Coalition. She denounced her opponents, Jane Byrne and Harold Washington, as agents of the conspiracy. In Minnesota, LaRouche supported the 1982 congressional bid of Patrick O'Reilly, a leader in the radical American Agriculture Movement (the farmers who rode their tractors to Washington, D.C., in 1980, demanding more federal support for agriculture). O'Reilly's campaign slogan was You Don't Have to Be Gay and Kill Babies to Be a Democrat. He blamed farmers' economic problems on the conspiracy and held a pig roast to raise money. The animal was said to be an effigy of Henry Kissinger.

In the summer of 1982, *New Solidarity* announced plans to "draft LaRouche" for president in 1984. The movement's supporters included an unusual combination of leaders of Hispanic groups, farm organizations, and labor union locals (though the AFL-CIO opposes LaRouche), as well as Baptist ministers and a few engineers and college professors. The roster included a woman identified as an official of the National Black Women's Political Leadership Caucus and a leader of the Student Government Association at Tuskegee Institute in Alabama.

While LaRouche made plans for another presidential campaign, his wife, Helga Zepp-LaRouche, headed a slate of thirty European Labor Party candidates in 1982 elections in the state of Hesse, West Germany. They supported Helmut Schmidt as the German leader most likely to oppose the conspiracy.

POSTSCRIPT

Because of his complex and chameleonlike politics, LaRouche is an easy target for both leftists and rightists who want to weave his organizations into their own conspiracy theories. In 1975, the U.S. Communist Party's newspaper, the *Daily World,* published articles claiming the LaRouchies were agents of the CIA. An article in *Overthrow,* published by the anarchist Yippies, denounced LaRouche as part of a plot "to prepare America for takeover by the forces of international fascism." After their encounter with the Fusion Energy Foundation demonstrator, Kissinger and his wife are reported to have told guests at a cocktail party in Washington, D.C., that they wouldn't be surprised if LaRouche were getting money from the KGB.

Because of the ambiguity of the life and mind of Lyndon LaRouche, scenarios could be constructed to lend credence to these allegations. But trying to discover a completely coherent explanation for his bizarre ways is probably futile. Despite his obsession with systematizing everything, he is, like other conspiracy theorists, motivated by irrational drives. Any attempt to impose too rigid a system on the chaos of LaRouche's hates and fears is bound to be as unsuccessful as explaining the world with a conspiracy theory.

Ultimately, what is significant about LaRouche is that he serves as a reminder that even the highly educated can be manipulated by a man who seems to offer the ultimate system. The LaRouchies fervently discuss the complexities of philosophy, science, and music. They are conversant in obscure details of ancient and medieval history. But their talk never strays beyond the edges of the network they have stamped on reality. They are like the sailors of old who insisted the world was flat, then navigated carefully lest they disprove their illusion.

Conclusion: Seeing the Light

"Let him who seeks continue seeking until he finds. When he finds, he will become troubled. When he becomes troubled, he will be astonished, and he will rule over all things."

—Jesus,
in the Gnostic *Gospel of St. Thomas*

The Illuminati conspiracy theory, in all its guises, reflects the centuries-old ideological war between the upholders of orthodoxy and those they condemn as heretics. "Orthodox" comes from the Greek words *orthos,* which means "straight," and *doxa,* or "doctrine." The word conjures images of boxes, right angles, rigidity—like the lines and squares of the Illuminati conspiracy theory charts. "Heresy" is a derivation of the Greek *hairein,* "to choose." Over the centuries, the word has come to connote a wild, flowing spirit that cannot be caged by the squares of dogma, a force that escapes the walls of orthodoxy, like light through the cracks of a box.

Many of those who have been called Illuminati—Gnostics, Cathars, Knights Templar, Rosicrucians, Freemasons, Enlightenment philosophers—were groups the Catholic church considered heretics. After the Protestants rebelled against the Catholics, they inherited the Vatican's enemies list and supplemented it with some new additions: Catholics and Jews. In the United States, those whose orthodoxy is patriotism consider

211

internationalists to be heretics. All these self-appointed guardians of the faith agree that secular humanists, who oppose the
right of any orthodoxy to enforce its ways on nonbelievers, are
the most dangerous heretics of all.

The opposite of Illuminati, the enlightened, would be
Obscurati, the benighted. While the various factions of Obscurati fight among themselves to defend their own absolutes,
they share the belief that truth comes from on high, and that
mankind's own attempts at understanding are inferior to the
wisdom promulgated by God. Accordingly, the most basic
Obscurati dogma is the legend of the Fall: that mankind fell
from its original state of grace because a serpent tempted Eve to
spurn God by eating the fruit of the tree of knowledge. Thus,
civilization, the embodiment of human thought, was damned
to a decline that will end in cataclysm, the death of secularism,
and the return of unquestioning obedience to the supernatural.

The people cast as villains in the Illuminati conspiracy
theory are the heretics, who in every century have opposed the
legend of the Fall with a more optimistic view of mankind's
ability to seek knowledge on its own. One of the earliest of
these groups, the Gnostics, taught that the snake was the hero
of the Garden of Eden and condemned Yahweh as a jealous
tyrant for greeting man's enlightenment with anger. The Gnostics believed salvation came not by faith in orthodoxy, as the
Catholic church decreed, but by *gnosis,* the Greek word for
knowledge, which the Gnostics equated with light.

The Gnostics, who lived during the first few centuries
A.D., believed the purpose of life was to *know,* to discover truth
through individual exploration instead of accepting the dogmas
of organized religion. They believed each human had the
power of his own salvation. *Gnosis* was a more mystical kind of
knowledge than that of later heretics such as the Enlightenment
philosophers, Freemasons, and secular humanists. But all these
groups shared a spiritual affinity as victims of what has become
an Obscurati tradition: extinguishing the flame of those who
find their light within instead of through the circuitry of an
ecclesiastical hierarchy.

When it came time for the Catholic church to decide
which books would be codified as the Bible, the gospels of the

Gnostics were excluded. Most copies were destroyed. For centuries, historians knew of the group mostly through the writings of its enemies—the leaders of the orthodox church. In 180 A.D., the Catholic bishop, Irenaeus, complained of heretics who "boast that they possess more gospels than there really are." "They imagine that they themselves have discovered more than the apostles . . . that they themselves are wiser and more intelligent."

What was it that the Gnostics claimed to know? Historians were able to piece together some of the beliefs from Catholic documents and a few Gnostic texts that had surfaced on the antiquities blackmarket during the eighteenth and nineteenth centuries. Then, in 1945, a group of peasants, digging for fertilizer near their village in northern Egypt, uncovered a jar that had been buried for 1500 years. Inside were thirteen papyrus books containing Coptic translations of Gnostic writings. The mother of one of the discoverers burned some of the manuscripts for kindling, and it took almost three decades of competition among academicians, the Egyptian government, smugglers, and black marketeers before the remaining texts were easily available for study by scholars. Finally, within the last two decades, the message of the Gnostics has found its way back into history. It is now easy to see why the fledgling church considered Gnosticism a threat.

In the orthodox *Gospel of John,* when the disciples asked Jesus how they could know "the way," he answered: "*I* am the way, the truth, and the life; no one comes to the Father, but by me." In the Gnostic *Gospel of St. Thomas,* Jesus answered the same question in a different manner: "There is light within a man of light, and it lights up the whole world." To orthodox Christians, Jesus was the light. Believe in him, obey the church, and you would enter the Kingdom when you died. But to the Gnostics the light was an inner force, the *gnosis* each person could find within. As Jesus said in the Gnostic *Dialogue of the Savior,* "the lamp of the body is the mind."

"The mind is the guide, but reason is the teacher," the Gnostic teacher Silvanus wrote. "Live according to your mind. . . . Acquire strength, for the mind is strong. . . . Enlighten your mind. . . . Light the lamp within you."

Allogcncs, another Gnostic teacher, wrote, "[I was] very disturbed, and [I] turned to myself. . . . [Having] seen the light that [surrounded] me and the good that was within me, I became divine."

The Catholic church claimed to be the one true religion because it traced its authority back to the original twelve apostles—those who, according to the orthodox gospels, saw Christ in the flesh after he was bodily resurrected. Jesus appointed Peter his successor, and "upon this rock," the Bible says, Peter founded the church. Its dogma and structure were to be in place until the Second Coming. Christ visited the twelve, disappeared, and that was it. The line of authority was established. The Church was rooted in the past with an absolute truth by which to measure heresy. It was a church that was indeed set in stone.

To the Gnostics, this literal interpretation of the resurrection was the "faith of fools." They believed Jesus didn't really rise bodily from the grave and return to earth. The Resurrection story was a way of saying that Christ's spirit lived on. To the Gnostics, Jesus was inside everyone. Anyone could be an apostle. Paying tithes to the priest and celebrating Mass would not lead to salvation, they said. People had to look inward, not upward, to find the light.

In the Gnostic *Apocalypse of Peter,* the "resurrected" Christ told Peter that those who "name themselves bishop, and also deacon, as if they had received their authority from God," are "waterless canals." They "do not understand mystery" but "boast that the mystery of truth belongs to them alone." They have set up an "imitation church."

The Gnostics were not pluralists, since they too believed they were on the path to the one truth. But, unlike the orthodox, they did not believe any specific doctrine could ever be more than an approximation of the way the world worked. They didn't even consider their own gospels to be sacrosanct. These writings were creations, art inspired by the Gnostic muse.

"Like circles of artists today, gnostics considered original creative invention to be the mark of anyone who becomes spiritually alive," Elaine Pagels wrote in her book, *The Gnostic Gospels:*

> Each one, like students of a painter or writer, expected to express his own perceptions by revising and transforming what he was taught. Whoever merely repeated his teacher's words was considered immature. . . . On this basis, like artists, they express their own insight—their own *gnosis*—by creating new myths, poems, rituals, "dialogues" with Christ, revelations, and accounts of their visions. . . . Just as many people today assume that the most recent experiments in science or psychology will surpass earlier ones, so the gnostics anticipated that the present and future would yield a continual increase in knowledge. . . . On this theory, the structure of authority can never be fixed into an institutional framework: it must remain spontaneous, charismatic, and open.

It is no wonder that the Gnostic gospels were suppressed. "Other religions are in varying measure God-centered," wrote R. M. Grant, another student of Gnosticism. "The Gnostic is self-centered." The 1980 edition of the *The Modern Catholic Dictionary* still lists Gnosticism as "the invariable element in every major Christian heresy."

It would be a mistake to equate the Gnostics with modern rationalists. They were not philosophers but mystics, and their teachings were as veiled in myth and allegory as those of other religions. They rejected the material world as evil—something to be escaped through inner knowledge. They saw their bodies as prisons for the pure spirit that belonged in the higher spheres of creation, but had fallen and become trapped in flesh. The myths were used not to obscure, however, but "to express and illuminate [the Gnostic's] understanding of himself," Grant wrote. "Gnostics were ultimately devoted not to mythology but to freedom. Speculation and mythology were aspects of this freedom, which involved freedom from astral spirits, from the god of the Old Testament, from the tyranny of the creation, from Old Testament law or any law."

Some Gnostic sects believed enlightenment would come

by transcending the moral law; they advocated complete sexual freedom. Other sects fought what they saw as the evils of flesh by practicing strict asceticism. The most radical Gnostics refused to procreate and bring more beings into the world to suffer. In a way, the Gnostics were like modern-day existentialists: they felt the alienation of being trapped in a world that was to them absurd; they sought transcendence through the self.

Gnostics have been dismissed in modern times as pessimists. But the orthodox church was at least as pessimistic in its belief that the human race is imbued with Original Sin. The Gnostics believed it was the material world, not mankind, that was inherently evil. While the orthodox taught that transcendence would come through obedience, the Gnostics believed humans could achieve it on their own.

To the conspiracy theorists, *gnosis* is the Illuminati light, the secret knowledge passed from elite to elite: from the Egyptian sun worshipers to the Pythagoreans to the Eleusinians to the Gnostics, Cathars, Knights Templar, Rosicrucians, and Freemasons. Although the notion of an ongoing brotherhood of Illuminati that extends to the beginning of civilization is a myth, some of these groups did have something in common. Like the Gnostics, they believed faith in doctrine was less important than personal spiritual experience.

We don't know if the Cathars of southern France inherited ideas directly from followers of the Gnostics. The two groups held similar beliefs: Yahweh was a lesser god who erred in creating the material world; Jesus was more important as a spirit than a human; bodily resurrection was a myth. The Catholic church was more severe in its dealings with the Cathars than it was with the Gnostics, perhaps because the Cathars were so successful in spreading their religion—they had their own bishops and church. By labeling this opposing religion a heresy and sending soldiers to massacre members by the thousands, Pope Innocent II ensured that Catharism would be remembered only as a cult. Two hundred Cathars were burned to death, after a ten-month siege at their temple in Montsegur, because they refused to admit they were wrong.

The Knights Templar became "Illuminati" when King

Phillip of France and Pope Clement charged the order with heresy, arrested its members, and seized its wealth. Although some of the knights were tortured and confessed to heretical practices—devil worship, sexual perversion, et cetera—fifty-five, including leader Jacques DeMolay, maintained they were innocent and were burned to death.

Later groups, such as the Rosicrucians, Freemasons, and Enlightenment philosophers, weren't slaughtered *en masse,* but they too were denounced by the Vatican for challenging orthodoxy with the notion that mankind could look beyond the church for knowledge. Earlier villains in the Illuminati legend, such as the Eleusinians and Pythagoreans, predate Christianity; the Obscurati made them heretics in retrospect. But, in a sense, all these groups are connected—not as elements in a conspiracy but because they were either victims or opponents of orthodoxy. Some sought light through reason, others through mysticism.

At the root of the Illuminati legend is the myth of the light-bearer. To the Obscurati, the light-bearer is Lucifer, the fallen Angel of Light, who led Adam and Eve astray with the promise that, by eating the fruit of knowledge, they would be like gods. To the Illuminati, the light-bearer is the hero Prometheus, the Titan who stole fire from the heavens to give it to man.

Tracing secular humanists to Gnostics and Freemasons is as fanciful as tracing Freemasonry to ancient cults. But there is a common spirit. The Gnostic Monoimus almost sounds as though he is describing a modern humanistic religion when he advises:

> Abandon the search for God and the creation and other matters of a similar sort. Look for him by taking yourself as the starting point. Learn who it is who within you makes everything his own and says, "*My* god, *my* mind, *my* thought, *my* soul, *my* body." Learn the sources of sorrow, joy, love, hate. . . . If you carefully investigate these matters you will find him in yourself.

The Gnostic *Gospel of Phillip* stated, "God created humanity; [but now human beings] create God. That is the way it is in the world—human beings make gods, and worship their creation. It would be appropriate for the gods to worship human beings!"

Of course, there was no such thing as secular humanism in the days of the Gnostics—the distinction between secular and ecclesiastic knowledge had not been made. But it is easy to see why, to the Obscurati, Gnosticism, Freemasonry, and secular humanism form a chain.

The Illuminati were, in their different ways, championing the extraordinary powers of the mind, glorifying an inner spirit over an outer one. We have come to take reason so much for granted that we forget what a magical thing it is. Illuminism is something basic to the human mind, a curious fire that is ignited in every age, a rebellion against power that would limit us in following our explorations wherever they lead. Whether, like the Gnostics, we see the mind as a door to a spiritual world or, as rationalists, we see it as a repository of some indefinable force called reason, the light is in our heads and not off in some heaven. Whether our brains are moons reflecting the sun of a cosmic truth or are the generators of the illumination, the power of Illuminism is beyond the control of any state or church. Whether we seek the light as part of an inner journey or use it to explore the outside world, in either case, arbitrary power is threatened.

THE EYE IN THE PYRAMID

In the 1980s, the Obscurati, in the form of the New Right, have applied the legend of the Fall to American history. They look to the past as Eden, when America was strong and independent, unshackled by obligations to the world; when this was largely a white Protestant nation with a religion that was taught in school with the certainty of arithmetic. The Obscurati idealize the founding fathers as guardians of an idyllic America that existed before the fall caused by secular humanism. They forget that many of the founders of the Republic were champions of Enlightenment philosophy who believed in pluralism, cosmopolitanism, and a humanistic approach to religion. And, in constructing their conspiracy theories, the Obscurati ignore the fact that many of the founders were Freemasons.

On December 27, 1778, when George Washington's revolutionary army retook Philadelphia from the British, he celebrated by donning his Masonic emblems and leading a march of Freemasons through the streets of the city. At Valley Forge, he presided over the initiation of Lafayette into American Masonry. Alexander Hamilton, John Marshall, James Madison, Henry Knox, Ethan Allen, and generals Greene, Lee, Sullivan, and Steuben, as well as the majority of the Continental Congress, were Masons. Some historians believe the Boston Tea Party was carried out by Masons, who plotted the act in a Masonic lodge.

While Washington was commanding the Continental army, Benjamin Franklin was frequenting the Masonic Lodge of the Nine Sisters in Paris. From 1779 to 1781, he served as the lodge's Worshipful Master, using it as a vehicle to help influence members of the French nobility to support the American Revolution. In 1778, Franklin directed the initiation of Voltaire into the Nine Sisters. Franklin once asked the philosopher to bless his grandson in the name of liberty.

Other members of the Nine Sisters lodge included Bonneville and Marechal, two supporters of the French Revolution who were especially influenced by the Freemasonic fascination with ancient cults and geometric symbols. Marechal praised Franklin as "the Pythagoras of the New World." Thomas Paine, the pamphleteer of the American Revolution, lived for years with Bonneville and his wife. Paine's *Common Sense* and *The Age of Reason* are common fare in American history classes. Less known is his pamphlet *Origin of Freemasonry,* in which he approvingly traced the spirit of Masonry to the Druids, suggesting that their worship of the sun had its roots in ancient Egypt, Babylonia, and Chaldea. Pythagoras, Paine wrote, brought the religion to the West after learning it from the Zoroastrians, who worshiped the light god Mazda.

The American Revolution was, of course, no more a Masonic operation than was the French Revolution. As in Europe, American Masonry was not only a haven for freethinkers but also a social club for aristocrats. That so many of the founders of our country were Freemasons may attest as much to our roots as a country started by the rich as it does to our Enlightenment spirit.

But, to be consistent, the same standards of evidence that the Obscurati use to link their enemies to Adam Weishaupt could be used to conclude that the United States of America was founded as an Illuminati nation. The Enlightenment idealism that inspired the revolution was tempered with economic self-interest. However, the results of this complex mix of idealism and practicality—the Declaration of Independence, Constitution, and Bill of Rights—reflect ideals that would have been embraced by Weishaupt: egalitarianism, brotherhood, freedom of thought, religion, and speech. There may even have been a touch of the mystical in the founders' belief that the United States was the manifestation of a new, brighter vision of mankind.

On July 4, 1776, the Continental Congress approved the Declaration of Independence and appointed Franklin, Jefferson, and John Adams to devise a Great Seal of the United States. The three men retained an artist and, on August 20, submitted a design in which the Eye of Providence, enclosed in a triangle and radiating light, hovers above a shield and the words *E Pluribus Unum* (One out of Many). The recommendation was tabled and a new committee was appointed in 1780. A third committee took over the task in 1782. Finally, in June of that year, all the recommendations were turned over to Charles Thomson, Secretary of the Congress, who combined them into the present seal, with its eagle on the front and pyramid on the back, accompanied by the words *Annuit Coeptis* (He [God] Has Favored our Undertakings) and *Novus Ordo Seclorum* (A New Order of the Ages). "The pyramid," Thomson wrote, "signifies Strength and Duration: The Eye over it & the Motto allude to the many signal interpositions of providence in favour of the American cause." The design was accepted.

In 1935, Henry A. Wallace, vice-president of the United States under Franklin D. Roosevelt, convinced Secretary of the Treasury Henry Morgenthau that the pyramid should also appear on the back of the one-dollar bill. Wallace was a consummate Illuminatus: an intellectual whose idealism bordered on the mystical. Historian Arthur Schlesinger wrote:

The occult fascinated him. He saw special significance in the Great Seal of the United States, with its phrase *E Pluribus Unum* and its conception of unity out of diversity; even more in the reverse of the Seal—the incomplete pyramid, with its thirteen levels of stone and the apex suspended above in the form of an all-seeing eye. . . . He sold [the idea] to Secretary Morgenthau on the prosaic ground that *Novus Ordo* was Latin for New Deal, and for years afterward Morgenthau was beset by people who assumed that the appearance of the Great Pyramid on the currency signified his own attachment to some esoteric fellowship.

There was no occult secret society, of course. If Wallace, Washington, and Franklin shared a spiritual fellowship it was the age-old tradition of championing knowledge, whether Gnostic or rationalist, over dogma; dynamic humanism over static orthodoxy; the spirit of progress over the legend of the Fall.

Such ideals have yet to be fully realized in the United States or anywhere else. But we have been moving steadily in that direction. The first step toward pluralism came when the colonists decided to tolerate all Protestant sects. Later, the concept of toleration was enlarged to include Catholics, then Jews. Now we are trying to expand it to include Buddhists, Muslims, Hindus, and atheists. This ever-increasing pluralism hasn't been a smooth progression. Each time a new wave of immigrants arrives, our ideals are stretched a little further. At first, the newcomers are persecuted and feared. But in time our system grows to accommodate them. On the international scale, the belief in plurality has led to a greater awareness of the value of international cooperation. This cosmopolitan vision undergoes frequent setbacks, and we recoil into isolationism and cry, "America first." But progress is inevitable. The result will not be the kingdom of the Antichrist but a more peaceful, equitable world order.

As secular humanism, pluralism, and cosmopolitanism continue to dominate the culture, we must be careful that our Illuminism not become a new orthodoxy that treats its opponents as heretics. We must be careful not to deify reason. After all, there is a bit of Obscurati in all of us.

To some extent, this tendency to trust too completely the fruits of analysis is already happening. Government bureaucrats calculate costs and benefits, then manipulate the levers of the economy, hoping to maximize the reading on the gross-national-product gauge, minimize the reading on the inflation gauge. The measures become ends, not means, and we forget that an economy is supposed to be for all the people, even those who show up as numbers on the unemployment scale.

During the Vietnam War, an Ivy League elite of military analysts (the ones David Halberstam called "the Best and the Brightest") reduced war to formulas and calculated (incorrectly, it turned out) how many deaths it would take to win. The danger is that Illuminati can become what Theodore Roszak called *technocrats*—those who use their expertise to impose order.

Elitism has always been the dark side of Illuminism: the revolutionary vanguard that seizes control because it *knows* what's good for the people, the philosopher-king who *knows* the truth, the technocrat who *knows* how to run societies and wars—all try to hoard the light at the top of the pyramid. Reason, which can be used to rescue man from churches and kings, can also be used to enslave him with dogmas of its own. Knowledge is a power that can be abused. A true Illuminatus knows that nothing is absolute, not even his own assumptions.

Bibliography,
Notes, and Sources

Many of the characteristics of political paranoia were first examined in Richard Hofstadter's forty-page essay, "The Paranoid Style in American Politics," written in 1963 and republished in *The Paranoid Style in American Politics and Other Essays* (Chicago: University of Chicago Press, Phoenix Books, 1979). The book also contains essays on the radical right of the early 1960s. In an anthology called *The Fear of Conspiracy: Images of Un-American Subversion from the Revolution to the Present* (Ithaca, New York: Cornell, 1971), David Brion Davis, a Yale University historian, has collected writings from two centuries of American conspiracy theorists, illustrating them with comments about the eras in which they were written. The best book, by far, on right-wing extremism in the United States is Seymour Martin Lipset and Earl Raab's *The Politics of Unreason: Right-Wing Extremism in America, 1790–1977*, second edition (Chicago: University of Chicago Press, 1978). Other general sources I consulted include: Daniel Bell, *The Radical Right* (Garden City, New York: Doubleday, 1963); William C. Baum, "The Conspiracy Theory of Politics of the Radical Right in the United States" (doctoral dissertation, Iowa City: State University of Iowa, 1960); Richard O. Curry and Thomas M. Brown, editors, *Conspiracy: The Fear of Subversion in American History* (New York: Holt, Rinehart and Winston, 1972); Robert Eringer, *The Conspiracy Peddlers* (Mason, Michigan: Loompanics Unlimited, 1981); Phillip Finch, *God, Guts, and Guns—A Close Look at the Radical Right* (New York: Seaview/Putnam, 1983); R. A. Remington "The Function of the 'Conspiracy Theory' in American Intellectual History" (doctoral dissertation, St. Louis, Missouri: St. Louis University, 1965); and Laird M. Wilcox, editor, *Directory of the American Right* (Kansas City, Missouri: Editorial Research Service, 1980). Two skeptical students of political paranoia, Richard Gilman of Insights Research Service (Ann Arbor, Michigan) and Robert Hertz, publisher of *Conspiracies Unlimited* (St. Paul, Minnesota), are excellent sources for information on conspiracy theorists.

Conspiracy Digest (Dearborn, Michigan) provides a quarterly forum for conspiracy theorists. Another journal, *Critique* (Santa Rosa, California), publishes a fascinating mix of articles on conspiracy theory, occultism, metaphysics, and parapsychology.

CHAPTER 1. *THE ARCHITECTURE OF PARANOIA*

For details about the Duck Club, I interviewed White and some of his followers at the organizational meeting of the Minneapolis–St. Paul Duck Club, 10/31/81. Other information is from issues of the *Duck Book* (later renamed the *Duck Book Digest,* then the *Financial Security Digest*), September 1981 to June 1983, and mailings sent by White to subscribers. Many journalists have written about the duck movement. See, for example, *Esquire,* October 1981, and the *Chicago Tribune,* 9/9/81.

Epigraph: Hofstadter, *The Paranoid Style,* p. 40.

White described the incident with Carrington in a letter mailed to subscribers in September 1982.

"These pimps are stealing America": remark made at Minneapolis–St. Paul Duck Club meeting, 10/31/81.

Wall Street Journal article, 9/16/81.

"Born-again Carter"; "that pimp Nixon": speech at 10/31/81 meeting.

"I hope you ducks": *Duck Book Digest,* October 1982.

The Paranoid Style

Spotlight circulation: *Spotlight,* 2/23/81.

Headline from the *Torch,* October 1979.

Christian Vanguard Hitler article, April 1981.

Hollenbeck quotes: *Minneapolis Star–Tribune,* 2/15/82.

The Illuminati Legend

"Effete corps": from a speech delivered 10/19/69 in New Orleans.

"The rear occiput of the left lobe": Lipset and Raab, *Politics of Unreason,* p. 16.

Welch on Insiders and Illuminati: *American Opinion,* November 1966.

Birchers on Insiders and occult groups: *American Opinion,* June 1962.

The New Right

30 million fundamentalists: Lipset and Raab, *Commentary,* March 1981.

Late Great Planet Earth, best-seller of 1970s: *Atlantic,* June 1982.

Lindsey on Trilateral Commission: *The 1980s: Countdown to Armageddon* (New York: Bantam, 1981), pp. 117–128.

7 million to 10 million regular Christian broadcast listeners: Conway and Siegelman, *Holy Terror: The Fundamentalist War on America's Freedoms in Religion, Politics and Our Private Lives* (Garden City, New York: Doubleday, 1982), p. 42.

"Hidden persuaders": Schlafly, *A Choice, Not an Echo* (Alton, Illinois: Pere Marquette Press, 1964), p. 25.

"The focus of evil": Reagan speech to National Association of Evangelicals, Orlando, Florida, 3/8/83.

"Oh, those demonstrations": *The New Republic*, 1/20/82.

CHAPTER 2. *PHILOSOPHERS AND MAGICIANS*

For excellent descriptions of occultism and secret societies, written from a rational point of view, see the twenty-four-volume *Man, Myth & Magic: An Illustrated Encyclopedia of the Supernatural* (New York: Marshall Cavendish Corp., 1970), edited by Richard Cavendish. Other good general sources include: Kurt Seligmann, *Magic, Supernaturalism, and Religion: A History of Magic and Its Influence on Western Civilization* (New York: Grosset & Dunlap, 1968); Norman Ian MacKenzie, editor, *Secret Societies* (London: Aldus, 1968); Colin Wilson, *The Occult: A History* (New York: Vintage Books, 1973); Arkon Daraul, *A History of Secret Societies* (New York: Pocket Books, 1969).

Epigraph: Klaus Epstein, *The Genesis of German Conservatism* (Princeton, New Jersey: Princeton University Press, 1966), p. 91.

"An enthusiastic philanthropist": Vernon Stauffer, *New England and the Bavarian Illuminati* (New York: Columbia University Press, 1918), p. 312.

The Invisible College

Frances A. Yates has written several fascinating and thoroughly documented accounts of the effect of Rosicrucianism and the hermetic-cabalistic world view on Renaissance thought. See, for example, *The Rosicrucian Enlightenment* (London: Routledge & Kegan Paul, 1972) and *Giordano Bruno and the Hermetic Tradition* (Chicago: University of Chicago Press, 1964). For a detailed look at the cabala, see Leo Schaya, *The Universal Meaning of the Kabbalah* (New York: Penguin Books, 1973). For a description of modern-day Rosicrucian philosophy, see H. Spencer Lewis, *Rosicrucian Manual*, 27th edition (San Jose, California: Supreme Grand Lodge of AMORC, 1982).

Quotes from Rosicrucian manifestos: Yates, *Rosicrucian Enlightenment*, Appendix.

Horrible Pacts: ibid., pp. 103–104.

The Masonic Craft

The most complete account of Freemasonry and the secret societies and cults included in the Masonic myths is Robert Freke Gould's six-volume *The History of Freemasonry* (London: Thomas C. Jack, 1882–1887). There are a number of books by Freemasons on Masonry. See, for example, Albert Mackey's *Mackey's Symbolism of Freemasonry: Its Science, Philosophy, Legends, Myths and Symbols,* revised by Robert Ingham Clegg (Chicago: The Masonic History Company, 1945). For accounts of Freemasonry written by non-Masonic historians, see James H. Billington, *Fire in the Minds of Men: Origins of the Revolutionary Faith* (New York: Basic Books, 1980); J. M. Roberts, *The Mythology of the Secret Societies* (London: Secker & Warburg, 1972); and the general references listed at the beginning of the notes for this chapter.

"A science of morality": cited in numerous Masonic reference books; for example, in the introduction to Mackey.

"A moral meritocracy": Billington, *Fire in the Minds of Men,* p. 92.

Sixteen princes were Freemasons: Roberts, p. 28.

Catholic anti-Masonic law: canon 2335, cited in John A. Hardon, S.J., editor, *Modern Catholic Dictionary* (Garden City, New York: Doubleday, 1980), p. 221.

The Esoteric Tradition

Most of the groups in the myth of the esoteric tradition are described in the general references mentioned earlier in the notes to Chapter 2. In some versions of the myth, the secret protected by the various societies is equated with the Holy Grail. In a best-selling book, *Holy Blood, Holy Grail* (New York: Delacourt, 1982), Michael Baigent, Richard Leigh, and Henry Lincoln claimed to show that the secret guarded by the societies was that Jesus and Mary Magdalene had children, whose descendants supposedly were among the royalty of Europe. For a good description of the Knights Templar, see Norman Cohn, *Europe's Inner Demons: An Enquiry Inspired by the Great Witch-Hunt* (New York: Basic Books, 1975), pp. 75–98.

"For we be"; "that the Modern Green-ribbon'd": Yates, *Rosicrucian Enlightenment,* p. 211.

G-in-triangle symbol and Tetragrammaton: Mackey, p. 181.

Rosicrucianism and Newton; Descartes, Bacon, and the Royal Society: Yates, *Rosicrucian Enlightenment,* pp. 114–129, 171–192, 200–202.

The Order of the Illuminati

For general accounts of the history of the Bavarian Illuminati, see Vernon Stauffer, *New England and the Bavarian Illuminati,* vol. 82, no. 1 of *Studies in History, Economics and Public Law* (New York: Columbia University Press, 1918); Klaus Epstein, *The Genesis of German Conservatism* (Princeton, New Jersey: Princeton University Press, 1966); and the books by Billington and Roberts. These accounts are based largely on two standard sources: R. LeForestier's *Les Illumiéns de Bavière et la franc-maçonnerie allemande* and Leopold Engel's *Geschichte des Illuminaten-Ordens.*

"To encourage a humane": Epstein, pp. 89–90.

"Go into ecstasies," et cetera: Billington, *Fire in the Minds of Men*, p. 94.

"Their total confidence": ibid.

Mozart and Schiller as Illuminati: Roberts, p. 124.

The Illuminati Suppression

The Illuminati documents seized and published by the Bavarian government are available at some libraries under the titles *Einige Originalschriften des Illuminaten Ordens* and *Nachtrag von weiteren Originalschriften.*

Rosicrucian-Jesuit ties: Stauffer, pp. 188–189; Yates, *Rosicrucian Enlightenment*, p. 101.

Number of works on Illuminati: Roberts, p. 129.

Exposure of the Cosmopolitan System: described in Epstein, pp. 97–99.

CHAPTER 3. *THOMAS JEFFERSON, ILLUMINATUS*

Roberts's *Mythology of the Secret Societies* charts the rise of the Illuminati conspiracy theory in Germany and France. Stauffer's *New England and the Bavarian Illuminati* extends the story to the early years of the American republic. Billington's *Fire in the Minds of Men* describes the fascination many revolutionaries had for the geometric-occult symbols of Freemasonry. For a firsthand look at one of these early versions of the Illuminati conspiracy theory, see John Robison's *Proofs of a Conspiracy*, republished by the John Birch Society (Belmont, Massachusetts: Western Islands, 1967). For an entertaining overview of the Illuminati conspiracy theory, see *The Illuminoids* (Albuquerque, New Mexico: Sun Publishing Co., 1978), in which Neal Wilgus has compiled various versions of the legend, both contemporary and historical, into a single narrative complete with a chronological chart.

Epigraph: Stauffer, p. 251.

"Brought from the orient": Billington, *Fire in the Minds of Men*, p. 103.

"The title of citizen": ibid., p. 97.

"Magic circles": ibid., p. 102.

"The history of an entire people": ibid., p. 104.

"The company which": ibid., p. 98.

Examples of divisions within Freemasonry: Roberts, pp. 159, 164.

"That the innocent rich": Robison, pp. 120–131; also see pp. 252–253.

"*Entire, absolute and universal*": Stauffer, p. 223 (italics in original).

"As the plague": ibid., pp. 226–227.

The New England Illuminati Scare

The best description of the New England Illuminati panic is Stauffer's book. Brief accounts appear in Hofstadter's *The Paranoid Style* and Davis's *Fear of Conspiracy*. A good source on the philosophical differences between Federalists and Jeffersonians is Vernon L. Parrington, *The Colonial Mind, 1620–1800* (New York: Harcourt, Brace & World, 1927, Harvest paperback edition). For a description of occult beliefs in the early years of the United States, see Herbert Leventhal, *In the Shadow of the Enlightenment: Occultism and Renaissance Science in Eighteenth-Century America* (New York: New York University Press, 1976).

"Eternal and immutable": Parrington, p. 331.

"All communities": from Federal Convention Debates, cited in John Bartlett, *Familiar Quotations,* 14th edition (Boston: Little, Brown, 1968), pp. 484–485.

"The people is a great beast!": Parrington, p. 305.

"Those atheistical": Stauffer, pp. 100–101.

"As a faithful watchman": ibid., p. 11.

"Secret and systematic": Hofstadter, *The Paranoid Style,* p. 9.

"To root out": Stauffer, pp. 233–234.

"While deluding mankind": Davis, p. 52.

"Temples of reason": Stauffer, p. 250.

Theodore Dwight speech: ibid., pp. 252–253.

"The nefarious and dangerous": ibid., pp. 342–343.

"From *Anno Lucis*": ibid., p. 282.

"Wonderful power": ibid., p. 333.

"Most precious interests": ibid., p. 287.

"[T]he subtil and secret," et cetera: ibid., pp. 290–293.

"I suspect that I have disturbed": ibid., pp. 303–304.

"Robison and Barruel can deceive": ibid., p. 356.

"Ravings of a Bedlamite": ibid., p. 312.

The Legend Spreads

The influence of Masonic symbols and ideas in the spread of revolutionary secret societies is documented in Billington's *Fire in the Minds of*

Men; the simultaneous spread of the Illuminati conspiracy theory is described in Roberts' *Mythology of the Secret Societies*. For details of the American anti-Masonic movement, see Lipset and Raab's *Politics of Unreason*, pp. 39–47. Nesta Webster's *Secret Societies and Subversive Movements* has been republished in recent years by Christian Book Club of America, Hawthorne, California, and become a standard source for contemporary conspiracy theorists. The 1933 edition of Edith Starr Miller's *Occult Theocracy* was printed in France "under the auspices of the International League for Historical Research . . . posthumously for private circulation only." Gerald Winrod's *Adam Weishaupt, A Human Devil* is distributed in the 1980s by Sons of Liberty of Metairie, Louisiana.

"An intimate connection": Lipset and Raab, *Politics of Unreason*, p. 42.

"The serpent has already": Hofstadter, *Paranoid Style*, p. 20.

"The aim of the societies": Miller, Conclusion.

CHAPTER 4. *THE GREAT PYRAMID GAME*

Information on Des Griffin is based on interviews conducted in March 1982, when we attended John Townsend's speech in Van Nuys, California. To fill in gaps in Townsend's account of the Illuminati legend, I have supplemented it with information from Griffin's books: *Fourth Reich of the Rich* (1979) and *Descent Into Slavery?* (1980), published by Emissary Publications, South Pasadena, California. All Townsend's quotes are from a tape recording of his speech. In places, Townsend mixes his own words with quotations or paraphrases from Winrod's book.

Epigraph: Griffin, *Descent Into Slavery?*, p. 40.

"To most people": Griffin, *Fourth Reich*, p. 2.

"Did we fall": ibid., p. 14.

"If we were merely dealing": Gary Allen, *None Dare Call It Conspiracy* (Rossmoor, California: Concord Press, 1972), p. 8.

"You've got shrinks"; "I believe virtually everything": Interview with Griffin.

The World According to Townsend

Bible quotes: Isaiah 14 and Ezekiel 28, from *The New English Bible* (Cambridge: Oxford University Press, 1970).

Information on the contemporary Rosicrucian Order is taken from mailings sent to members and from Lewis, *Rosicrucian Manual*.

Solving the Puzzle

For the real history of the Rothschilds and an explanation of the mysteries of banking, see Virginia Cowles, *The Rothschilds: A Family of*

Fortune (New York: Alfred A. Knopf, 1973); John Kenneth Galbraith, *Money: Whence It Came, Where It Went* (New York: Bantam Books, 1980); and Anthony Sampson, *The Money Lenders: Bankers and a World in Turmoil* (New York: Viking, 1981). For a non-paranoid examination of the influence of financial and intellectual elites on American politics and foreign policy, see G. William Domhoff, *The Higher Circles: The Governing Class in America* (New York: Vintage Books, 1971). For a more conservative account, see Leonard Silk and Mark Silk, *The American Establishment* (New York: Discus/Avon, 1980).

CHAPTER 5. *THE COMPUTER IN THE VATICAN*

Information about Rivera is from an interview in March 1982 at Chick Publications' headquarters in Cucamonga, California; from *ALL,* the newsletter of the Anti-Christ Information Center (also called AIC Ministries) of Canoga Park, California; and from various books, tracts, and comics published by Chick Publications. Other information is from articles in *Christianity Today,* 3/13/81, 10/23/81; *Christian Century,* 1/20/82; and the *Los Angeles Times,* 8/9/80, 3/14/81, 10/27/81. An excellent source on the history of anti-Catholicism in the United States is Ray Allen Billington, *The Protestant Crusade, 1800–1860: A Study of the Origins of American Nativism* (New York: Macmillan, 1938). For more contemporary examples, see Lipset and Raab's *Politics of Unreason.* For a recent history of the Jesuits, see David Mitchell, *The Jesuits: A History* (New York: Franklin Watts, 1981).

Epigraph: Hofstadter, *Paranoid Style,* p. 21.

Los Angeles Times article on LaHaye: in San Diego County supplement, 2/22/81.

"religious hate literature": *Christian Century,* 1/20/82.

"immoral and indecent": *Los Angeles Times,* 10/27/81.

Cartoon Adventures

The account of Rivera's story is taken from *Alberto* and supplemented with information from my interview with him.

"I don't believe in accidents": interview with Rivera.

The Jesuit Plot

"Seditious machinations": Mitchell, p. 180.

"Set the fashion"; "the darkness of": ibid., pp. 217–218

Adams-Jefferson correspondence: ibid., p. 223.

"Break the Pope's Neck"

"None who profess": Billington, *Protestant Crusade,* p. 6.

"To cut the throats": ibid., p. 10.

"The average Protestant": ibid., pp. 345–347.

"The abuse of the Catholics": ibid., p. 346.

"About seventy-five": ibid., p. 388.

"To exterminate all heretics": Lipset and Raab, *Politics of Unreason,* pp. 79–80.

"Telepathic thought waves": ibid., p. 139.

"A great man": ibid., p. 99.

The Rivera Hoax

"[O]nce that he pleads": interview with Rivera.

Christianity Today's investigation of Rivera was published 3/13/81.

"The [Jesuits] have been after," et cetera: interview with Rivera.

"The Pharisees couldn't": *ALL* (Rivera's newsletter), February 1981.

Christianity Today's investigation of John Todd was published 2/2/79.

Postscript

For details on Father Coughlin, see Sheldon Marcus, *Father Coughlin* (Boston: Little, Brown, 1973) and Lipset and Raab, *Politics of Unreason.* Information on Catholic traditionalists is from interviews in January 1982 with a priest from St. Pius X seminary, Oyster Bay Cove, New York, and several members of a St. Paul, Minnesota, church that follows Lefevbre. I also referred to literature distributed by several of the traditionalist groups named in the text and an article by novelist Mary Gordon that appeared in *Harper's,* July 1978.

"I'm a very orderly person": interview with traditionalist church member.

"Celebrate Black Masses": *Harper's,* July 1978.

"[I]f the impending doom": Kelly, *Conspiracy Against God and Man* (Boston: Western Islands, 1974), pp. 225–226.

CHAPTER 6. BANKERS, COMMUNISTS, AND JEWS

Information on Liberty Lobby is based largely on the group's promotional literature; its newspaper, *Spotlight;* a critical article in *National Review,* 9/10/71; and a report by the Anti-Defamation League, "Liberty Lobby and the Carto Network of Hate," *ADL Facts,* Winter 1982. An interview I arranged with Liberty Lobby officials at the group's Washington, D.C., office in March 1982 was canceled when I arrived; a request to reschedule the interview was denied.

Epigraph: in Curry and Brown, p. 103.

Populism "means government by those"; nationalism is "undiluted sovereignty": untitled Liberty Lobby pamphlet, circa 1981.

The Protocols

For a history of the *Protocols* and the myth of the Judeo-Masonic conspiracy, see Norman Cohn, *Warrant for Genocide* (New York: Harper & Row, 1966); Jacob Katz, *Jews and Freemasons in Europe: 1723–1939* (Cambridge, Massachusetts: Harvard University Press, 1970); and James Webb, *The Occult Establishment* (La Salle, Illinois: Open Court, 1976). Paperback editions of the *Protocols* are published by several extremist organizations such as Sons of Liberty of Metairie, Louisiana, and are usually based on an English translation by Victor Marsden. For information on worldwide uses of the *Protocols* today, see articles in the magazine, *Patterns of Prejudice* (London: Institute of Jewish Affairs), especially the November/December 1977 issue.

Description of *Hebrew Talisman* and *Secret of the Jews:* Webb, pp. 227–237.

"The evil principle": Cohn, *Warrant for Genocide*, pp. 179–180.

"Natural opponent"; "the circles of international": *Patterns of Prejudice*, November/December 1977.

"The best proof": Adolf Hitler, *Mein Kampf*, translated by Ralph Manheim (Boston: Houghton Mifflin, 1943), p. 307.

Hitler's conspiracy theory: *Mein Kampf*, pp. 308–328.

"In resisting"; "another power": *Mein Kampf*, quoted in Cohn, pp. 187, 189.

Henry Ford

For details on Ford and the *Protocols*, see Lipset and Raab, *Politics of Unreason*, pp. 135–138; and Cohn, *Warrant for Genocide*, pp. 156–164. Columns from the *Dearborn Independent* have been republished as *The International Jew: The World's Foremost Problem* (Hawthorne, California: Omni Publications, undated). For a general history of anti-Semitic conspiracy theories in the United States, see Lipset and Raab, Chapters 4, 5, and 6; Davis, *Fear of Conspiracy*, Chapters 6, 7, and 8; Hofstadter's essay on populism in Curry and Brown, *Conspiracy: The Fear of Subversion*, pp. 100–113. For an analysis of the role of Jews in recent American politics, see Stephen D. Isaacs, *Jews and American Politics* (Garden City, New York: Doubleday, 1974). For a discussion of Jews and American communism, see the article by Nathan Glazer in the *Jewish Journal of Sociology*, December 1969. Richard M. Gilman's *Behind World Revolution: The Strange Career of Nesta H. Webster*, vol. 1 (Ann Arbor, Michigan: Insights, 1982) provides a detailed description of the background of Nesta Webster and the influence of her books on twentieth-century political paranoia.

"Heinrich Ford": Cohn, *Warrant for Genocide*, p. 162.

Chicago Tribune article; *Christian Science Monitor* editorial: Lipset and Raab, p. 135.

Willis A. Carto

For background information on Yockey, see Carto's introduction to *Imperium: The Philosophy of History and Politics* (Sausalito, California: Noontide Press, 1969) and *National Review*, 9/10/71. For examples of Holocaust revisionist literature, see A. R. Butz, *The Hoax of the Twentieth Century* (Torrance, California: Institute for Historical Review, 1977); *The Journal of Historical Review* (Torrance, California: Institute for Historical Review); and *Spotlight*'s special supplement, "The Great Holocaust Debate," distributed by Liberty Lobby. *Patterns of Prejudice* regularly reports on Holocaust revisionism in the United States, England, France, West Germany, and elsewhere.

American Nazi and KKK statistics: *Patterns of Prejudice*, August 1979, March/April 1978.

"Racial mongrelization"; "niggerfication"; "There are 600 million": *National Review*, 9/10/71.

Yockey on the Holocaust: *Imperium*, pp. 598–606.

"I knew that I was": from the Introduction to *Imperium*, p. ix.

"Genetic Diseases Disprove"; "Rise of the Aryan": *American Mercury*, Winter 1976. (Carto sold the *Mercury* in 1979.)

"Probably the most": *ADL Facts*, Winter 1982.

Legion for Survival business license: *ADL Facts*, ibid.

Description of Liberty Lobby party: *Spotlight*, 2/23/81.

Dickinson, Collins, and Ervin quotes: Liberty Lobby pamphlet: *Who's your lobbyist in Washington?*

Warren Richardson incident: *Washington Post*, 4/17/81 to 4/26/81.

"Anti-Jewish"; "vicious racist": ibid.

The *True* magazine account was in the November 1970 issue; it is described in the *Washington Post* articles.

"I ought to be": telephone interview with *Spotlight* staffer, February 1982.

The Seamy Side of Christianity

Background on James K. Warner is from "The Christian Defense League," *ADL Research Report*, April 1978.

"Federal Reserve"; "greedy, usurious, scheming": *Christian Vanguard*, January/February 1981.

Church of Holy Brotherhood quotes are from an undated booklet, mailed in 1981 to people who answered the *Spotlight* advertisement.

Postscript

For information on Nazis and the occult, see Webb, Chapters 4 and 5.

"The frightening": cover of Antelman, *To Eliminate the Opiate,* vol. 1 (New York and Tel Aviv: Zahavia, 1974).

"Perhaps the most": Antelman, pp. 14–15.

CHAPTER 7. *THE INSIDERS*

The history of the John Birch Society is from Benjamin R. Epstein and Arnold Forster, *The Radical Right: Report on the John Birch Society and Its Allies* (New York: Random House, 1966); Lipset and Raab, *Politics of Unreason,* pp. 248–333; Bell, *Radical Right,* pp. 201–225; Davis, *Fear of Conspiracy,* pp. 327–339; and William W. Turner, *Power on the Right* (Berkeley, California: Ramparts Press, 1971). For a more contemporary perspective, see Alan Crawford, *Thunder on the Right: The "New Right" and the Politics of Resentment* (New York: Pantheon, 1980, paperback edition), pp. 94–97. For the society's own perspective, see Robert Welch, *The Blue Book of the John Birch Society* (Belmont, Massachusetts: Western Islands, 1961), and Gary Allen, *None Dare Call it Conspiracy* (Rossmoor, California: Concord Press, 1972).

Epigraph: Welch, pp. 30–31.

"Hundred Year Hoax": *American Opinion,* July/August 1959; "What's Right": February 1959.

Dondero account: in Davis, pp. 302–304.

"Reject the concept"; "to combat the activities": ibid., pp. 301–302.

"How can we account": *Congressional Record,* Senate, 6/14/51, p. 6602.

John Birch Society membership: *Wall Street Journal,* 8/29/79. After he was elected chairman of the society in early 1983, Representative Larry McDonald estimated membership at between 60,000 and 80,000.

John Birch Society budget: Crawford, p. 95.

Invasion from Within

The society's first meeting is detailed in Welch's *Blue Book.*

"Influential," "patriotic": Welch, p. 1.

"[T]he truth": ibid., p. 9.

"[T]he unions": ibid., pp. 21–24.

"With his death": Lipset and Raab, *Politics of Unreason,* p. 11.

Scoreboards appear in the July/August issues of *American Opinion.*

"Concentration camps": *American Opinion,* July/August 1962.

"Assorted Insiders": *American Opinion*, July/August 1982.

Invisible Empire

A discussion of the National Association of Manufacturers versus liberal groups appears in Domhoff, *Higher Circles*, pp. 186–195.

"To See the Invisible": *American Opinion*, October 1962.

Temple of Understanding article: *American Opinion*, June 1962.

"Hall of Illumination": Edith Kermit Roosevelt, quoted in Robert Keith Spenser, *The Cult of the All-Seeing Eye* (Hawthorne, California: Christian Book Club of America, 1964), p. 44.

U.N. meditation room: Spenser, pp. 7–21.

"Enlightenment mystics," et cetera: *American Opinion*, June 1962.

"It is entirely possible": *American Opinion*, March 1964.

"The veil of secrecy," et cetera: Davis, pp. 330–331.

Welch Illuminati article: *American Opinion*, November 1966.

"Communism is not": ibid.

"It took a tremendous": Lipset and Raab, *Politics of Unreason*, p. 253.

"The numerous vermin": *American Opinion*, February 1964.

5 million copies of *None Dare Call It Conspiracy*: statement on cover of book.

Another popular Trilateral Commission conspiracy book is: Antony C. Sutton and Patrick M. Wood, *Trilaterals Over Washington* (Scottsdale, Arizona: The August Corp., 1979).

"Who believe that major," et cetera: Allen, pp. 8–10.

U.S. News and World Report on Trilateral Commission: 4/7/80.

Forbes on Trilateral Commission: 11/24/80.

"Unreasonable and immoral": Allen, pp. 39–40.

"*Agents-provocateurs*": *American Opinion*, November 1966.

"If only by some miracle": Lipset and Raab, *Politics of Unreason*, p. 266.

"Divine Being": Welch, p. 146.

"Every great religion": ibid., p. 59.

Blacks in the John Birch Society: Lipset and Raab, *Politics of Unreason*, p. 267

Postscript

Soviet conspiracy theories: *Patterns of Prejudice*, January/February 1979.

CHAPTER 8. *THE DOOMSDAY PLOT*

For a history of fundamentalism and the intricacies of biblical prophecy, see George M. Marsden's *Fundamentalism and American Culture: The Shaping of Twentieth Century Evangelism, 1870–1925* (New York: Oxford University Press, 1980). Other good sources include Richard Hofstadter's *Anti-Intellectualism in American Life* (New York: Vintage Books, 1962), pp. 55–141, and C. Allyn Russell's *Voices of American Fundamentalism: Seven Biographical Studies* (Philadelphia: Westminster, 1976). For an account of fundamentalism by fundamentalists, see Ed Dobson and Ed Hindson's *The Fundamentalist Phenomenon: The Resurgence of Conservative Christianity*, edited by Jerry Falwell (Garden City, New York: Doubleday, 1981). Dozens of books on fundamentalist prophecy are available in Christian bookstores. For this chapter, I relied on Hal Lindsey's *The 1980s: Countdown to Armageddon* (1981) and *The Late Great Planet Earth* (1970), both published by Bantam, New York; Bill Maupin's *The "Key" to the Book of Daniel and 40 Year Generation* (Tucson, Arizona: Lighthouse Gospel Tract Foundation, 1981); and Mary Stewart Relfe's *When Your Money Fails . . . the "666 System" is here* (1981) and *The New Money System . . .* (1982), both published by Ministries Inc., Montgomery, Alabama. Biblical doomsday prophecy also inspired religious movements in an earlier age; see Norman Cohn's *The Pursuit of the Millennium: Revolutionary Millenarians and Mystical Anarchists of the Middle Ages*, revised edition (New York: Oxford University Press, 1970).

Epigraph: Lindsey, *Countdown to Armageddon*, p. 128.

Bible quotes are from *The New English Bible*.

"[A]t the sound": 1 Thessalonians 4.

"I'd like to see you": interview with Maupin.

"As things were in Noah's days": Matthew 24.

More than 15 million copies of *Late Great Planet Earth*: *New York Times Book Review*, 3/15/81.

"Yes, I am coming": "the hour of fulfillment": Revelation 1 and 12.

"I tell you this": Matthew 24.

"The Illuminati": Maupin, p. 81.

Lindsey scenario: from *Late Great Planet Earth*.

"[The Beast] worked": Revelation 13.

Statistics on Relfe book: Relfe, *The New Money System*, p. 253.

Premillennialism

Every "pastor, evangelist, missionary": Russell, p. 18.

Statistics on *Scofield Bible*: *Atlantic*, June 1982.

"One of the principal *architects*," et cetera: Marsden, pp. 44–47 (italics added).

"It makes no difference": Hofstadter, *Anti-Intellectualism*, p. 85.

"[A]s iron shatters": Daniel 2.

Daniel's dream: Daniel 7.

Fundamentalist Politics

For details on McIntire, Hargis, and the Church League of America, see Erling Jorstad, *The Politics of Doomsday: Fundamentalists of the Far Right* (Nashville, Tennessee: Abingdon, 1970) and Gary K. Clabaugh, *Thunder on the Right: The Protestant Fundamentalists* (Chicago: Nelson-Hall, 1974). For details on the Church League's espionage activities, see Frank J. Donner, *The Age of Surveillance: The Aims and Methods of America's Political Intelligence System* (New York: Vintage Books, 1981), pp. 421–425.

"Will hate you": Matthew 24.

"The church in America": Hofstadter, *Anti-Intellectualism*, p. 116.

"When the word": ibid., p. 122.

"It would be better": ibid., p. 125.

"Modern Tower of Babel": Jorstad, *Politics of Doomsday*, p. 41.

"Roman Catholic terror"; "a master plan"; "superchurch"; "pacifist propaganda": ibid., pp. 49–51.

"America used the atomic bomb": ibid., pp. 147–148.

"House of red Babel": ibid., p. 86.

Budget for 20th Century Reformation: ibid., p. 61, 83.

"Called of God to launch": ibid., p. 71.

"A group of Harvard radicals": ibid., p. 82.

"Sound film footage": *The Church League of America Story* (pamphlet distributed by the organization in 1982).

McIntire's financial problems: *Christianity Today*, 8/17/79.

Hargis resigns: *Time*, 2/16/76.

Hargis fund-raising letters: mailed to supporters in 1982 and 1983.

James Watt and biblical prophecy: *Newsweek*, 6/29/81.

Robertson on Lebanon: *Newsweek*, 7/5/82.

"God has raised up America": *Humanist*, June 1982.

Falwell and Begin incident: ibid.

The Survivalists

Information on the Christian-Patriots Defense League is from the group's literature, an interview with Harrell, and an article in *Time*, 11/5/79. Information on McKeever is from his newsletters and his book *Christians Will Go Through the Tribulation—And How to Prepare For It* (Medford, Oregon: Omega Publications, 1978). Information on Posse Comitatus is from articles in the *Minneapolis Star–Tribune*, 2/15/83, 2/16/83, 2/18/83, 3/9/83, 3/14/83, 5/29/83, 6/4/83, 6/7/83; the *Milwaukee Journal*, 7/27/80 to 7/31/80; and the group's *Posse Noose Report*.

Parable of the virgins: Matthew 25.

"You can't make a mess," et cetera: interview with Harrell.

Wickstrom quotes from *Posse Noose Report:* July 1981, April/May 1982.

Kahl letter: *Minneapolis Star–Tribune*, 3/9/83.

"A legend and a martyr": *Minneapolis Star–Tribune*, 6/4/83.

Postscript

For details on the British-Israel movement, see Charles Samuel Braden's *These Also Believe: A Study of Modern American Cults & Religious Movements* (New York: Macmillan, 1949), pp. 385–402. For a book by a leader of the movement, see William J. Cameron's *The Covenant People* (Merrimac, Massachusetts: Destiny Publishers, 1966). For examples of conspiracy theories that include British-Israelites, see *Don Bell Reports* (MARAH Inc., Palm Beach, Florida), 2/12/65, 2/19/65, 2/26/65, and the description of a book called *Union Jack* in *Suppressed Truth Review*, 1982, a booklist published by *Conspiracy Digest*, Dearborn, Michigan.

CHAPTER 9. *THE NEW RIGHT*

For a critical look at the New Right, written by a former insider, see Alan Crawford's *Thunder on the Right: The "New Right" and the Politics of Resentment* (New York: Pantheon, 1980, paperback edition). Other sources include Erling Jorstad, *The Politics of Moralism: The New Christian Right in American Life* (Minneapolis: Augsburg, 1981) and Flo Conway and Jim Siegelman, *Holy Terror: The Fundamentalist War on America's Freedoms in Religion, Politics and Our Private Lives* (Garden City, New York: Doubleday, 1982). For books presenting the New Right's point of view, see Richard A. Viguerie, *The New Right: We're Ready to Lead* (Falls Church, Virginia: The Viguerie Co., 1981) and Robert W. Whitaker, editor, *The New Right Papers* (New York: St. Martin's Press, 1982). For two perspectives on Schlafly, see Carol Felsenthal's admiring biography, *Phyllis Schlafly: The Sweetheart of the Silent Majority* (Chicago: Regnery Gateway, 1981), and Frances Fitzgerald's critical article in the *New York Review of Books*, 11/19/81. Schlafly describes her conspiracy theories in such works as *A Choice Not an Echo* (Alton, Illinois: Pere Marquette Press,

1964), *The Gravediggers* (Alton, Illinois: Pere Marquette Press, 1964), and *Strike From Space: How the Russians May Destroy Us* (New York: Devin-Adair, 1966). The latter two books are written with coauthor Chester Ward. The New Right's view of secular humanism as a one-world plot is described in Tim LaHaye's *The Battle for the Mind* (Old Tappan, New Jersey: Fleming H. Revell Co., 1980) and Claire Chambers's *The SIECUS Circle: A Humanist Revolution* (Belmont, Massachusetts: Western Islands, 1977). A good profile of Tim LaHaye was published in the San Diego edition of the *Los Angeles Times*, 2/22/81.

Epigraph: Crawford, p. 310.

"There are more"; *New York Times*, 7/31/80.

"Culturally destructive": Whitaker, p. 53.

"Controlled by our adversaries": ibid., p. 31.

"Christ is our chairman": from *Christian Voice*'s "Statement of Purpose," 1979.

"It is basic": Whitaker, p. 62.

Anti–New Right conspiracy charts: see, for example, the booklet *The New Right Takes Aim*, published by the United Auto Workers.

"We believe that": from *Christian Voice*'s "Statement of Purpose."

"The bleeding heart": *Minneapolis Star*, 8/29/80.

"The humanistic/atheistic/hedonistic": Crawford, p. 161.

"The focus of evil," et cetera: Reagan speech to National Association of Evangelicals, Orlando, Florida, 3/8/83.

"The international communist"; "master scheme": in Reagan's *Where's the Rest of Me?* (New York: Karz, 1981), pp. 158, 162.

"A debt to"; "many of the Catholic": Whitaker, pp. 50, 52.

Weyrich article: *American Opinion*, April 1982.

"The New Right leaders": Crawford, p. 96.

National Review on John Birch Society: 10/19/65.

"A small group of secret"; "can it really be": Schlafly, *A Choice, Not an Echo*, pp. 25, 102.

Atheistic Secular Humanism

"Well-concealed humanist": Chambers, p. xi.

"Two more cogs": ibid., p. 389.

"An international subversive movement," et cetera: ibid., pp. 393–394.

"An invisible enemy": LaHaye, inside front cover.

"Humanism is," et cetera: LaHaye, pp. 25–27.

Creationism

The classic account of creationism is *The Genesis Flood: The Biblical Record and Its Scientific Implications* (Phillipsburg, New Jersey: Presbyterian and Reformed Publishing Co., 1961) by John C. Whitcomb and Henry M. Morris. Many shorter works are available, including David C. C. Watson, *The Great Brain Robbery: Studies in Evolution* (Chicago: Moody Press, 1976). For information on later developments in creationism, I attended two seminars in St. Paul, Minnesota, in 1981: "In the Beginning . . . ," held November 21 at the Fourth Baptist Church, supported creationism; "Evolution and Public Education," held December 5 at the University of Minnesota, St. Paul campus, opposed creationism. The seminars are summarized in Walter T. Brown, *In the Beginning,* second edition, (Naperville, Illinois: Institute for Creation Research Midwest Center, 1981) and *Conference on Evolution and Public Education: Resources and References* (Minneapolis: University of Minnesota, Department of Conferences, 1981). I also relied on articles in *Bible-Science Newsletter* (Bible-Science Association, Minneapolis); literature from the Institute for Creation Research in San Diego; and interviews with creationists at the Bible-Science Association. For the history of Protestantism and science, see Marsden's *Fundamentalism and American Culture* and Stephen F. Mason, *A History of the Sciences* (New York: Collier, 1962), pp. 175–191. For details of the "Great Chain of Being," see Arthur O. Lovejoy, *The Great Chain of Being* (Cambridge, Massachusetts: Harvard University Press, 1973).

"Two premises were": Marsden, pp. 14–15.

"The genetic information": Brown, p. 3.

Ark calculations: ibid., p. 11.

Creationists on radioactive decay rates: *Bible-Science Newsletter,* August 1981; Whitcomb and Morris, Chapter 7.

Creationist atomic model: *Bible-Science Newsletter,* December 1981.

Creationists on thermodynamics: Whitcomb and Morris, pp. 222–227.

Attempt to disprove Hubble and Einstein: *Bible-Science Newsletter,* August 1981, December 1981.

"To the person": James Hanson, *A New Interest in Geocentricity* (Minneapolis: Bible-Science Association, undated).

Postscript

For details of Wilson's life and theories, see his autobiographical book, *Cosmic Trigger: The Final Secret of the Illuminati* (New York: Pocket Books, 1977), and his collection of essays, *The Illuminati Papers* (Berkeley, California: And/Or Press, 1980). The *Illuminatus!* trilogy *(The Eye in the Pyramid, The Golden Apple,* and *Leviathan)* was published by Dell, New

York, in 1975. I supplemented these sources with material from an interview with Wilson, March 1982, in San Francisco.

The *East Village Other* chart is reprinted in *The Eye in the Pyramid*, p. 97.

Garrison and the Illuminati: *New Yorker*, 7/13/68.

Wilson quotes are from *Cosmic Trigger*, pp. 48–53.

Principia Discordia quote: ibid., p. 479.

"Maybe the secret": ibid., p. xviii.

CHAPTER 10. *THE "NEW DARK AGES" CONSPIRACY*

LaRouche's conspiracy theory is described in his organizations' many books and periodicals. Two of the most complete accounts are Carol White's *The New Dark Ages Conspiracy: Britain's Plot to Destroy Civilization* (New York: The New Benjamin Franklin House, 1980) and "The Secrets Known Only to the Inner Elites," an article by LaRouche published in his magazine *Campaigner*, May/June 1978. I also referred to *Dope, Inc.: Britain's Opium War Against the U.S.* (1978), by Konstandinos Kalimtgis, David Goldman, and Jeffrey Steinberg, *Carter and the Party of International Terrorism* (1976), and the following books by LaRouche: *Basic Economics for Conservative Democrats* (1980), *How to Defeat Liberalism and William F. Buckley* (1979), *The Power of Reason: A Kind of an Autobiography* (1970), *What Every Conservative Should Know About Communism* (1980); all are published by LaRouche's New Benjamin Franklin House. To keep up on the latest twists of the conspiracy theory, I read the twice-weekly newspaper *New Solidarity* from May 1982 to May 1983 and issues of the organizations' other periodicals: *Fusion, War on Drugs, Campaigner, Investigative Leads,* and *Executive Intelligence Review*. For the early history of the organization, I relied on articles in *Solidarity* and *New Solidarity*, which are available at the New York Public Library; LaRouche's autobiography, *The Power of Reason;* and articles in the *New York Times*, 1/20/74, 10/7/79, 10/8/79.

The one person who has probably spent the most time investigating LaRouche is Dennis King, a New York City free-lance writer. King's findings were published in an eleven-part series in the New York City newspaper *Our Town*, beginning 9/2/79, and in *Nazis Without Swastikas: The Lyndon LaRouche Cult and Its War on American Labor* (New York: League for Industrial Democracy, 1982). Another veteran LaRouche watcher, Chip Berlet, works with the National Lawyers Guild of Chicago and has published LaRouche articles in the *Chicago Sun-Times*, 6/17/79, and the Chicago *Reader*, 3/7/80. Another booklet good for historical information on LaRouche is *NCLC: Brownshirts of the Seventies* (Arlington, Virginia: Terrorist Information Project, 1977), available through the National Lawyers Guild. Articles have also been published in *Inquiry*, 2/15/82, *Mother Jones*, January 1982, *New West*, 3/24/80, *National Review*, 3/30/

79, *Business Week,* 10/2/78, *The Public Eye* (National Lawyers Guild), Fall 1977, and the *Washington Post,* 2/17/74. I supplemented these sources by interviewing LaRouche and several of his followers in New York City in January 1981.

Epigraph: interview with Fay Sober, January 1981.

Opening scene, quotes, and description of headquarters: visit by author, January 1981.

$200,000-a-week budget: interview with Sober, January 1981.

Fonda incident: *New York Times,* 7/27/81, 10/28/81.

Nancy Kissinger incident: *Washington Post,* 6/11/82.

"We're not very nice": interview with Goldstein, January 1981.

The Philosophy War

Platonic solids: in his dialogue *Timaeus,* Plato associates the five solids with earth, air, fire, water, and the cosmos and explains how reality supposedly is constructed from them.

"From their standpoint"; "it's done through": interviews with LaRouche and Goldstein, January 1981.

"The fallacy of": *New Solidarity,* 10/8/78.

LaRouche on Holocaust: ibid.

History of a Cult

"A brilliant synthesizer": *New York Times,* 1/20/74.

"Poetry Must Begin": *Fusion,* October 1978.

"The third grade," et cetera: *Power of Reason,* pp. 39–42.

"A battery of": ibid., p. 43.

"Intellectually I almost": ibid., pp. 57–58.

"He is one," et cetera: interview with Rose, fall 1980.

"Usually [LaRouche's] goon squads": 1976 private intelligence report prepared for AFL-CIO.

"They disrupt meetings": *Public Eye,* Fall 1977.

White incident: *New York Times,* 1/20/74.

"An eight-cycle": ibid.

Enforcing Reality

Rose's quotes are from interviews in fall 1980. Rose's experiences are also described in an article he wrote for *National Review,* 3/30/79.

"The fundamental tendency," et cetera; "the result": from a 1979 statement by former LaRouche followers obtained by the *New York Times* and National Lawyers Guild.

Strange Alliances

Former members on right-wing allies: former members' statement, 1979.

"Once we have won": *National Review*, 3/30/79.

Senior party member advocates assassination: former members' statement, 1979.

LaRouche in Mexico and India: *New York* magazine, 6/21/82.

Details of LaRouche-supported campaigns: reports in *New Solidarity*.

Postscript

Daily World article: 9/18/75.

Overthrow article: reprinted in *Conspiracies Unlimited* (St. Paul, Minnesota), vol. 4, no. 1, 1983

CONCLUSION. *SEEING THE LIGHT*

Elaine Pagels's *The Gnostic Gospels* (New York: Vintage, 1981) is an excellent introduction to the controversy between the orthodox Catholic church and the Gnostics. For an English translation of the gospels of the Gnostics, see James M. Robinson, general editor, *The Nag Hammadi Library* (San Francisco: Harper & Row, 1981). Other good books on Gnosticism include: Hans Jonas, *The Gnostic Religion: The Message of the Alien God and the Beginnings of Christianity,* second edition, (Boston: Beacon Press, 1963); R. M. Grant, *Gnosticism and Early Christianity* (New York: Columbia University Press, 1959); and Jean Doresse, *The Secret Books of the Egyptian Gnostics* (New York: Viking, 1960). Jacques Lacarricre's *The Gnostics* (London: Peter Owen, 1977) is a beautifully written essay evoking what it might have felt like to be a Gnostic in the early centuries A.D. In *Pagan and Christian in an Age of Anxiety* (London: Cambridge University Press, 1965), E. R. Dodds describes the mystical world views of the Gnostics, early Christians, Neoplatonists, and pagans.

Epigraph: Pagels, p. 153.

Legend of the Fall: according to various interpretations, the fruit represents secular thought, universal wisdom, moral knowledge, or the discovery of the pleasures of sexual intercourse. See *The Interpreter's Dictionary of the Bible* (New York: Abingdon Press, 1962), vol. 4, pp. 695–697.

"Boast that they possess": Pagels, p. xv.

"They imagine that": ibid., p. 25.

"*I* am the way": John 14 (italics added).

"There is light": Pagels, p. 144.

"The lamp of the body": "the mind is the guide": ibid., p. 153.

"[I was] very disturbed": ibid., p. 166.

"Faith of fools": ibid., p. 12.

"Name themselves bishop," et cetera: ibid., p. 29.

"Like circles of artists," et cetera: ibid., pp. 22–30.

"Other religions are": Grant, p. 8.

"The invariable element": *Modern Catholic Dictionary*, p. 232.

"But only because," et cetera: Grant, pp. 9–12.

Gnostics as libertines, ascetics, and existentialists: Jonas, pp. 270–277, 320–340.

"Abandon the search": Grant, p. 9 (italics added).

"God created humanity": Pagels, p. 147.

The Eye in the Pyramid

For an interesting but exaggerated account of the role of Freemasonry in the American Revolution, see Bernard Fay, *Revolution and Freemasonry: 1680–1800* (Boston: Little, Brown, 1935). For information on the effect of Enlightenment philosophy on the founding of the United States, see Henry Steele Commager, *The Empire of Reason: How Europe Imagined and America Realized the Enlightenment* (Garden City, New York: Anchor Press, 1978).

"The Pythagoras of the New World": Billington, *Fire in the Minds of Men*, p. 103, footnote 100.

Paine on Freemasonry: Thomas Paine, "Origin of Freemasonry," in William M. Van der Weyde, editor, *The Life and Works of Thomas Paine*, vol. 9, (New Rochelle, New York: Thomas Paine National Historical Association, 1925).

History of Great Seal: Harriet P. Culley, editor, *The Great Seal of the United States* (Washington: U.S. Department of State, July 1980).

"The pyramid signifies": ibid., p. 5.

"The occult fascinated him": Arthur M. Schlesinger, *The Coming of the New Deal*, vol. 2 of *The Age of Roosevelt* (Boston: Houghton-Mifflin, 1959), p. 31.

"The Best and the Brightest": David Halberstam, *The Best and the Brightest* (New York: Random House, 1972).

Technocrats: Theodore Roszak, *The Making of a Counter Culture* (Garden City, New York: Anchor Books, 1969).

Index